Edward S. Eunson

Hope you [...] Kick out of this [...] blaq.

Oct '42

EX LIBRIS

E. S. EUNSON

SABOTAGE!

We may be sure that Hitler and Japan will cooperate to do the unexpected. . . . In any event, the psychological and sabotage offensive in the United States and Latin America will be timed to coincide with, or anticipate by a few weeks the height of the military offensive.

We must be especially prepared to stifle the fifth columnists in the United States who will try to sabotage not merely our war material plants, but even infinitely more important, our minds.

Vice-President Henry A. Wallace

May 8, 1942.

SABOTAGE!

THE SECRET WAR AGAINST AMERICA

By MICHAEL SAYERS
and ALBERT E. KAHN

HARPER & BROTHERS PUBLISHERS

NEW YORK AND LONDON

SABOTAGE! The Secret War Against America

To

the late Moritz Kahn

and to

Phillip Sayers

FOREWORD

The contents of this book may at first seem incredible to the American reader. An almost identical book might have been published a few years ago in Europe, and its contents would have seemed incredible to most Europeans. Today, the Europeans know better. They are only too tragically familiar with the subject of this book.

This book is about Axis sabotage. It deals with a weird political underworld of spies and saboteurs. It portrays the agents and conspiracies of a system, reaching into the United States, which relies upon wrecking, terror and treachery as major weapons in its war to enslave the world.

Sabotage is not a new device in war. The use of arson, explosives and assassinations to strike at the enemy's home front has been common to all modern wars. Until recently, however, sabotage was regarded as an auxiliary weapon. Even in the First World War, the Imperial High Command never gave more than lukewarm support to von Papen's sabotage ring in the United States.

But with the Nazis, sabotage became state policy.

Nazi Germany itself is the creation of professional spies and saboteurs. The ex-Reichswehr spy Adolf Hitler came to power by means of a secret bargain struck with the former arch saboteur, Franz von Papen, in the home of the democracy-hating Cologne banker Baron Kurt von Schroeder. The consolidation of Nazi power was achieved with history's supreme act of sabotage: the burning of the German Reichstag by Hermann Goering's arsonists.

Criminals like Dr. Robert Ley, terrorists like Julius Streicher, espionage agents like Captain Fritz Wiedemann, assassins like Baron Manfred von Killinger are the acknowledged leaders of the Nazi State. The same gangster types head the government in Fascist Italy under the dictatorship of Benito Mussolini, and in Japan under the rule of the Japanese warlords, whose secret Black Dragon Society paved their way to power with a series of political murders.

There is no device of sabotage which the professional wreckers of the Axis have not mastered. They have raised the weapon of sabotage to a new level in modern warfare. Their saboteurs assume the importance of a Second Army, operating within the borders of other nations, wrecking, disrupting and undermining morale.

Sabotage on a world scale; sabotage of industry, agriculture, transport, the press, finance, labor, the armed forces, politics; sabotage striking into the very minds of the opposing peoples; sabotage incessant and universal: *this* is the "secret weapon" of Axis war.

This weapon can function with full effect only as a *secret* weapon. Understanding it is the first step toward nullifying its potency.

Axis saboteurs are at work in the United States today. They seek to cripple American war production and to undermine American morale. It is impossible to understand the workings of these saboteurs without a full awareness of Axis plotting in America during the years that preceded the attack on Pearl Harbor, and without recognizing the role that certain Americans, some of them still prominent in public life, played and are still playing—some wittingly, some unwittingly—in aiding Axis sabotage.

It is in the hope of bringing about this understanding, and of thus contributing to the war effort, that this book has been written.

The Authors, New York, July 1942

TABLE OF CONTENTS

PART II

PSYCHOLOGICAL SABOTAGE

LIST OF ILLUSTRATIONS

PART I

PHYSICAL SABOTAGE

CHAPTER ONE

THE GHOSTS THAT WALK AGAIN

I. *The Ghost of a Firebug*

It was 9:15 P. M.. March 16, 1941. The Cleveland-Pittsburgh Express was thundering across the snow-blanketed Pennsylvania countryside on the last lap of its 400-mile run. Rushing alongside the black streak of the Ohio River at a speed of sixty-five miles an hour, the train neared the little town of Baden. Periodically, the engineer poked his head from his window and quickly jerked it back into the cab. The night was bitter cold. The locomotive's great beam bored into clouds of falling snowflakes. Eerie and shrill, the engine whistle sounded across the white fields.

Suddenly, without warning, the giant engine swayed violently, and, with a furious grinding roar, it leaped from the tracks and hurtled down the river bank. Behind the locomotive, the passenger cars were catapulted one after another into the dark icy water, twisting and turning, and crumpling like toys. As the deafening cacophony of ripping metal subsided, there came a deep gasp of steam from the overturned engine, as if it were breathing its last. Then could be heard the piercing, terrible screams of the injured. . . .

Five persons were killed. One hundred and twenty-one were injured.

Pennsylvania Railroad officials said, "Definitely caused by sabotage!" The Interstate Commerce Commission reported the results of its investigation on May 8: "malicious tampering with the track" had caused the wreck.

3

At the Interstate Commerce Commission hearing, experts expressed the belief that the derailment plot was aimed at the 13-car Manhattan Limited which had passed over the same tracks eighteen minutes before the disaster occurred. A group of United States Army men were aboard the Manhattan Express, and the train carried forty-four Soviet representatives, part of a delegation of engineers and diplomats who had arrived at San Pedro, California, from Vladivostok on March 12.

Fascist Ukrainian saboteurs, working for the Nazis, were suspected of having caused the wreck. . . .

An anti-fascist newsletter published in New York City, *The Hour*, revealed that the Pittsburgh industrial area was infested with cells of a fascist Ukrainian terrorist organization, operating under the Intelligence Service of the German War Office. Captain Leonid Klimenko, a fascist Ukrainian emissary from the German War Office, had arrived in the United States a short time before the train wreck and had held secret conferences with key fifth columnists working in the Pittsburgh area. At the time of the wreck, Klimenko was already on his way back to Berlin. *The Hour* urged Federal authorities to investigate the Pittsburgh friends of Captain Klimenko.*

On April 24, a shabbily-dressed, gaunt-faced man with long white mustaches and short-cropped white hair strode into the office of *The Hour*. He was admitted to the editor and stood staring down with fanatical, cat-like eyes.

"You write about me in *Hour*," he said haltingly, with a guttural, foreign accent.

There was something hauntingly familiar about the face of this strange visitor.

"What's your name?" the editor asked, quite certain he had seen the man's face before.

The visitor shook his head, without replying.

"Who are you?" The editor named various individuals who

* The results of the subsequent investigation were not made public.

had been mentioned in *The Hour's* recent exposés. The visitor just stared, unblinkingly.

"Are you Fiodore Wozniak?"

"Yah," said the visitor. "Me Wozniak."

As he spoke he stretched his arm with a loose, quick gesture, and something slipped from his sleeve and dropped with a faint clatter to the floor. Quickly, he stooped and picked it up. It was the serrated blade of a hack saw, about a foot long.

With some show of embarrassment, Wozniak tucked the blade in the newspaper he was carrying. Backing away, he said in a low threatening voice, "You write no more about me and sabotage, All lies. See?" He turned and hurried from the office.

Fiodore Wozniak!

The name may mean little to the reader in 1942. Yet back in 1917, Fiodore Wozniak helped to make some of the most sensational headlines that ever blazed on American newsstands.

How many Americans recall the sabotage terror of the great Kingsland Fire?

For four terrifying hours, on the afternoon of January 11, 1917, the inhabitants of New York City, New Jersey, Westchester and Long Island listened to the roar of 500,000 three-inch, high-explosive shells being discharged in a continuous bombardment. The disaster occurred in the shell-assembling plant of the Agency of the Canadian Car and Foundry Company near Kingsland, New Jersey, about ten miles from the great docks in New York Harbor. Suddenly and inexplicably, fire had broken out in Building 30, where thousands of high-explosive shells were being assembled. Within a few minutes the whole plant was ablaze. As the flames reached each case of shells and exploded the projection charges, the missiles leaped high up in the air and then hurtled down in and around the factory.

When the din, smoke and fire subsided, it was found that 275,000 loaded shells, 300,000 cartridge cases, 100,000 detonators, 440,000 time fuses, huge stores of T.N.T., and over a million unloaded shells were completely destroyed. Luckily the shells had not yet been equipped with their detonating fuses; otherwise the casualties would have been immense. As it was, the shells fell back as so much deadweight metal, and the men, women and children in the neighborhood escaped in the nick of time without casualties. After four hours of incessant explosions and raging fire, it was found that material damage amounting to $17,000,000 had been accomplished by one of the most successful acts of sabotage ever perpetrated against a nation's war industry. That was the Kingsland Fire.

Investigation quickly established that the blaze had originated at the work bench of the very man, then a worker in the Kingsland Plant, who twenty-four years later walked into the office of *The Hour* and introduced himself with the words, "Yah. Me Wozniak."

In 1917 American investigators coined a nickname for Fiodore Wozniak: they dubbed him "The Firebug." Yet it was not until many years later that the United States Government was able to track down all the evidence to prove conclusively that the Kingsland disaster was an act of German sabotage, and that "The Firebug," Fiodore Wozniak, working under German instructions, had started the fire at his work-bench either by the use of an incendiary pencil or with rags saturated with phosphorus dissolved in some solvent. It is the boast of German sabotage agents that their "techniques" leave no trace and can never be fully explained.

It was not until June 1939, two months before the outbreak of the Second World War, that United States Supreme Court Justice Roberts was able to hand down the decision that Germany (1) waged undeclared war by sabotage on the United States from 1914-17; (2) caused the famous Black Tom and Kingsland disasters; and (3) by continuously presenting per-

jured testimony through its Foreign Office officials, tried for
22 years to hide the proof of its guilt. . . .*

In the hectic interlude between September 1, 1939, when
Germany marched on Poland, and December 7, 1941, when
the Japanese bombers winged out of the gray dawn over
Hawaii, it seemed to many Americans that history was being
rewritten by that mystical-minded old philosopher, Hegel,
who said, "History always repeats itself." Once again, the
United States was reluctantly girding itself in face of the
threat of war. Once again, an aggressive, imperialistic Germany was employing every device of diplomacy, propaganda
and sabotage to isolate the United States from its potential
allies abroad and to cripple American production. History
was repeating itself—but on a gigantic scale which exaggerated
the past and magnified its tragedies and melodramas.

Fiodore Wozniak, "The Firebug," walking the streets of
New York, consorting with fascist Ukrainian terrorists whose
cells were active in vital American industrial regions, seemed
like a ghost from a nightmarish past. Yet there were other,
more potent ghosts emerging from the sinister legends of
World War I.

---

* Supreme Court Justice Roberts handed down this decision as Umpire at the
Mixed Claims Commission hearings held at The Hague, Holland. The Mixed
Claims Commission was an international court established in 1921 for the pur-
pose of adjudicating American and German claims for damages arising out of
the First World War. Each country appointed a Commissioner and these two
Commissioners selected a neutral Umpire. The three officers constituted the
Commission. Supreme Court Justice Roberts became Umpire in 1931.

In 1933, Fiodore Wozniak confessed that he had been in contact with German
secret agents prior to the Kingsland sabotage fire. Wozniak produced a letter
which he had written to Franz von Papen complaining that his services had
been ill-rewarded by the German Government. In 1937, Wozniak admitted that
the fire broke out at his bench in the Kingsland Plant, that he had received
an incendiary pencil from German sabotage agents and had discussed plans
for sabotaging the Kingsland Plant. The United States Government took no
legal action against Wozniak, who served as an important witness during the
Mixed Claims Commission hearings. However, Wozniak's petition for naturali-
zation, filed in 1937, was denied.

In July 1942, as this book was going to press, Wozniak was taken into custody
by the FBI.

II. *The Ghost of Handsome Franzi*

The Kaiser's Germany launched its "Great War" without taking American resources into consideration. German strategists then, as now, dreamed of *blitzkrieg* victory. They based their plans on a rapid and overwhelming defeat of the Allied forces in Belgium and northern France. Only after the setback at the first crucial Battle of the Marne did the Kaiser's High Command realize it faced a long struggle in which economic strength would be the decisive factor and American resources might be the key to victory. Hastily, and belatedly, the High Command turned its attention to crippling American war production. Germany was already cut off from American ports by the British blockade. There was no way of shipping large numbers of saboteurs across the seas. So Germany was forced to rely on her diplomatic representatives in the United States to organize the secret war against American resources.

On January 26, 1915, the Intelligence Service of the German High Command sent a secret code message to the German Embassy in Washington. It read:

> For Military Attaché: You can obtain particulars as to persons suitable for carrying on sabotage in the U. S. and Canada from the following persons: one, Joseph MacGarrity, Philadelphia; two, John P. Keating, Michigan Avenue, Chicago; three, Jeremiah O'Leary, 16 Park Row, New York. One and two are absolutely reliable and discreet. Number three is reliable but not always discreet. These persons were indicated by Sir Roger Casement. In the U. S. sabotage can be carried out in every kind of factory for supplying munitions of war. Railway embankments and bridges must not be touched. Embassy must in no circumstances be compromised. Similar precautions must be taken in regard to Irish pro-German propaganda.
>
> ZIMMERMAN

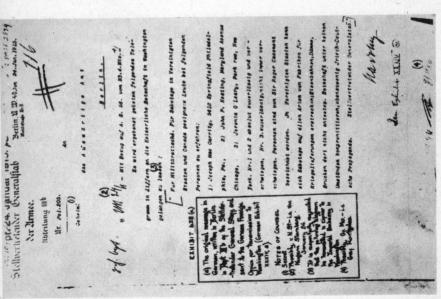

Left: the original message dated January 24, 1915, from *Section IIIB* (German Military Intelligence) concerning sabotage operations in the United States. *Right:* a section of message in code as transmitted by Zimmerman of the German Foreign Office to the Embassy in Washington; above the code numbers is *Section IIIB's* message decoded into German. These documents were introduced as evidence in the Mixed Claims Commission Hearings on German sabotage in the United States during first World War.

Zimmerman was the Kaiser's Minister of Foreign Affairs.

The Military Attaché at Washington, to whom the secret code message was addressed, was Captain Franz von Papen, first of Germany's saboteur-diplomats. He was very popular in Washington circles before America entered the First World War. Young, wealthy, aristocratic, "handsome Franzi" gave the appearance of being a man utterly fearless and frank. Only a certain narrowness about the eyes suggested the other aspect of the man's character: his evil genius for intrigue. Captain von Papen was given the task of organizing German sabotage in the United States.

G. Amsinck & Company, a New York firm which von Papen purchased, became the front for the sabotage work. From here, the Military Attaché dispatched his agents—professional wreckers, American pro-German agitators, Irish anti-British terrorists, hired criminals and malcontents. Von Papen's men penetrated everywhere: they were employed in American munitions plants, on docks, in ships, on farms, in detective agencies. Von Papen even contrived to insert some of his agents into United States Government offices. To pay for this secret army on American soil, von Papen spent $40,000,000 which has been traced, and probably millions more.

America was not prepared for this sort of thing. The combination of diplomacy and sabotage which von Papen had worked out scored some amazing successes in the early months of the war. Later, when the United States Government fully realized with what it was dealing, American counter-sabotage squads went to work and von Papen's hastily improvised sabotage ring was quickly smashed. But those early successes went to the young Military Attaché's head. He felt he could do anything with these "idiotic Yankees," as he contemptuously described the American people. He drew up a wild plan for a German invasion of Canada—incidentally, the first invasion plan calling for the use of an organized fifth column; and he was quite chagrined when the German Ambassador Count

Johann Heinrich von Bernstorff dismissed the scheme as "foolhardy." Von Bernstorff was more receptive to von Papen's plans for blowing up the Welland Canal, for firing vital munitions depots in American ports, for poisoning American cattle destined for Allied consumption, and for spoiling American crops. All of these schemes were undertaken by von Papen's agents with results so gratifying to the Imperial High Command that Captain von Papen's reward, after his expulsion from the United States, was promotion to the rank of Major and a personal commendation from Kaiser Wilhelm himself.

In all, von Papen's sabotage ring cost the United States more than $150,000,000 in direct physical damage done to essential war resources. More than forty industrial plants and freight yards were wrecked, not to mention the forty-seven ships in which fire-bombs had been planted before they left American ports.

The abdication of the Kaiser did not end von Papen's plotting. In the following years he worked tirelessly at sabotaging and undermining German democracy. As Chancellor of the Weimar Republic, he paved the way for the Nazis coming to power, and thereafter devoted his perverted talents to furthering the cause of the Swastika.

Recent history has familiarized millions with the name Franz von Papen: a name that has weaved in and out of contemporary events like a sinister spell, always conjuring in its wake, in Germany, in Poland, in the Balkans, in Turkey, a nightmare of intrigue, sabotage and murder.

As Nazi Germany's leading diplomat, von Papen helped to reorganize the entire German diplomatic service. Henceforth, all German diplomacy was to be modeled on his own activities as Military Attaché in the United States. Von Papen transformed the German diplomatic service into a corps of Nazi saboteur-diplomats who carried on his sinister intrigues in every nation in the world.

These saboteur-diplomats started coming to the United

States in 1933 and, operating under their diplomatic immunity, entangled the forty-eight states in a web of secret destruction. After the German consulates were closed down in 1941, their work was carried on through the innumerable subversive agencies they had organized on American soil.

The type of official representatives sent to America during the years 1933-41 by the Nazi Foreign Office would alone be enough to indict the system which bred them.

There was the dandily-dressed Baron Manfred von Killinger, who came to the United States in 1937 to be Nazi Consul General in charge of the West Coast region. In pre-Hitler Germany, von Killinger was a pioneer Storm Troop chief. He arranged the murder of the Catholic Minister Matthias Erzberger, was tried and escaped conviction only because of his high connections with the growing Nazi movement. Subsequently, von Killinger was convicted of complicity in several other assassinations; he received the extraordinarily mild sentence of eight months imprisonment—which, again because of his excellent Nazi connections, he never served. With Hermann Goering, Ernst Roehm and other Nazi leaders, von Killinger helped plan the Reichstag Fire. Von Killinger wrote a book entitled, *Ernstes und Heiteres aus dem Putschleben* (Gay and Serious Moments in the Life of a Putschist), in which he described his exploits as a Nazi. He gleefully recalled how he treated a trade union girl, "I gave the signal and the brigadiers laid the she-goat across a wagon-shaft and stroke by stroke with a horse-whip painted her back red till not a streak of white showed." In his official capacity in the United States, von Killinger set up special West Coast units of the German American Bund in preparation for the coming Nazi espionage-sabotage offensive against American shipping and aircraft industries.

There was the hefty, dark-browed, lantern-jawed Captain Fritz Wiedemann who replaced von Killinger when the latter's subversive activities were exposed. Adolf Hitler had served as corporal in Wiedemann's company during World War I, and an intimate friendship had sprung up between the two. At San Francisco, Wiedemann directed the Nazi espionage-sabotage ring on the West Coast and established collaboration with the Japanese machine. He also set about creating a "Cliveden Set" in America with the aim of defeating repeal of the Neutrality Act, then hampering American aid to the democracies abroad. Hitler reportedly wired Wiedemann, congratulating him on "your fine work in defeating repeal of the Neutrality Act." Wiedemann was the paymaster for Nazi underground activity in the United States, and, according to a report in the *New York Times* on February 20, 1941, paid out more than $5,000,000 to various agents.

There was Baron Edgar von Spiegel, New Orleans Consul General, a former U-boat commander now turned Nazi saboteur-diplomat. Von Spiegel's crude attempt to blackmail an American newspaper in his territory brought about a State Department investigation.

There was suave, amiable Dr. Herbert Scholz, Consul at Boston, later revealed to be a representative of Heinrich Himmler's Gestapo in the United States. Scholz's job was to bring pressure on German-Americans and to force them to assist the Bund and the Nazi secret service. Scholz set up an intricate espionage-sabotage network along the Boston waterfront.

In Washington, San Francisco, New York, Baltimore and other American cities, the ghost of "handsome Franzi," diplomat and saboteur, was walking again.

III. *The Ghost of the Silent Colonel*

The man who was responsible for the supreme direction of German espionage-sabotage activity in the Allied countries during World War I was Colonel Walther Nicolai, chief of *Section IIIB* (Intelligence) of the German High Command. Nicolai was a Ludendorff man. He shared the General's fanatical belief in the supremacy of the German *volk*. In later years, he also shared Ludendorff's obsession that Germany had been defeated because the Kaiser's strategists had failed to wage war with sufficient ferocity against the Allies' home fronts. The "Silent Colonel," as Nicolai was called by his staff, also shared Ludendorff's faith in a certain little loud-mouthed anti-Semitic Austrian agitator named Adolf Hitler.

Nicolai and Ludendorff spent much time together during the years 1918-32—those crucial years when the struggling German democracy was being undermined and wrecked by a cabal of army leaders, industrialists and professional spies. The German secret service was supposedly disbanded after the war; but Ludendorff approached Alfred Hugenberg, financial backer of the Nazi party, and, with funds supplied by Hugenberg, Nicolai was privately able to reorganize *Section IIIB*. Nicolai placed his trained spies and saboteurs at the disposal of the Hitlerite conspirators who were then planning the destruction of the German Republic.

With the triumph of the Nazis, Colonel Walther Nicolai became the man behind the secret service of the Third Reich, which retained the title of the old German Military Intelligence, *Section IIIB*.

In the spring of 1936 a young German-American came upon a fascinating book in the New York Public Library. It narrated the successes of German espionage in Europe and America during the First World War. The story so impressed the young German-American that he decided to become an espionage agent in the service of this seemingly all-powerful *Section IIIB*. The young man was twenty-seven years old, a deserter from the United States Army, and the son of a minor functionary in the old Imperial Austrian consular service. His name was Guenther Gustav Rumrich.

Returning home, he sat down and wrote a letter to the author of the book which had so impressed him. He described himself as a former lieutenant in the United States Army who had seen service in the Air Corps both in Panama and Hawaii. If the German War Office could make use of him, he wrote, it should communicate with him by inserting an advertisement addressed to "Theodore Koerner" in the Public Notices column of the *New York Times*. Rumrich addressed his letter to:

Colonel Walther Nicolai,
c/o Voelkischer Beobachter,
Berlin, Germany.

The *Voelkischer Beobachter* is the official newspaper of the Nazi party. Rumrich's letter got to Colonel Nicolai without delay. On April 6, 1936, a Public Notices item in the *New York Times* instructed "Theodore Koerner" to communicate with "Sanders" at "Post Office Box 629, Hamburg, Germany." Rumrich did so, and subsequent communications to him from "Sanders" were postmarked New York City. Eventually, the would-be spy was told to present himself on a certain evening at the Hotel Taft, Seventh Avenue and 50th Street, New York City. Rumrich was sent a carefully drawn plan of the hotel lobby. An X indicated the exact spot where "Sanders" would be sitting. "Sanders" turned out to be a tall, dark-haired German, aged forty-five, named Dr. Schmidt. He showed Rumrich an envelope containing two $1,000 bills—payment due a Nazi spy in Brooklyn, he said, for having stolen war secrets from the Sperry Gyroscope plant. More $1,000 bills were available for Rumrich if he could "produce."

A somewhat bewildered American public was made aware that the forgotten Colonel Nicolai of World War I was still very much alive when, on October 14, 1938, Guenther Gustav

Rumrich was brought to trial in New York City. Actually, Nicolai's *Section IIIB* itself was placed on trial and charged with directing sabotage and espionage against the United States; but in 1938 American counter-sabotage and counter-espionage forces were still inadequate to cope with the Nazis. Of the eighteen saboteurs and spies named in the Federal indictment, only four faced American justice in the dock: Guenther Gustav Rumrich and three petty accomplices. The big fish had slipped through the FBI net and were already back in Berlin, reporting to the Silent Colonel. Dr. Schmidt, alias "Sanders," had vanished, along with his fellow spies: Captain Lieutenant Erich Pfeiffer, "in direct charge of all espionage in North and South America," and Dr. I. Griebl, the organizer of a ring of saboteurs in key American defense factories. At the trial it was revealed that Griebl's agents had been at work in the Hall Aluminum Company, which was manufacturing a "torpedo bomber" for the U. S. Navy, in the Sperry Gyroscope plant which was producing a special bombsight, in the Buffalo Curtiss-Wright aircraft plant, in the Long Island Seversky aircraft plant, as well as in other important plants, docks and airports.*

Three years later another of Colonel Nicolai's agents was caught in the United States. This was the veteran saboteur-spy, Frederick Joubert Duquesne, head of a ring of 33 Nazi spies and saboteurs arrested by FBI agents in June 1941. Duquesne had worked under the Silent Colonel in World War I.

---

*At the trial, Rumrich pleaded guilty and became the key witness for the Federal prosecution. He was sentenced to serve two years in prison. His three accomplices were found guilty of espionage on behalf of the German Government. Johanna Hoffman, who had worked as a hairdresser aboard the trans-atlantic liner *Europa*, was sentenced to four years imprisonment. Otto Hermann Voss, one of Dr. Griebl's agents employed at the Seversky aircraft plant at Farmingdale, Long Island, received a six-year prison sentence. Erich Glaser, a private of the Eighteenth Reconnaissance Squadron stationed at Mitchell Field, Long Island, charged with having stolen an Air Corps code, received a two-year prison sentence.

He had been in charge of German sabotage of British shipping in South American ports. He was arrested in the United States in 1918 and charged with murder in connection with the sinking of the British ship *Tennyson*. He later escaped from the United States authorities. In 1941, Duquesne was ordered to start sabotage operations in the United States against electric power and gas plants. Colonel Nicolai's theory is that sabotage of public utilities is advantageous from two points of view: it slows down war production by cutting off power and it also undermines public morale. The Silent Colonel was preparing for an all-out sabotage offensive in the United States. Rumrich and Duquesne were only two, and by no means the most important, of his agents in this country. . . .

IV. *A Phantom from the Moscow Trials*

In November 1941, the authors of this book received an anonymous tip that "a very interesting fellow" named Paul Scheffer could be found at a certain house on East 51st Street in New York City. We went to this address. It was a large old house with its windows boarded up, obviously unoccupied. Thinking we had been misled, we started away, when the doorman of the apartment house next door asked us if we were looking for someone. We told him we were looking for the occupant of the deserted house. "A smart dresser with a foreign accent?" asked the doorman. He told us that such a man periodically came to this house, apparently to collect his mail.

The next time Paul Scheffer came to the deserted house, we were waiting for him. When he left, we followed his taxicab to a smart apartment house at 227 East 57th Street. We learned that Scheffer was living there in Apartment No. 3G.

Paul Scheffer was not at all inclined to be interviewed, but we finally persuaded him. He told us that he was in the United States as a "special correspondent" for *Das Reich,* Dr. Goebbels' own newspaper. He did not tell us, but we soon found out, that he was in touch with the Nazi agents and "newspaper-men," Rudolf Mattfeldt in Washington, and August Halfeld and Herbert Gross in New York. We also uncovered some interesting biographical details about Paul Scheffer, a man with quite an extraordinary career.

Under the Weimar Republic, Paul Scheffer had the reputation of being one of the foremost liberal journalists in Germany. He wrote regularly for the famous *Berliner Tageblatt*. At the same time, according to subsequent revelations, he was reporting to *Section IIIB*. In fact, the "liberal" journalist, Paul Scheffer, was later disclosed to be a Nicolai spy, a paid agent of the Reichswehr faction then working to secure the downfall of German democracy. Scheffer worked directly under Colonel Oberhaus, one of Nicolai's lieutenants in *Section IIIB*.*

Shortly before Hitler came to power, Paul Scheffer traveled to the Soviet Union as "foreign correspondent" for the *Berliner Tageblatt*. Scheffer's orders were to contact Mikhail Alexandrovich Chernov, who then headed the Peoples' Commissariat of Trade in the Ukraine and was soon to become head of the Peoples' Commissariat of Agriculture of the entire U. S. S. R.

Chernov was already in the pay of the German Intelligence, receiving an average of 4,000 rubles a month in return for providing the Germans with Russian military and trade secrets. Scheffer's password to Chernov was "Reinhold"—the pseudonym by which Chernov was known in the files of *Section IIIB*.

---

* These and the facts that follow about Paul Scheffer are revealed in the record of the Court Proceedings in the case heard before the Military Collegium of the Supreme Court of the U.S.S.R. in Moscow, March 2-13, 1938. Two years before those court proceedings took place, the late United States Ambassador to Germany, William E. Dodd, wrote in his diary, on November 15, 1936, "I have been watchful of this Scheffer who was a Social Democrat a few years ago, was several years in the United States as correspondent for the German free press and is now a good Nazi."

Even at this early date the German High Command was planning a vast campaign of sabotage against Soviet agriculture and industry. Chernov later admitted that Scheffer used him to organize a ring of saboteurs among opposition elements in the Soviet Union. Scheffer operated from the Moscow offices of the *Berliner Tageblatt*. He still posed as a liberal.

"I had a number of periodical meetings with Scheffer," Chernov later testified before the Supreme Court of the U. S. S. R. "I transmitted information to the German Intelligence Service, and through him received instructions from the latter about the organization of wrecking work. I had an especially long conversation with Scheffer on the organization of wrecking work in the sphere of grain collections and grain supplies. The chief task assigned to me by the German Intelligence Service at that time was to arrange to spoil grain within the country. . . . Those commissions that Scheffer gave me I carried out."

The complete record of the sabotage carried out by Chernov in Soviet Russia during 1930-36 is too long to give here in its entirety. These are just a few of his accomplishments:

> creating a discrepancy between grain collections and storage space, thus spoiling the grain and arousing the indignation of the peasants who saw their products ruined;
> arranging for the wholesale contamination of storehouses by pests, particularly by the corn beetle;
> carrying on wrecking activities in such fields as seed, crop rotation, machine and tractor stations;
> killing off pedigree breed-stock and raising cattle mortality by preventing the development of fodder resources and especially by artificially infecting cattle with various kinds of bacteria;
> effecting a shortage of the serum to counteract epidemics of anthrax (in one case, 25,000 horses perished as a result of Chernov's sabotage in this field);
> infecting tens of thousands of pigs with erysipelas and with

certain plagues by having virulent bacteria placed in medicinal serums . . .

On March 2, 1938, Soviet justice caught up with the saboteur-spy Mikhail Chernov. He was tried in Moscow, along with twenty other Soviet citizens, on charges of "treason to the country, espionage, committing acts of diversion, terrorism, wrecking, undermining the military power of the U. S. S. R." The Soviet Supreme Court sentenced Chernov to be shot.

Some time before the trial began, the Soviet authorities had ordered Paul Scheffer to leave the country. He returned to Berlin and stayed for a while in the Third Reich. He began working for Dr. Goebbels, whose Propaganda Ministry has its own espionage division called the *Abwehr* (Counter-Action) Department. Its function is to coordinate propaganda, sabotage and espionage work in foreign countries. In 1938, the very year Chernov was standing trial in Moscow, Paul Scheffer came to the United States. For three years he remained in the United States, reporting regularly to Dr. Goebbels' newspaper, *Das Reich.* . . .

When Nazi Germany declared war on the United States, Paul Scheffer was quietly picked up by the FBI and interned as an enemy alien.

Could such wholesale sabotage of agriculture, as took place in the Soviet Union, take place in the United States? To many Americans the testimony at the 1938 Moscow Trials, especially the repeated references to the use of disease germs and poisons against cattle and crops, seemed utterly fantastic. Yet this diabolical sabotage was actually practised by German saboteurs in 1915 in the United States of America.

Anton Dilger, a German-American medical graduate from Johns Hopkins University, was in Germany when the First

World War broke out. He offered his services to the Kaiser, and was promptly detailed by Colonel Nicolai to do secret service work in the United States. Dilger returned to America with a supply of cultures of glanders and anthrax germs. Financed by von Papen, he set up a laboratory in Chevy Chase, near Washington, and started breeding germs on a large scale for infecting mules, horses and cattle awaiting shipment to the Allies.

By the fall of 1915, Anton Dilger had prepared enough germ cultures to initiate an extensive disease-spreading campaign. The actual inoculations were carried out by an American citizen who had been hired by the von Papen ring. This man organized a band of some twelve assistants to travel around the country, carrying Dilger's germs in small glass phials stoppered with corks through which a needle extended. This roving band jabbed their deadly needles into the livestock. They also spread germs by placing them in fodder and drink. Thousands of soldiers, as well as horses and cattle, died as a result of Dilger's germs. At last Dilger himself revolted against his mission of silent death. He was murdered by German spies a few months before the end of the war.

Could it happen here? It did happen here!

Out of the political underworld of twenty-odd years ago, the ghosts of secret destruction are walking again through the American countryside and stretching forth their hands from across the seas into American farms and factories and ships and mines. . . .

The Kaiser's Germany was unprepared for America's entry into the conflict. Adolf Hitler's Germany, after nine years of criminal intrigues seeking to isolate America from her Allies, was not caught unprepared by America's entry into the war. Hitler had plans already drawn up to deal with that emergency.

CHAPTER TWO

SABOTEURS AT WORK

I. *The Memorandum and the Index*

In September 1941 the Federal Bureau of Investigation conclusively established:

> that the German Government had laid extensive plans for the launching of a campaign of sabotage against American defense industries, transport and shipping;
> that German money was pouring into the United States through Dutch, Spanish and South American banks for the purpose of financing spies and saboteurs;
> that the Nazis maintained a special radio station at Hamburg which was in regular communication with secret shortwave stations in the United States, and that vital information about American defenses was being sent to Germany through these stations;
> that Axis spies and saboteurs were employed in key positions in American defense plants and on U. S. steamship lines;
> that these spies and saboteurs were in possession of detailed accounts of U. S. fortifications, airfields, ports and other vital defense centers.

An extraordinary document entitled *Memorandum of Instruction to Saboteurs* had been circulated among foreign agents in the United States. It contained full instructions for sabotage against American industry and transport. Couched in military language which suggested that it emanated from the German War Office, the *Memorandum* listed various methods of crippling railroad cars and engines, burning out boilers of locomotives, blocking and destroying rights of way, and even the "deterioration of the underground high-tension cables" on electric railroads.

The FBI uncovered further evidence of Axis sabotage preparations when it found that the Axis governments had compiled a special *Index of American Industry*. According to J. Edgar Hoover, the nature and purposes of this *Index* were revealed through the arrogance of a certain "foreign industrialist" in the United States who unguardedly stated that he could get confidential information on all American manufacturing and commercial activities. Not realizing he was talking to a Federal agent, he boasted that he could obtain a detailed report on any American defense factory within twenty-four hours.

As a test, the Federal agent named a certain factory producing important war materials. The very next day, the Federal agent was shown a dossier which not only gave a comprehensive summary of the factory's business, but also *"named and classified each individual worker politically, racially, and religiously, set out what each had done in the past, what he was doing at present, and what he might be used for in the future. Opposite each name were notations of the worker's loyalty and international sympathies."* Subsequent investigation revealed that this information—obtained by a foreign industrialist within twenty-four hours—was in many respects more detailed than could be found in the American factory's home offices or anywhere else in the United States.

Clearly, the very existence of such an *Index* indicated that a staggeringly large Axis espionage apparatus was at work, and that a sabotage network of ominous proportions was being organized.

The interlocking of Nazi espionage and sabotage work in the United States was dramatically revealed in the strange case of William G. Sebold.

II. *The Case of William G. Sebold*

During the First World War, William G. Sebold was a corporal in a machine-gun unit of the German Army on the Western Front. He came to the United States soon after the war and managed to get work as a machinist. The tall, 200-pound German liked America and decided to become an American citizen. He got married and worked hard at various jobs, earning excellent pay. It was not until 1939 that he thought of returning to his native land on a trip to Mülheim-Ruhr, his birthplace. In the summer of that year he took a leave of absence from his job at the Consolidated Aircraft Company in San Diego, California, and sailed for Germany.

The simple-seeming German-American whose passport read "airplane mechanic" strongly appealed to the Gestapo agent at Mülheim. He promptly reported Sebold's arrival to his superiors. The Gestapo placed Sebold under observation. They trailed him on his visits to his mother, his brothers and sisters, all of whom lived in Germany. They carefully studied the postcard messages he sent back to his wife in California.

Shortly before Sebold was preparing to return to America, a Gestapo official visited him at his hotel room.

The Gestapo official was very polite, very smooth and very ominous. He knew all about Sebold—more, in fact, than Sebold knew about himself. "So you wish to return to America? That corresponds exactly with our plans. We can use men like you in America. . . ."

The bewildered mechanic gradually realized he was being asked to become a Nazi spy. "But I am an American citizen," he protested.

The Gestapo official cut him short. Sebold was told that he was a German and, more to the point, that he was now in the Third Reich.

The Gestapo official clicked his heels and departed. Sebold hastily started packing. It was only then that he discovered that he had lost his American passport. The Gestapo had stolen it.

When the Gestapo official returned several days later, Sebold was scared and attentive.

It was September 1, 1939. The loud-speakers in the cobbled streets of Mülheim were blaring the news of the march on Poland. . . .

Sebold was sent first to Cologne where he was interviewed by other Gestapo officials. At Cologne, in a desperate effort to break through the Gestapo trap, Sebold furtively made contact with certain United States consular representatives. He told them he had lost his American passport.

"You are in a tough spot," one of the United States representatives said.

Sebold was in Gestapo hands from that day on.

They sent him to a school in Hamburg. Here, under the supervision of Nazi secret police, Sebold was trained in the use of the Leica camera and the making of microphotographic reductions. He was taught the use of codes, telegraphy, short-wave radio, and secret inks. Other students at the Hamburg school were being trained in the arts of sabotage and studying the effects of various explosives and poisons.

Sebold was taught the divisions of the Nazi spy system: the *collectors,* the *transmitters,* the *couriers,* the *drops* and the *specialists.*

Collectors got hold of desired information.

Transmitters forwarded the data to Germany, by coded mail or shortwave radio.

Couriers worked on steamship lines and transatlantic clippers, and carried special messages to and from Germany.

Drops were innocent-seeming addresses of business houses or private individuals, usually in South American or neutral European ports. Reports were sent to these addresses for forwarding to Germany.

Specialists were expert saboteurs.

Sebold was trained to be a *transmitter*. He was kept at the Hamburg school for four months. On January 27, 1940, he was called in to be interviewed by the school's chief, Dr. Nicolaus Adolf Fritz Ritter,* who questioned Sebold closely on his knowledge of American industry.

"What do you know about the Norden plant which manufactures the special American bombsight?" Sebold was asked.

"I never heard of it," he confessed. Thinking to make a good impression, Sebold added, "But I can find out about it when I get back to America. I might even be able to lay my hands on the blueprints."

Dr. Ritter smiled. "Don't you worry about that," he said. "The blueprints of the Norden bombsight are already in our possession."

He then handed Sebold a tiny slip of tissue paper on which were written four names:

Herman Lang: 59-36 20th St., Woodbridge, Long Island, in care of C. I. Norden Company, New York City
Else Weustenfeld: 312 West 81st St., New York City
Lily Stein: 127 East 54th St., Merrick, Long Island
Frederick Joubert Duquesne: in care of Air Terminals Building, New York City

On February 8, 1940, one William G. Sawyer arrived in the United States aboard the American liner S. S. *Washington* which had sailed from Genoa, Italy. Concealed in the back of his watchcase were five lengthy documents reduced by microphotography to the size of a postage stamp. The microscopic documents contained detailed instructions to Nazi spies and saboteurs in the United States. In William G. Sawyer's pocket was $910, the remainder of the $1,000 which the Gestapo had given him before he left Hamburg.

---

*Dr. Ritter headed the Hamburg division of the Gestapo. He visited the United States in 1938 and, operating under the name of "Dr. Rankin," laid the groundwork for special espionage activities in the New York area.

William G. Sawyer was William G. Sebold.

Sebold was to set up an office as a front for his espionage work. To finance him, Dr. Ritter sent $5,000 through a Mexican branch of the Chase National Bank in December 1940. Two months later, Sebold received another $5,000; and $10,000 more at intervals during the next six months. With this money, Sebold rented an office in the Newsweek Building at 152 West 42nd Street, New York City. Painted on the office door was the sign, "Diesel Research Company."

Meanwhile, Sebold sought out the four contacts given him by Dr. Ritter. Herman Lang had moved to 74-36 64th Place, Glendale, Long Island. Sebold visited him there on March 23, 1940. Lang turned out to be a stocky, dark-haired, self-assured fellow with bushy eyebrows and sparkling brown eyes. A naturalized citizen, Lang was an expert draftsman and an inspector, employed at the Norden plant. Sebold greeted him with the spy password, "I bring you greetings from Rantzau, Berlin and Hamburg."

Lang told Sebold that he had fought as a Nazi Storm Trooper with Adolf Hitler between 1923 and 1927 and that he knew Hermann Goering personally.

"You know, Goering considers the Norden bombsight the most important thing in the world," said Lang. "In 1938 I memorized the blueprints and carried them over to Germany in my head. I got 10,000 marks for that job."

The second contact, Else Weustenfeld, turned out to be a heavily-built middle-aged divorcée working as a stenographer and Notary Public in a law office in the building which housed the German Consulate at 17 Battery Place. She had been born in Essen, Germany, on April 16, 1889, and had been a naturalized American citizen for some 14 years. She worshipped Adolf Hitler and talked a great deal about "our Nazi boys."

The third contact, Lily Barbara Carola Stein, whom Sebold found in her apartment at 232 East 79th Street, New York City, was a good-looking, plumpish artist's model with plucked eyebrows, blonde hair and heavily rouged lips. She was the link between the German Military Intelligence and its agents in the United States. Money came to her regularly through Amsterdam and South American banks, and she passed it on as directed. Lily Stein was well versed in the mysteries of codes and secret inks. She moved in high circles and used her good looks to advantage in striking up acquaintances with Americans who might have valuable information.

Most interesting of Dr. Ritter's four "contacts" was Frederick Joubert Duquesne. He was the brains of the New York ring. He arranged for Sebold to meet him at the Little Casino Restaurant, a small side-street *beerstube* at 206 West 85th Street. While drinking light beer, Duquesne regaled Sebold with colorful anecdotes drawn from his experiences in two world wars. Duquesne was an animated fleshynosed man with wavy white hair and squinting watery eyes. He was enormously talkative and conceited. He told Sebold that he had been born in South Africa sixty-two years ago, and had entered the German secret service during the Boer War. He boasted that he was an expert saboteur and the inventor of many new types of bombs currently being used by saboteurs in the United States.

Sebold told him about his "research" office. Duquesne nodded, "That's good, that's very good. That's the kind of business that will cover up almost any kind of sin."

Later, when they were alone in Duquesne's comfortable apartment at 24 West 76th Street, Sebold extracted a minute square of microfilm from his watchcase and handed it to Duquesne, who began to study it with the aid of a powerful magnifying glass. It took him fifteen minutes to read all the instructions.

The United States war secrets which the German Military Intelligence asked Duquesne to report on included: Americantested methods of bacteriological warfare, the new American gasmasks, anti-fog devices, anti-aircraft shells, automatic range-finders and coaxial cable. The Germans also wanted specific details on:

an International Telephone and Telegraph Company device by which one ray directs bombers to objectives while a second ray releases bombs directly over targets;

textiles for Army uniforms that neutralize mustard gas, said (according to Nazi instructions) to have been perfected by a "Professor Bullard" of Hobart College;

"trench crushers" believed to be able to destroy trenches by overriding them (Duquesne was instructed to furnish the names of the manufacturers, the size of deliveries and for whom they were being made);

the "latest developments" in gun-turret design for Sunderland flying boats.

"How is this stuff to be sent over?" Duquesne asked when he had read all the instructions. Sebold explained that Dr. Ritter had ordered him to build a special short wave radio station for this purpose.

It took Sebold some time to buy all the necessary radio equipment. Dr. Ritter lodged a large sum to his account at the Chase National Bank to pay for it, and also for the small house which Sebold rented at Centerport, Long Island. Here Sebold installed an expensive short-wave radio transmitting and receiving apparatus capable of communicating with Germany.

Late in April, 1940, Sebold received a coded letter from Germany outlining the final details for the establishment of communication between Centerport and Hamburg. The German station was to use the call letters AOR. Starting on May 15, Sebold was instructed to try to get Hamburg every evening at 6 P.M.,E.D.T., using the call letters CQDXVW-2 and a wavelength of 14,300 to 14,400 kilocycles. "A great deal will depend on atmospheric conditions," the letter stated. "Don't become impatient even if it shouldn't work for days."

Sebold faithfully carried out the Hamburg instructions. On May 31, 1940, the first full-length coded message came through clearly to Sebold at his Centerport station. The message was:

> Need urgently from all friends monthly production of air-plane factories, exports to all countries, especially England and France; number, type, date of delivery by steamer or air, armature and armament; payment cash and carry or credit. Rose has $200 for you. . . . Greetings.

"Rose" was the pseudonym of the spy chief in Hamburg.

Sebold was in constant communication with his superiors in Germany during the following months. The spies brought him their data and once or twice a week he radioed it to Germany or mailed it via the *couriers* and *drops.*

Sebold soon realized that he and his four "contacts" were not alone. There were many other agents operating under Nazi instructions in the United States. Duquesne had at least thirty spies and saboteurs working with him. By the spring of 1941, Sebold was acquainted with many of them.

There was "Heinrich," a glib, suave, cosmopolitan fellow who turned out to be Carl Edmund Heine, former foreign manager of the Ford and Chrysler Motor Companies. Heine had his headquarters in Detroit where he "collected" American aircraft secrets and sent them to Lily Stein for transmission to Germany.

There was the chief *courier,* Heinrich Carl Eilers, who was a library steward on the United States transatlantic liner, S. S. *Manhattan.*

There was Duquesne's girl-friend, the smart, bohemian, Arkansas-born Evelyn Clayton Lewis, who combined espio-nage with sculpture and playwriting.

There was the Hamburg-trained saboteur, Carl Alfred Reuper, who had managed to get himself employed in Air

Associates, Inc., of Bendix, New Jersey, where airplane parts were being manufactured.

Sebold learned that there was another group of spies and saboteurs working independently in the New York area under the leadership of a man named Kurt Frederick Ludwig, forty-eight-year-old American citizen of German extraction, who posed as a salesman of leather goods. Ludwig reported at regular intervals to Heinrich Himmler, head of the Gestapo in Germany, forwarding detailed information on ships entering and leaving the port of New York.

Working with Ludwig was a pretty eighteen-year-old blonde named Lucy Boehmler who had been a member of the Queens, New York, unit of the German American Bund. Her regular duties as Ludwig's assistant included maintaining a permanent card file on United States army camps, disposition of United States military forces, troop movements and arms production.

Another of Ludwig's "contacts" was Rene Charles Froehlich, a soldier at Fort Jay, Governors Island.

The Ludwig group covered United States fortifications, flying fields and naval bases along the Eastern seaboard, taking photographs and gathering material for the use of saboteurs and for the German Military Intelligence abroad.*

---

* As United States Attorney Mathias F. Correa established at the trial of Ludwig and six of his co-workers, the real leader of Ludwig's ring was Ulrich von der Osten, a high officer of the German Military Intelligence, who arrived in the United States from Japan on March 16, 1941. Von der Osten's mission was to coordinate the work of the various espionage-sabotage groups in the New York area. He traveled under a Spanish passport, registering at the Hotel Taft, New York City, as Julio Lopez Lido from Shanghai, China. Two days after his arrival, while walking with Ludwig in Times Square on March 18, von der Osten was struck and killed by a passing taxicab. In his baggage at the Hotel Taft, clues were found which enabled the FBI to identify him. The FBI obtained a highly confidential report which von der Osten had prepared on the defenses of Pearl Harbor and Hickham Field. The Nazi agent had written at the bottom of this report that the information would be very interesting to "our yellow friends." After the death of von der Osten, Ludwig took over as leader of the spy ring.

On the evening of June 28, 1941, the greatest spy roundup in American history was started off by a series of sudden FBI raids. The entire Duquesne ring in New York was taken into custody. Later, all members of the Ludwig group were arrested by Federal agents.

The Nazi agents were astounded. How had it happened? They had thought their intricate system was impregnable. There must have been a leak. But how?

It was not until they faced trial that the bewildered Nazi spies and saboteurs discovered that their tireless co-worker, William G. Sebold, was actually an agent of the United States Federal Bureau of Investigation!

Sebold had been working under FBI supervision ever since he had gone to the United States consular representatives in Cologne to complain about his lost American passport. From the moment he arrived in the United States aboard the S. S. *Washington* in February, 1940, Sebold had been in daily contact with United States Department of Justice officials. The FBI agents drafted the letters which Sebold sent to his "superiors" in Hamburg. They also supervised Sebold's short-wave radio station, subtly falsifying the reports which he broadcast to Germany so as to render them useless to the Nazis.

III. *Spy Letters*

The letters which are reproduced on the following pages were mailed in New York City on April 16 and on April 22, 1941, by the Nazi spy Kurt Frederick Ludwig. They were addressed to Heinrich Himmler, the chief of the Gestapo in Germany, through "drops" in Madrid, Spain, and in Lisbon, Portugal. These two letters never reached their destinations. They were intercepted at Bermuda by officers of the British Intelligence and handed over to the United States Department of Justice.

Laboratory experts at Bermuda subjected the letters to certain tests which revealed—on the reverse side of the letters—invisible writing containing highly confidential information about American and Allied shipping, troop movements and war production. The invisible messages had been written with a toothpick dipped in an aqueous solution of pyramidon.

A commemorative stamp ·on each envelope indicated to Himmler that the letter was important. Each letter was also numbered with a pencil notation under the stamp. Ludwig usually signed himself "Joe."

This is the envelope which Ludwig mailed on April 16, 1941, in New York City. "Manuel Alonso" was Heinrich Himmler's personal "drop" in Madrid, Spain. Ludwig's espionage data was forwarded from there to Himmler in Germany.

On cursory inspection, Ludwig's letters to Himmler appear to be innocent business communications from a New York exporter to one of his customers abroad, but even the typed portions of Ludwig's letters contained important communications to Himmler. Part of the letter Ludwig mailed in New York City on April 16, 1941, is printed in the left-hand column below; on the right we give the meaning as it would have been understood by Himmler:

Ludwig's "Doubletalk"	*What It Meant*
"Your order 5 is rather large—and I with my limited facilities and funds shall never be able to fill such an immense order completely. But I have already many numbers in stock, and shall ship whatever and whenever I can. I hope you have no objections to part shipments."	"Your instructions to me in communication No. 5 call for a lot of work and will take some time to execute. Remember that I have only a few people working for me, and not too much money. I already have some of the information you want, and shall send it at once. The rest will follow as fast as I can get it."

IV. *Devices of the Saboteurs*

Through the work of espionage agents, the saboteur is supplied with information concerning those defense centers or transport facilities which are most vital, and therefore most important for him to attack. Having selected his objective, the next step for the saboteur is to choose his sabotage device. A vivid illustration of the whole process was provided at six-thirty o'clock, on the evening of June 25, 1941, when the Nazi saboteur-spy, Frederick Joubert Duquesne, entered the "research" office of William G. Sebold in the Newsweek Building in New York City.

Sebold was sitting at his desk in his shirtsleeves, chewing a piece of candy, when Duquesne came in. They greeted each other, shook hands, and settled down to business. Unknown to Duquesne, Sebold had arranged for United States Federal agents to be secreted in an adjoining room, equipped with microphones and motion picture cameras to record every word and action that was to take place.

Duquesne bent down, took off his left shoe, and drew from his sock a long white envelope, which he handed to Sebold. The envelope contained material on United States Army weapons which Duquesne had gathered while attending the

Dear Sir:

About a week ago already I received (indirectly) a cable announcing the settlement of the affair with Bill's papers till the 20th inst. Let us hope they
are made out this time to me personally - so that we have here no difficulties with them. May I state in this connection here again that my name was
not mentioned as the first papers were returned five weeks ago. In any case
I wish to thank you for your valuable assistance in this delicate matter.
The receipt of your letter of March 8th was acknowledged some weeks ago already. You mentioned in it a letter from me dated January 7th, but on this
day I wrote no letter - apparently you mean the one from January 5th which
you should have received long ago.
In the meantime I made offers to all three of the mentioned prospective customers, and I hope you will hear from them soon too. As I have still too much
work here, you would certainly greatly oblige me if you would have the kind-
ness to get in touch with my customers, and give them a detailed instructions for the various shipments. Sometimes I even don't know in what language
to write them, or to whom I should refer to.
Concerning your various orders and inquiries mentioned in your letter of
March 8th I wish to state the following:
Re: point 1 and 2 not much known here - these numbers are not on the market
yet, and so I did not bother about them before I received your letter. As far
as I am informed samples of the numbers given in "1" are shipped already since
last year directly, without any stops. Of course there are plans for sending
smaller articels the way mentioned in your letter - but the preparations for
it are just beginning.
About points 3 and 4 I wrote a few times already - only recently I found some
additional parts, and I hope to be able to send you this month a more or less
complete sample of both numbers. But the exact answer to your wishes I did
not find yet. The customer mentioned in 4 ordered last year seven and later
eleven - but these orders are apparently not completed yet (model A).
Till the middle of February seven have been sent directly to the other customer (3) - but these were obviously brand new samples with large deliveries to
follow soon. So far as I know nothing has been shipped from the old stock of
this number.
Your order 5 is rather large - and I with my limited facilities and funds
shall never be able to fill such an immense order completely. But I have already many numbers in stock, and shall ship whatever and whenever I can. I
hope you have no objections to part shipments.
As I have here really too much work, I advise sometimes the manufacturers that
they ship directly to the customers. Of course it would be of no use whatsoever to write to these concerns, as they most likely would not forward my
mail to me. My friend out west discontinued to conduct his business from an
office, as the turnover was very small, and I am not in a position now to pay
part of the rent, as I did during the last half-year. So in case you want to
make him some new offers, please address your mail to his home, as you did
last year already.
As I wrote you already some time ago, my aunt sold her store, and is out of
business for the time being. As she did not get any shipments or mail from
me you for many weeks, I guess you received the announcement of the sale in
time, to make your arrangements accordingly.
Did Bill write you about Pauline - she is a rather nice girl (or as she puts
it a "young lady") - she as well as her friends and relatives are helping me
lately in many ways, and so you would do me a very great favour by writing her
a few encouraging lines.
My friend Henry - mentioned in my last letter to my wife - left already and
intends to visit my wife during the first part of June. There is a possibility that he may call on you before - I gave him Phil's old address who certainly would be able to show him to your office.

This is the letter Ludwig mailed in New York City on April 16, 1941. The back of the
letter was perfectly blank—until the British Intelligence officers at Bermuda treated
it with certain chemicals. Turn the page and you will see what the British Intelligence
officers found on the reverse side of Ludwig's letter. . . .

On April 14 was at pier 97 (Manhattan) the Norwegian M.S. TAI SHAN - 6.801 tons - gray superstr # at pier 90 was a Dutch freighter - ~ 6000 tons - gray hull - yellow superstr - cannon aft - looked very neglected # at pier 90 was the English ship SOUTHERN PRINCESS ~ 7000 tons - built like a midocean ferry steamer . two black funnels aft # at pier 88 north is still the NORMANDIE - at pier 88 south are now only the MONT EVEREST and ÎLE DE NOIR MENTIER # at pier 86 was the British freighter EMPIRE SWAN ~ 6000 tons - black hull, reddish - brown superstr - loading at pier 54 (south) was a British freighter - about 4.500 tons - black hull - yellow superstr - cannon aft - at the piers of the U.S. Lines and at pier 54 were no enemy vessels # at the piers of the Holland - America - Line and south of them were many enemy ships - among them: a Dutch tanker about 8000 tons - black hull - buff superstr # and an English freighter ~ 5000 tons - black hull - red superstr # at the pier of the GDYNIA - line was a Polnish freighter ~ 3.500 tons - 10 cm cannon aft # On Hoboken was at pier 16 an English tanker ~ 7000 tons - black hull - buff superstr # at pier 14 (Hoboken) were on April 14 two Norweg. tankers ~ 6.500 tons - at the Hoboken piers were also many other enemy ships - among them a British freighter, and also a Polnish freighter (in repair?) of ~ 3000 tons # the Dutch steamer BLOMMER - DIJK - 6855 tons - arrived here in New ...

Subjected to chemical tests by British Intelligence at Bermuda, the invisible writing on the back of Ludwig's letter to "Manuel·Alonso" (Heinrich Himmler) becomes visible.

My wife knows quite a lot about him, if you call her up, she might be able to give you also the address of his parents from whom you could get additional information. Even if he did not do much lately, he brought me during 1939 and 1940 in contact with some business people who were able to further my efforts considerably. So it would be really a very good idea if you or one of your business friends would interview Henry. Of course I did not give him any merchandise for you nor for any of our customers or friends.
As I wrote to my wife already it is advisable not to believe everything he might tell you - especially about his own business activities which were very limited indeed, as he did not want to take any risks or to work hard - like most of them imported fellows.
He expects to get a position with a similar concern for which he worked here, and he claims he has very good references. In one of my next letters I'll write you more details about Henry, who knows me since 1927 and at least some of my local business friends.
On February 5th you ordered some merchandise of which I sent you samples already last year. The # 852, 853, 854, & 857 I am sending whenever I am able to get them, as they are not so very easy to obtain now. The # 813, 842, 872, & 879 you should get regularly and in sufficient quantities, if not, please let me know about the delay immediately. The other number (861) is ordered - but so far I did not get even a sample. Sometimes I sent you and our customers also some new samples and merchandise on approval; you would greatly oblige me by writing me what you think about such numbers.
Since over half a year I am sending also regularly some merchandise which Bill ordered for you - but as I am having sometimes difficulties with him, you would do me a very great favour by letting me know at your earliest convenience whether you are really interested in such numbers as 097, 390, 191, 192, 195, 196, and 331 to 340. These I have to buy specially, and in case you want me to continue to handle such expensive merchandise, I should be obliged for any information about payment - as from Bill I can't expect any money.
One of the cheapest articles is number 487 which really is for my wife. Last year I was sending sometimes this number directly to my wife but she never received a single piece of it. Therefore you would greatly oblige as well me as my family by forwarding this number to my wife - no hurry about it.
The numbers 271 and 617 were ordered by Phil, and he wrote me last year I should send at least 271 by airmail - but he never mentioned who would pay for the postage. As it is rather high on such articles I discontinued very soon to ship anything by airmail.(outside of small articles of course).
Concerning the accident I wish to inform you that the public administrator still has Phil's belongings. The matter could have been settled already if at least one of Phil's relatives would have written me a few lines - so we don't know anything, and can't do much either. For the time being friends are taking care of the grave. In case Phil's relatives want to have the body shipped to Europe that still could be done - but I don't know whether a navicert is necessary for it. In case you or Phil's relatives want some additional information I am only to glad to give it to you - so please write about anything which should not be perfectly clear to you.
In one of my former letters I mentioned something about two friends who wish to return immediately (I should like to go back too) - as they are asking me time and again whether I could help them, you would greatly oblige me by answering (if possible by cable) as soon as possible whether and what you could do for them. It really would increase my prestige considerably, and also further business activities in many ways - if something could be done for these two friends. Of course I know (and I told them so too) that neither you nor I could do anything directly - but you certainly know somebody who would be able and willing to give the necessary advice and assistance.
The next letter will be again exclusively for my wife - but as it might contain also some information of value to you, I am taking the liberty of sending it to you, and you would oblige me by forwarding it (or the copy).

Sincerely yours, Je.

This is the second page of Ludwig's letter to "Manuel Alonso." Turn the page again, for the secret writing which was on the reverse side.

... the Ville de Liog (American Farmer) arrived at Boston from England on Wed and went out with 2,657 lbs DICHLOR BENZALCHLORIDE # in hold # 6.
British battleship MALAYA arrived here on April 7 - 9 number off St. George Staten Island - two U.S. Navy tugs (?) on each side and protected by a Coast Guard cutter # off Staten Island were also same enemy tankers # On April 7 were at the Morse Dry Docks Brooklyn, two British tankers and two enemy freighters in a pair at the U.S. Army base was the WASHINGTON and also some Staaten transports
At pier S was a steamer from the Prince-line ~ 6,500 tons ~ # an other British freighter - black hull - buff superstr. a funnel # at pier 4 (Furness-Prince line # were two British freighters # at pier 3 were 3 British and a Dutch freighter - all painted gray # A Scotchman working on an "enemy" vessel were may sited; as soon as the "enemy" vessels are getting near the American "continent" the Polish, Czech, and other foreign crew members are stocked in below-deck - and are only allowed to come on deck again after the vessels are well out on the open sea. Only trusted English sailors are permitted to go ashore pier. The reason for this precautionary measure is that too many Foreign sailors des enlist once they were on American Soil; # On the English coast US freighters have in anchor off shore because most of the English harbours are heavily damaged. In England maybe the Batteships now the foreigners are allowed to go ashore - the morale of the crews is very low - can't you do something about it? On the then passenger brutem ...

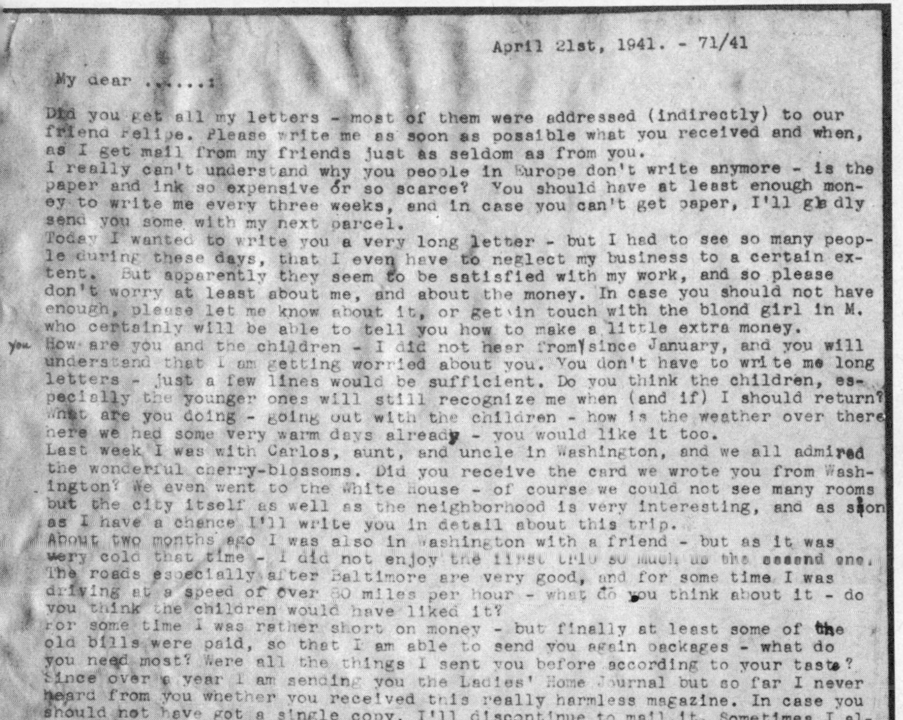

April 21st, 1941. - 71/41

My dear ......:

Did you get all my letters - most of them were addressed (indirectly) to our friend Felipe. Please write me as soon as possible what you received and when, as I get mail from my friends just as seldom as from you.
I really can't understand why you people in Europe don't write anymore - is the paper and ink so expensive or so scarce? You should have at least enough money to write me every three weeks, and in case you can't get paper, I'll gladly send you some with my next parcel.
Today I wanted to write you a very long letter - but I had to see so many people during these days, that I even have to neglect my business to a certain extent. But apparently they seem to be satisfied with my work, and so please don't worry at least about me, and about the money. In case you should not have enough, please let me know about it, or get in touch with the blond girl in M. who certainly will be able to tell you how to make a little extra money.
How are you and the children - I did not hear from you since January, and you will understand that I am getting worried about you. You don't have to write me long letters - just a few lines would be sufficient. Do you think the children, especially the younger ones will still recognize me when (and if) I should return? What are you doing - going out with the children - how is the weather over there here we had some very warm days already - you would like it too.
Last week I was with Carlos, aunt, and uncle in Washington, and we all admired the wonderful cherry-blossoms. Did you receive the card we wrote you from Washington? We even went to the White House - of course we could not see many rooms but the city itself as well as the neighborhood is very interesting, and as soon as I have a chance I'll write you in detail about this trip.
About two months ago I was also in Washington with a friend - but as it was very cold that time - I did not enjoy the first trip so much as the second one. The roads especially after Baltimore are very good, and for some time I was driving at a speed of over 80 miles per hour - what do you think about it - do you think the children would have liked it?
For some time I was rather short on money - but finally at least some of the old bills were paid, so that I am able to send you again packages - what do you need most? Were all the things I sent you before according to your taste? Since over a year I am sending you the Ladies' Home Journal but so far I never heard from you whether you received this really harmless magazine. In case you should not have got a single copy, I'll discontinue to mail it. Sometimes I also sent the Saturday Evening Post which especially for ladies is very interesting but I guess you have not enough time to read such periodicals.
Our friend Henry is leaving ... isit you early
...ot everything)
... will be able to
...nce many months,
... much easier. So
... was more interes-
... And please don't

... also but I'll
...ring you anything
... you directly.
... all? This week
...ontents for the
...t were four packag-
...ou easily will be
...aving soap for
...soaps (7 large &
...f Lifeboy soap
...of toilet soap

... to all your poor H.

PAR AVION
NEW YORK, N.Y. APR 22 1130 PM 1941 CHURCH ST. ANNEX
C.A.
VIA AIR MAIL
Miss Isabel Machado Santos
Rua Marquez da Fronteira 175
(a Campolide)
L i s b o n , Portugal

This spy letter was addressed by Ludwig in the envelope here reproduced to a "Miss Isabel Machado Santos" in Lisbon, Portugal, another Nazi "drop." Turn the page and you will see, in secret writing as developed by the British at Bermuda, Ludwig's espionage data on the reverse side.

+ their British forces arrived ready even on Iceland + The S.S. VILLE DE LIEGE.
too was sunk about April 14 - many thanks + Types of airplanes flown to Eng
216 land (continued from letter 62) - 3.) BOEING B-17C (model 299 T)

twenty were ordered by the U.S. Army to Britain on Nov 20, 40 + 13 B-17C
+ reassembled on Nov 16/41 at McChord Field, Wash. with British markings - later
some B-17C were seen at Vancouver, B.C. on route to Gandar Lake,

N.F. - arrived in England some weeks ago + seven or eight B-17C reached
North Africa till the beginning of April 41 + forty-one (41) B-17C were
delivered to the U.S. Army (without engines) till Nov 40 + during 1940 the
U.S. Army ordered ... B-17C which are apparently all delivered (part
of them to England) + B-17B - at the end of Sept 40 the U.S. Army had
54 (fifty-four) B-17B (299 M) which may be used for transports (2 to or
for Britain?) + According to British publications Boeing is since months
manufacturing B-17B which I doubt very much - apparently newer mod
as are mont - either B-17D or B-17E of which the U.S. Army had
ordered over 500 + Production of B-17 was: Sept 40 one in four days +
Oct to Jan 41 one in two days; Febr to March 41 one every day +
The Penn Central Airlines sold four 247 - D in Aug 40 and ten additional in Sept 40 to Canada for training pilots + One Boeing 3/4
was delivered to Britain Apr 41 - the second one will be ready in
June 41; and the third during summer 41 - each costs ~ one million $

recent maneuvers in Tennessee. The material included photographs of the new Garand rifle, a baby tank, a large tank, a secret anti-tank invention, and a photograph of a Navy speedboat. The Nazi spy boasted that he had obtained the last from "the Navy Department in Washington." He requested Sebold to pass on this material to Germany, and then proceeded to the real purpose of his visit.

"I want you to get me some dynamite caps and a slow-burning fuse," said Duquesne, explaining that he had "looked over" the General Electric plant at Schenectady and that he "could do the job with a slow-burning fuse."

While Duquesne outlined his plan for blowing up the General Electric plant, Sebold was unwrapping a small piece of candy. Duquesne pointed to the candy and said, "If that piece of candy was broken in two," he took the candy from Sebold and demonstrated, "and some combustible phosphorus were placed inside it, it would make a very effective, though small, incendiary bomb."

"But a better bomb," said Duquesne, "could be made from chiclets." By chewing the gum thoroughly, he said, and then folding it around a certain phosphorous compound, one would have an effective incendiary device which could then be planted on docks or elsewhere "through a hole in the pocket of one's coat."

Duquesne was very proud of his "chiclet bomb." He told Sebold he had employed the device with great success in the past. Among its advantages, he added, were its "inability to explode in temperatures under 72 degrees" and the fact that it could be planted "while speaking to the boss."

However, in spite of all these novelties, Duquesne confessed to a partiality for the traditional "lead-pipe type of bomb." In the end, it was more reliable and gave better results. He repeated his request for some dynamite caps and the slow-burning fuse. . . .

Duquesne's list of bombs, which he obligingly recited that evening for the benefit of the concealed FBI agents, by no means exhausts the number of unusual devices used by the saboteurs. The files of the FBI are filled with descriptions of extraordinary devices used by saboteurs to start fires, set off explosions or cause the wreckage of intricate machinery.

Devices for starting fires have always been in high favor with saboteurs. Arson accomplishes at one stroke three most important ends: it destroys the object of attack; it is likely to obliterate any clues by which the saboteur might be apprehended; and it is demoralizing. Thus there are a host of devices for starting fires. The most widely used of all these devices was invented by a German chemist in the United States during the last World War.

Early in 1915, Dr. Walter T. Scheele was assigned by the German Government to undertake research into explosives and chemicals which could be utilized by von Papen's saboteurs. Dr. Scheele had a perfect front for his work in the New Jersey Agricultural Chemical Company of which he was president. After a brief period of experimentation, Dr. Scheele quickly evolved what, in various improved forms, is still the saboteur's favorite weapon: the "fiery cigar."

The original Scheele fiery cigar consisted of a lead tube with a copper disc which separated sulphuric acid from either potassium chlorate or picric acid. For incendiary purposes, Dr. Scheele usually used picric acid, and the ends of the tube were sealed with wax. The "cigar" started to work as soon as it was filled, for the sulphuric acid immediately began eating its way through the copper disc. When the sulphuric acid reached the picric acid, a chemical reaction took place which resulted in the emission of a white, hot flame.

This was the incendiary device which von Papen's "firebugs" used to start the great conflagrations in American munitions plants in 1915-17. It was also used by the German saboteurs to start fires in ships loaded with war-aid for the Allies.

An improvement on the fiery cigar was the "fire-pencil," an ordinary pencil from which the lead had been removed and a glass tube filled with incendiary chemicals substituted in its place.

The fire-pencil is still in use; but thermite revolutionized the primitive instrument of Dr. Scheele. Thermite generates on ignition an almost instantaneous heat of some 3,000 degrees. It was loaded into the Nazi fire-bombs which started the huge city-wide fires in London in the fall of 1940. Flames generated by thermite cannot be extinguished by any of the usual fire-fighting methods. Water poured on thermite causes it to explode, and thus increases the incendiary effect.

The modern thermite fire-pencil, first used by saboteurs in the United States in 1939, consists of a thin aluminum tube loaded with the incendiary material. Externally identical in every way with an ordinary pen or pencil, two or three of these instruments can be carried in the saboteur's pocket without attracting any undue attention. The thermite pencil can be regulated to go off at any time; the process is started simply by breaking the tip. The intense heat generated by the thermite pencil usually completely destroys all traces of the substance of its case, thus making it almost impossible to prove that an act of sabotage has taken place. A favorite method of using the thermite pencil is to leave it in the pocket of a coat, sometimes soaked in oil and always left hanging near inflammable material.

Another incendiary device was discovered in 1941 when the FBI began investigating a series of mysterious fires on ships carrying lend-lease materials to Britain and China. This device resembles an ordinary paper envelope such as anyone might openly toss into a wastebasket or place in a ship's mailbag. But this "envelope" was found to contain two sections, with certain chemicals in each section. When the chemicals mingled, intense fire started.

Then there is the "Zepplinite," an incendiary device invented during the last World War, but recently adopted for the starting of forest fires near Army camps and warehouses. The Zepplinite is a tiny balloon, usually filled with hydrogen gas, to which a delayed-action fire-pencil is attached. The balloon is released when winds are favorable, and it descends many miles from the point of release. A Zepplinite was found by the New Hampshire state police on May 1, 1942, during an investigation of a series of destructive forest fires which had suddenly broken out in the New England area, destroying much property, and timber already cut for army use.

Next to fires, explosions are most popular among the saboteurs. The traditional explosive device is a time-bomb such as was used by the terrorists who attempted to destroy the British Pavilion at the New York World's Fair on July 4, 1940. All kinds of variations of the time-bomb have been found by the FBI. One of the cleverest is an exact duplicate of a can of food. It is intended particularly for ships' galleys, but it can be equally effective in a factory commissary. When the cook opens it, it explodes.

Another variation of the time-bomb, used by saboteurs in the United States, is the "cabbage-bomb." In this case, the time-bomb is camouflaged to represent a vegetable, usually a head of cabbage. One of these "cabbage-bombs" was found in a ship's larder on the West Coast in 1941. Still another variation, in the shape and color of a piece of coal, was found about the same time on a ship in an East Coast port.

The "cracker" is one of the most recently discovered sabotage devices being used by Axis saboteurs in the United States. It is a small instrument resembling an ordinary spark plug. When screwed into an airplane motor, it permits the plane to take off and acquire considerable altitude before exploding through extreme heat. The resultant blast is large enough to ignite the gasoline fumes, and usually causes the destruction of the plane and its occupants.

Sabotage of industrial goods at the source of production is also carried on by the use of many devices evolved by painstaking experimentation in Berlin and Tokyo. Special acids have been developed which cause the rapid deterioration of cloth. Since such vital items as parachutes, airplane fabrics, machine belts, machine-gun clips, uniforms and army blankets are made wholly or largely of cloth, these acids, according to a report by J. Edgar Hoover, are coming into considerable favor with adept saboteurs.

Poisons were first utilized on a large scale by von Papen's saboteurs in the last World War when they attempted to poison canned foodstuffs being prepared for the Allies. In 1940 the FBI found that sugar stores aboard a large American steamship had been treated with a poisonous chemical ordinarily used as a water softener or cleaning agent. The officers and crew, who were using the sugar, began to suffer from gastro-intestinal ailments which led to the FBI investigation. Luckily, the poison was detected in time, and no one suffered any serious injuries.

All sorts of devices are used to ruin military equipment. In gun-foundries, for instance, the saboteur has only to spill a little hot coffee or tea down the cooling barrel of a big gun. So finely tempered is the steel used in these cannons that, after they have been sabotaged in this way, the barrels will crack upon the first discharge. At the Glenn L. Martin bomber plant in Baltimore, in October 1941, a Nazi saboteur was caught who had damaged a number of planes by cutting their communication lines, placing sections of rubber tubing in the gasoline tanks, and crushing metal tubing.

The word sabotage itself derives from the sabots (wooden shoes) which nineteenth century French weavers flung into their looms to smash the machinery which they believed would rob them of their jobs. Wrecking machinery remains one of the most common forms of sabotage. There are in-

numerable ways in which this can be accomplished. In November 1940, for example, emery dust and ground glass were
found in costly drills and lathes at the Todd shipyards in
Seattle, Washington. At the Federal Shipbuilding and Drydock Company in Kearney, New Jersey, Frederick W. Bilgeshouse, a German-born worker, was arrested in May 1942,
on charges of deliberately ruining valuable dies and punches.
Fellow workers reported having seen him damage dies by
loosening the set screws holding them, as well as by placing
a putty knife across dies as the press punch was being lowered.
A Federal Jury found Bilgeshouse guilty of sabotage.

A no less effective device for sabotaging war production is
that of stirring up dissension among the workers and thus
cutting down their output. The Hamburg-trained Nazi saboteur, Carl Alfred Reuper, was sent into the United States in
1939 with orders "to create discord and bad feeling" among
defense workers.

Carl Alfred Reuper was not the only Nazi saboteur in this
field.

V. On the Production Line

One of the purposes for which the German American Bund
was organized was to help the Nazis recruit spies and saboteurs
in key jobs in American industries. The Bund Fuehrer Fritz
Kuhn had once been a chemist at the Ford Motor Company
in Detroit. Many of his followers were pro-Nazi German-
Americans employed in important factories. Neil Howard
Ness, a former Bund member in Los Angeles, told a Congressional investigatory committee that at secret Bund meetings "we discussed what we would do towards helping Germany, such as blowing up waterworks and munitions plants
and docks . . . we planned on paralyzing the Pacific Coast from
Seattle to San Diego."

Many Bundists were trained to make use of explosive and incendiary sabotage devices. They were also taught to carry on more subtle forms of sabotage on the production lines. Two favorite Bundist devices for interrupting the supply of war materials are artificially incited slowdowns and strikes. In order to sabotage production by these means, the saboteurs must first gain some influence among the workers, or occupy strategic positions within the plants. The Nazis had taken care of that too.

In April 1942, four months after the Axis declared war on America, the former New Jersey state-treasurer of the German American Bund, Herman von Busch, was found to be holding a supervisory position in the vital Harrison, New Jersey, gas works of the Public Service Corporation, which was supplying gas to a large section of New Jersey's defense industries. Von Busch was thus in a perfect spot to commit sabotage. He was not alone. The chief still operator at the Harrison gas works was Wilhelm Koehne, also a member of the Bund. The general foreman was Fritz Kunze, who had been dismissed from the same plant in World War I because of his pro-German sympathies. John Wilkins, a blower-room operator at the Harrison works was found to have a son in the Nazi Army; and the chief purification operator, George Haag, openly kept a large picture of Adolf Hitler at his work bench. These Bundists and pro-Nazis had been provoking disputes and discontent among the Harrison workers, thus interfering with production. They were ordered 'dismissed from the gas works after a New York newspaper exposed their pro-Nazi records and printed the complaints of their fellow-workers.

This state of affairs was found to be duplicated in other important industrial plants. At the New York Liquidometer plant, Bundists on the production line had organized a slowdown to interrupt the flow of warship and aircraft parts urgently required by the United States Army and Navy.

While armed guards were patrolling the outside of the
Liquidometer plant to prevent entry of spies and saboteurs,
the Nazi Bundists were actually hampering production inside
the plant. The first-class machinist Julius Weber, who served
on a German minesweeper during World War I, was publicly
giving the Nazi salute and telling his fellow-workers, "Hitler
is the greatest man in the world." The department supervisor
John Blaeser was telling the fifteen men working under him,
"Don't worry about production so much," and spreading pro-
Hitler, anti-American propaganda. The foreman Joseph Feilzer sat under a red,white and blue poster which proclaimed,
"*Time is Short*," reading a German newspaper during working hours. On March 20, 1942, when two new men were
assigned to Feilzer's department and were waiting to be put
to work, Feilzer said, "Let them wait. I have all day." Certain
vital plane parts produced at the Liquidometer plant under
these conditions were later found to be defective—although
stamped with the official naval stamp which is used to indi-
cate the product is in good working order.

Similar conditions prevailed at the Brewster Aeronautical
plants where Bundists openly heiled Hitler, wandered
around the departments chatting in German during working
hours and did everything they could to slow down production. On April 20, 1942, the United States Navy was forced
to take over the four Brewster plants which had failed to
deliver a single plane to the United States armed forces. Five
supervisory employees and twenty-seven other workers were
discharged after Federal authorities had investigated their
pro-Axis records.*

To secure effective control of the American labor movement has long been the aim of Nazi agents in the United

---

* One Bundist in a Brewster plant was found to have purchased over $7,500
worth of *Rueckwanderer Marks,* which were special marks sold at a discount by
Nazi Germany, deposited to the purchaser's account in a German bank and
usable only in the Third Reich.

States. The first attempts were staged in the strategic industrial center of Detroit early in 1939. There the German American Bund helped to form an organization called the National Workers League, the chief object of which was to recruit large numbers of workers from the auto plants. The Nazis hoped that by involving sufficient auto workers in this organization they would soon dominate the unions in the industry and, eventually, be able to sabotage production through slowdowns and strikes.

Parker Sage, an American citizen who had for some time been closely associated with the German American Bund, was chosen to head this "labor" organization in Detroit. Sage had been previously expelled from the Chevrolet Gear and Axle local of the United Automobile Workers (CIO) on charges of being a professional labor spy.

One morning in the spring of 1939, workers in the Packard plant found that thousands of little cards had been mysteriously placed in their lockers and along the production lines. The cards carried printed messages urging "Christian American workers" to join the National Workers League for the purpose of "Protecting the Jobs, Happiness and Welfare of the American Gentile."

This propaganda barrage was followed up by a succession of public rallies at which Sage was the chief speaker. Workers were urged to join the National Workers League to fight the "Jew bosses." Aiming his propaganda at the many Detroit workers who had migrated from the South, Sage declared that Negroes were "being smuggled into Detroit" in a plot to lower the wages of the auto workers. "America for Americans!" the pro-Nazi propagandist Parker Sage shouted to his audiences.

For a while, Sage's campaign met with a certain amount of success. During 1940 his organization penetrated the Ford, Chrysler, Plymouth, Hudson and Packard auto plants, as well as the U. S. Rubber, Murray Body and Motor Product companies. Much discord and dissension was stirred up among the workers before the true character of Parker Sage and his National Workers League became apparent.

When the auto workers themselves finally recognized what lay behind Sage's agitation, they launched a vigorous counter-campaign through their union locals to expose the National Workers League as a Nazi-inspired fifth column. Thereafter, Sage was forced to restrict his organizational activity, and to limit his disruptive efforts to spreading pro-Axis racial propaganda among the workers. He was still kept supplied with enough money to carry on his propaganda work on a large scale. During the last six months of 1941, his National Workers League spent $15,000 on pro-Axis propaganda.

The failure of the National Workers League to grow into a powerful pro-Nazi "labor" organization did not end the plot to control the American labor movement. The Nazis turned to those native fascist organizations which in their opinion exercised some influence among the workers. A Nazi agent approached Hiram W. Evans, the Imperial Wizard of the Ku Klux Klan, with an offer of $75,000 for a controlling voice in Klan affairs. Evans reportedly rejected this offer. After Evans was succeeded as Imperial Wizard by James A. Colescott, hooded Klansmen entered into collaboration with the German American Bund. This new relationship was cemented at the joint Bund-Klan rally held at the Nazi Camp Nordland at Andover, New Jersey, on August 18, 1940.

The Klan abruptly reversed its traditional line of open opposition to organized labor. Imperial Wizard Colescott told his followers:

> Get into every [union] local, every department, division and plant. . . . The UAW and CIO leaders are all Reds. We must Americanize them through Kluxing every white, Protestant, Gentile American.

The Klan invasion of the labor movement was under way. After Pearl Harbor, the Klan activity in this field became intensified, especially in Detroit. Here, working with Nazi agents, the Klansmen tried to capture executive positions in the auto workers union. They spread pro-Axis racial propaganda aimed at disrupting the unions and succeeded in provoking slowdowns and occasional wildcat strikes to sabotage war production. Inside the plants and at union meetings, the Klansmen campaigned against the union's Victory Program and tried to stop the sale of United States Defense Bonds.

The Klan penetration assumed particularly serious proportions in the Packard plant where marine and aircraft motors were being manufactured for the United States and British armed forces. The Klan put on a high-pressure lavishly-financed recruiting campaign among the 15,000 Packard workers. The situation became so bad that on April 12, 1942, the Trial Board of the UAW Packard local took action and expelled a Klansman named Frank Buehrle from the union. He was found guilty of "actively building the Ku Klux Klan" in the Packard plant and of stirring up dissension and sabotaging the morale of the Packard workers.

Perhaps the most successful act of Klan sabotage in Detroit was the riot which it incited at the Sojourner Truth Settlement, a defense housing project designated by the United States Housing Authority for occupancy by Negro defense workers and their families. At clandestine meetings, the Klansmen received orders to keep the Negro workers from entering their new homes. The National Workers League cooperated with the Klan in preparing and staging the subsequent riot in which scores of people were injured.

The purpose behind the Klan-incited riot was made doubly clear when from Berlin and Tokyo lurid accounts of the affair were broadcast to India and South America. The Axis radio commentators said the Sojourner Truth riot showed the discrimination against colored people within the democracies. Pamphlets following the same propaganda line were distributed among Negro defense workers in Detroit. Negro members of the auto workers union charged that Japanese agents were collaborating with the Nazis in seeking to turn them against the war effort and to recruit them as propagandists in the factories.

CHAPTER THREE

SABOTAGE BY CARTEL

During the First World War, von Papen's ablest associate and rival—for the political underworld has its rivalries, too—was Captain Franz von Rintelen whose motto went, *"Ich kaufe was ich kann; alles andere schlage ich kaput!"* ("I'll buy what I can, and blow up what I can't!").

As for the "blowing up," von Rintelen personally claims responsibility for the sabotage of some thirty-six American and Allied ships loaded with war materials. Von Rintelen also claims to have conceived the first large scale plan of economic sabotage by creation of artificial scarcities. Actually, the credit for this sabotage technique should go to Dr. Heinrich Albert, the ruthless little mild-mannered Commercial Attaché at the Washington Embassy. . . .

Equipped with a forged Swiss passport, a $500,000 credit note, an impeccable Oxford English accent, and a super-secret code concealed in two tiny glycerine pellets (for swallowing in an emergency), von Rintelen landed in the United States on March 22, 1915. He proceeded to put into effect the first half of his motto: "I'll buy what I can."

Von Rintelen's plan was simply to buy up vast quantities of munitions in the United States, and so to keep the American supplies from the Allies. He talked it over with the mild little German Commercial Attaché, Dr. Heinrich Albert. To Von Rintelen's surprise, Dr. Albert had already put such a scheme into operation in the key munitions center of Bridgeport, Connecticut.

Just nine days before von Rintelen arrived in the United States, Dr. Albert had created a large fake munitions con-

53

cern, the Bridgeport Projectile Company, which he incorporated with funds supplied by the German Foreign Office. Through his secret service channels in Washington, Dr. Albert spread the false information that the Bridgeport Projectile Company was a British-financed corporation. The object of the fake munitions concern was to tie up urgently needed machinery, machine tools, powder and other supplies.

The wily Dr. Albert, who was kept well informed by his trade investigators and secret agents on the production-rates and available stocks of war products required by the Allies, was purchasing vital materials essential to the war industries. Each month, for example, he was buying up fifty tons of liquid chlorine. As the Allies had only a small chlorine factory in France and an even smaller one in England, these purchases were sufficient to embarrass the Allies seriously. Dr. Albert also succeeded in buying up considerable stocks of another much-needed product: carbolic acid.

Dr. Albert's plan was exposed by the United States secret service, and the Commercial Attaché was expelled along with von Papen from the United States.* Von Rintelen remained behind, posing as a British businessman.

Operating out of the downtown New York firm of E. V. Gibbons, Inc., and supplied with unlimited funds by the German Foreign Office, von Rintelen began buying up large amounts of ammunition in the hope of creating a serious scarcity. However, he found it was impossible to divert sufficient quantities of American supplies really to hurt the Allies. The daily production of munitions in the United States was so great that von Rintelen discovered, as he later confessed, "If I had bought up the market on Tuesday there would

---

* In the spring of 1940 Dr. Albert's law partner, Dr. Alois G. Westrick, arrived in the United States from Nazi Germany (via Japan) to carry out assignments of economic sabotage almost identical to those undertaken by Dr. Albert in World War I. Dr. Westrick was exposed by the *New York Herald-Tribune,* and he left the country in the summer of 1940.

still have been an enormous fresh supply on Wednesday. . . ."

Von Rintelen soon abandoned his schemes of economic
sabotage and returned to the traditional time-bomb and fire-
pencil. But von Rintelen's motto was not forgotten. *"Ich kaufe
was ich kann; alles andere schlage ich kaput!"* was destined
to become the official economic policy of the Third Reich. . . .

No incendiary device or high explosive, however destructive, can wipe out an entire branch of industry. Yet this is
precisely what the Nazi economic saboteurs of World War II
tried to accomplish in the United States. They actually
"bought up" whole industries and so diverted essential products from the armed forces of the United States and its Allies.
The Nazis achieved this colossal economic sabotage through
their ruthless manipulation of international partnerships,
cartels and patent pools.

American businessmen, who did business with German
firms, were caught in a trap of swindling and commercial ruth-
lessness backed by all the economic might of Nazi power.
Old-established American corporations, lured into partnerships, patent pools and cartels with German trusts, found
themselves the unwitting puppets of the Nazi Government,
which used them, without their own knowledge and even
against their own interests, as fronts for Nazi espionage and
economic sabotage in the United States and in South America.
By means of these international agreements, the Nazis were
able to bring about drastic shortages of vital war materials—
such as military optical instruments, synthetic oil and rubber
—in the United States.

Most of the cartel agreements were formed between American and German firms long before Hitler came to power.
The cartel which made possible the Nazi sabotage of American
production of military optical instruments was formed back
in 1921 between Bausch and Lomb Optical Company of

Rochester, New York, and Carl Zeiss of Jena, Germany. The agreement gave Bausch and Lomb the American monopoly rights on patents for the production of such vital war items as bombsights, range-finders, periscopes, altimeters, torpedo directors, gunsights and telescopes. But the agreement also stipulated that:

> Bausch and Lomb's military department was to be headed by a person acceptable to the Germans;
> Bausch and Lomb was to pay royalties to the Germans on all military optical goods, including sales to the United States Government.*

These arrangements enabled the Nazis, when they came to power in Germany, to determine what the United States Army and Navy were buying in the way of military optical instruments. The Nazis also had a controlling influence in American production. When the British and French Governments tried to order $1,500,000 worth of range-finders and other instruments from Bausch and Lomb in 1935, the American company turned down the orders. The United States Department of Justice when it acted to break the cartel in 1940, found that these agreements with the Nazis had prevented the United States from building up a military optical industry with sufficient plants and skilled men to meet the war emergency.

Further evidence of Nazi economic sabotage of American war industry was spread on the record of the Senate Patents Committee in April 1942. Some of the evidence concerned tetracene, a chemical compound used as the priming in machine gun, rifle and pistol ammunition. Non-poisonous to handle, non-corrosive and inexpensive, tetracene gets results vastly superior to other priming materials.

------

* The sources for these facts and those that follow are public records of the Department of Justice, the Senate Patents Committee and the Senate Truman Committee investigating the National Defense Program.

Tetracene was invented in Germany and patented in the United States in 1922. The patent was sold in 1929 to Remington Arms which was persuaded to enter into a cartel agreement with the giant German trust, I. G. Farbenindustrie. As part of this cartel agreement, Remington Arms promised its German partner:

> not to license the United States Government to make tetracene ammunition in its own arsenals unless the Germans approved the arrangement;
> not to sell any of this new ammunition to countries within the British Empire.

The Germans also induced Remington Arms to promise:

> to pay royalties to the Germans even on ammunition sold to the United States Government in time of war;
> to make statements to the Germans covering the extent of American production of the ammunition.

In February 1941, the A. C. Spark Plug Company went to Remington Arms for aid in making machine guns for the United States Government. A. C. Spark Plug wanted tetracene priming for the guns because it was non-poisonous to handle and non-corrosive, and because its use would "eliminate the work and expense" of the barrel cleaning necessary when the older types of chlorate priming were used. A. C. Spark Plug was informed by the Remington Arms attorney that they would be permitted the use of tetracene, providing this priming was not used in "ammunition sold to the British Government or to any of the countries of the British Empire." The Remington Arms attorney said that the German agreement prohibited sales to the British countries. His memorandum was dated February 10, 1941, more than seventeen months after the war began. Even at the time of the writing of this book, despite the vast superiority of tetracene ammunition, it has not yet been generally adopted by the United States armed forces because of the Nazi economic sabotage. . . .

The same story can be told of beryllium, the "magic metal," two per cent of which mixed with copper makes a metal stronger than most steels; combined with steel, it is almost unbreakable.

Germany was the first to recognize the value of beryllium alloys. By 1938 the Nazis were using 15,000 beryllium bushings on plane propellers. They showed no sign of wear after 12,000 hours. Ordinary bushings last only 300 hours.

By 1934 the Beryllium Corporation of America had independently developed the beryllium alloy process. Three years later the Beryllium Corporation entered into an agreement with the German firm of Seimens and Halske. This agreement gave the American company the exclusive right to produce beryllium for America, while the Nazis reserved exclusive rights for Europe, including England. It caused artificially high prices and limited production in America, which was what the Nazis wanted. It also enabled the Nazis, after the war started in 1939, to order their American partner to refuse to ship any products to England.

Magnesium is a vital war metal one-third lighter than aluminum. It is made from sea water and readily available ores. Documents seized by the Senate Patents Committee from the files of ALCOA (Aluminum Corporation of America) showed that, by virtue of a clever cartel agreement, the Nazis held American annual production of magnesium down to 2,500 tons before 1940, while German production soared to several times that level. In 1940, one year after the outbreak of War, the Nazis produced 19,000 tons of magnesium, or almost half the world's output; that same year America produced 5,680 tons, or 14 per cent. The agreement which ALCOA had with the Nazi trust I. G. Farbenindustrie granted ALCOA a monopoly of the American market but gave the Nazis veto power over American production.

By means of a similar agreement with ALCOA, American aluminum production was drastically restricted, so that when the war came Germany was producing one-third to one-half more aluminum than America.

The same was true of tungsten carbide *(Carboloy)* which is a vital element in machine tool manufacture. According to the Department of Justice, an agreement between General Electric and the German Krupp trust gave the Nazis veto power over American production. Nazi Germany was producing twenty times as much tungsten carbide as America in 1940.

Back in 1930, Standard Oil of New Jersey and the German trust I. G. Farbenindustrie organized a chemical company in America called Jasco, Inc., which was to develop and exploit new processes for making chemical products out of natural and refinery gases. Although this joint enterprise was ostensibly a partnership, it was in fact under German control. Jasco built a plant at Baton Rouge, Louisiana, and, as a result of joint German-American experimentation, a new process for making acetylene was developed. Acetylene is a component of acetyl acid used as a raw material in making rayons, plastics, film, paints, varnishes, pharmaceuticals and dyestuffs. The new process resulted in what Standard regarded as the cheapest and best product in the world. Under German orders, the experimentation at Baton Rouge was discontinued in 1935, and all further work was carried on in Germany. The American company was not even kept informed of subsequent improvements, and it was prohibited from conducting further experiments here. On September 6, 1939, immediately after the outbreak of war in Europe, the Germans ordered Standard to dismantle the plant at Baton Rouge. Standard tried vainly to get I. G. Farbenindustrie's consent to make a variety of different products at Baton Rouge, but the Germans refused, and the plant was dismantled. "The German Government, through I. G. Farben, was undoubtedly anxious to facilitate the destruction of any plant in the United States which might be useful in war production," an official of the United States Department of Justice told the Senate Patents Committee in 1942, commenting on this typical example of Nazi economic sabotage in America.

According to evidence submitted to the Senate Truman Committee in March 1942 by Thurman Arnold, Assistant Attorney General in charge of anti-trust prosecutions, development of synthetic rubber and oil production in the United States was delayed because of German agreements with Standard Oil of New Jersey. Thurman Arnold disclosed that Standard had helped the Nazis in 1939 to design their plant facilities in Germany for manufacturing synthetic aviation gasoline, while at the same time the American company was induced to withhold essential information necessary for the building of synthetic oil and rubber plants in the United States. Standard defended itself against these charges, but on the basis of documents subpoenaed from Standard's files, the Truman Committee reported: ". . . the conclusion remains that whether or not Standard so wished, it put itself in the position of furnishing information to the German company, through which it would be available to the German Government, while withholding the same information from the United States."

The cartels, partnerships and patent pools were used by the German Government as espionage channels, which enabled the High Command to learn many of the military secrets of the United States.

Chemnyco, Inc., of New York, an American representative of I. G. Farbenindustrie served as an agent for collecting all manner of information on American war production useful

to the German Government and to Nazi saboteurs in the
United States. When Treasury agents raided the New York
headquarters of Chemnyco in February 1942, they found a
complete espionage file "on all American industry" in the
Nazi company's vaults.*

Bendix Aviation, a General Motors affiliate, entered into a
patent pool with the Robert Bosch Company of Stuttgart,
Germany, under which the American company was obli-
gated to send information of possible military value to the
Nazis as late as May, 1940. The letter containing this information was intercepted by the British naval authorities. In
1942 the House Naval Affairs Committee read into its records
this Bendix inter-office memorandum, which had been sent
by company official R. P. Lansing to his colleague, N. B.
McLeah:

> How do we send (blueprints) to Bosch, Germany? (By air?)
> I suppose you know boat mail was captured and showed up
> in England?

The parentheses were in the original memorandum.

On April 22, 1942, President Roosevelt moved to free
American war production from the sabotage of Nazi cartels
and patent pools. He ordered the seizure of all patents controlled directly or indirectly by the enemy.

On that same day the Senate Patents Committee began
considering legislation prohibiting any future secret international cartels.

---

* This was quite possibly a copy of the *Index of American Industry,* referred to
on page 23, which the FBI had learned about in 1941 through the indiscretion
of a certain "foreign industrialist."

CHAPTER FOUR

TOKYO TERRORISTS

I. The Claws of the Black Dragon

The city of Los Angeles, together with its war industries, is dependent on a water supply reaching it by means of an aqueduct system. Sabotage of this system would effectively cripple the chief city of the West Coast. . . .

On June 29, 1934, Mr. H. A. Norman, the chief engineer and general manager of the Los Angeles Bureau of Water Works and Supply, received a polite request from the Japanese Consulate for information about the Los Angeles water supply system. The Chancellor at the Japanese Consulate, K. Kagayama, wrote:

> If you have any books or pamphlets covering the water system of this city, we shall appreciate it very much if you will kindly forward us copies of same.

More specifically, Kagayama added:

> We should like to have information that will explain every point of the system, including reservoirs, quantity of water supply, number of consumers, filtering, purifying, pipe pressure, kinds of pipes used, office organization, number of employees, etc. . . .

As soon as he received this letter, Mr. Norman consulted the U. S. Department of Justice and military authorities. Kagayama got no information from Mr. Norman. . . .

CONSULATE OF JAPAN
820 CHAMBER OF COMMERCE BLDG
1151 SOUTH BROADWAY
LOS ANGELES, CALIFORNIA

June 28, 1934.

Mr. H. A. Van Norman,
Chief Engineer and General Manager,
Bureau of Water Works & Supply,
209 South Broadway Street,
Los Angeles, California.

Dear Sir:

If you have any books or pamphlets covering the entire water system of this city, we shall appreciate it very much if you will kindly forward us copies of same.

We should like to have information that will explain every point of the system, including reservoirs, quantity of water supply, number of consumers, filtering, purifying, pipe pressure, kind of pipes used, office organization, number of employees, etc.

We shall be glad to defray any expenses in this connection.

Thanking you for your kind attention to our request, we are

Very truly yours,

CONSULATE OF JAPAN

By: K. Kaguyama,
Chancellor.

HC

A polite request from the Japanese Consulate for certain highly important information.

But the Japanese were not to be so easily put off. There was already one Japanese-American on the payroll of the Los Angeles Department of Water and Power. Soon after Kagayama's request for information had been turned down, twelve more Japanese-Americans were placed on the Department's payroll. According to subsequent Congressional investigation, Kiyoshi P. Okura, a Japanese-American who for some time was chief examiner of the Los Angeles Civil Service Commission, helped place them there. . . .

One night in Los Angeles, a few years ago, there was a street-fight. When the police arrived they found a wounded Japanese lying in the gutter. He had been stabbed in the stomach. The police arrested another Japanese on suspicion that he was the assailant. It turned out that both men were members of the Black Dragon, a secret Japanese terrorist society which, in addition to its functions in Asia, carried on espionage-sabotage work in the United States. In the locked bedroom of Buichiri Abo, the man charged with the street stabbing, the Los Angeles police found a short-wave radio set, expertly-drawn maps of Hawaii's fortifications—and the complete plans of the Los Angeles water supply system. . . .

The German and Japanese Intelligence Services began an intimate collaboration shortly after Hitler came to power. In 1934, Colonel Walther Nicolai sent his *Section IIIB* aide, Major General Eugene Ott, to Tokyo. Major General Ott was one of Germany's most resourceful secret service men. He helped the Japanese to reorganize their espionage and sabotage activities in Asia and the Americas. El Salvador became the chief base for joint Nazi-Japanese operations in the Western Hemisphere. Ott, who later became the German Ambassador to Tokyo, took a special interest in the work of the powerful Society of the Black Dragon, which by 1936 was virtually in control of the Japanese Government and High Command.

An emissary of the Black Dragon Society came to Los Angeles in 1937. Working out of the Japanese Consulate, this man, whose name was Tadaaiki Iizuka, organized the Japanese Military Servicemen's League, which by 1941 had 7,200 members, and the Imperial Comradeship League, which by 1941 had 4,800 members. Both of these organizations were controlled by the Black Dragon, and served as schools of espionage and sabotage. They operated chiefly among the Japanese-American communities on the West Coast and in Hawaii.

In the years before Pearl Harbor, potential Japanese saboteurs moved in by droves to take up residence and carry on business in the immediate vicinity of important United States military establishments, oil storage tanks, oil wells, harbors and forts in California. On the strategic Terminal Island at the entrance to Los Angeles Harbor, 3,000 Japanese were living. After December 7, when FBI agents made a series of raids on these Japanese communities, they uncovered caches of guns, ammunition, explosives, maps, charts, highpower cameras, signaling devices, short-wave radios, and other equipment of spies and saboteurs.

Following the Nazi pattern, the Japanese Consulates in American cities had been converted at an early date into centers of espionage-sabotage activity. The Consulates on the West Coast were in constant communication with the innumerable Japanese "fishing" fleets which infested the United States Pacific waters. These "fishing" fleets, equipped with powerful engines, short-wave radios and intricate sounding devices, were officered by agents of the Japanese Naval Intelligence, and were used for gathering data helpful for sabotage and for possible future military invasion of United States territory.

A constant stream of information was fed into the offices of the Japanese Army and Naval Intelligence by Japanese export and import companies in the United States. These companies accumulated information on the location of essential supplies of war materials and prepared detailed reports helpful to saboteurs.

On June 25, 1940, Mr. Russell Palmer of the trade journal *Petroleum World* received a typical request for "information" from the manager of the San Francisco branch of Mitsubishi Shoji Kaisha, Ltd. The manager of the Japanese firm politely wrote:

> In reference to many of your articles concerning alkylation and iso-octane plants, will you be kind enough to let us know for our information the following:
>
> (1) Name of companies that have alkylation and/or iso-octane plants in California, its capacity (each) and date of construction.
> (2) By whom and how many are in the process of being constructed in California, when will it be completed and its capacities.

The Japanese Intelligence had long recognized the necessity of hiring non-Japanese agents for underground work in the United States. This was made clear enough to Americans by newspaper headlines in 1936.

On July 2, 1936, Harry T. Thompson, a former yeoman of the United States Navy, was tried and found guilty of having sold United States naval secrets to a Japanese agent. Thompson was sentenced to fifteen years imprisonment.

On July 14, 1936, Lieutenant Commander John Somer Farnsworth was arrested on charges of selling confidential United States Navy documents to the Japanese Embassy in Washington. Farnsworth was sentenced to from four to twelve years in the penitentiary. There were a number of similar cases.

There was the case of the Japanese-American, Torichi Kono, who for eighteen years had been secretary and valet

June 25, 1940   NO. PET-484

Mr. Russell Palmer
Petroleum World
412 W. Sixth Street
Los Angeles, Calif.

Dear Sir:

      We are subscribers to your "PETROLEUM WORLD" and
find the magazine very interesting and of value. We hope
that you will continue to make the magazine of more value by
your constant researches.

      In reference to many of your articles concerning
alkylation and iso-octane plants, will you be kind enough to
let us know for our information the following:

   (1) Name of companies that have alkylation and/or
       iso-octane plants in California, its capacity
       (each) and date of construction.

   (2) By whom and how many are in the process of
       being constructed in California, when will it
       be completed and its capacities.

      You will kindly let us know as soon as possible,
if such information is available. Even an estimate of the
capacity for the above will be appreciated.

      Yours truly,

      MITSUBISHI SHOJI KAISHA, LTD.

TI:MK   MANAGER, SAN FRANCISCO BRANCH

According to the report of a congressional investigatory committee, this is how
a Japanese business firm in the United States sought information useful to the
Tokyo Military Intelligence and to Tokyo's saboteurs in this country.

to Charles Chaplin. Kono worked with Commander Itaru Tatibana, an agent of the Japanese Naval Intelligence who was posing as a student at the University of California. During the early part of 1941, Kono and Tatibana enlisted the services of a former yeoman of the United States Navy. They financed this ex-yeoman on two trips to Pearl Harbor where he secured for them certain information concerning the U.S.S. *Pennsylvania*, flagship of the United States Fleet, and other important war vessels. The plot was exposed on June 10, 1941, when Federal agents arrested the spies.

In spite of such setbacks, Tokyo secured enough information from its spies in the United States to prepare, just before Pearl Harbor, a 200-page handbook filled with photographs and technical details about the United States Navy. Among other things, the handbook contained a large map showing the location of all major United States airfields and bases, including those recently acquired from Britain. This handbook was distributed to Japanese agents in the United States. Congressional investigators later described it as "the answer to a saboteur's dream."

The Japanese spies and saboteurs, firmly entrenched through their Black Dragon Leagues and other Tokyo-controlled organizations in Japanese-American communities on the West Coast, received a major setback on February 20, 1942. On that date President Roosevelt issued an executive order authorizing the Army to evacuate anyone, alien or citizen, from military areas. A mass evacuation of Japanese and Japanese-Americans was found necessary, and was undertaken throughout the entire West Coast area.

After the mass evacuation, Tokyo was forced to rely almost entirely on her non-Japanese agents to carry out espionage-sabotage assignments in the United States. While Tokyo could count on the use of the vast Nazi underground machine, nevertheless certain specific tasks could be accomplished only

Japanese spy map secured by congressional investigators. The numbers appearing on this map identify barracks, forts, ship yards, air fields, army camps, aviation schools and naval bases in California.

by trusted Japanese-employed and Japanese-trained agents. The largest group of these was composed of certain White Russian fascists who had been under Japanese command for years.

The American leader of the Japanese-controlled White Russian fascists was Anastase Andreivitch Vonsiatsky of Thompson, Connecticut. Certain details of this man's spectacular career as master spy and saboteur in three continents are worth recording at some length.

II. Millionaire Saboteur

About sixty miles from Hartford, Connecticut, the town of Thompson is hidden away among gently rolling hills. The town is so small that most maps fail to mention its name. Driving on State Highway 193, you are through the hamlet almost before you have noticed the little cluster of houses and the quaint old Inn. The only thing about Thompson that might impress you is its quiet, peaceful atmosphere and the loveliness of its surroundings. Yet, unknown to its residents, this quiet Connecticut town has for years been a center of international intrigue and a rendezvous for notorious spies, saboteurs and assassins.

Thompson, Connecticut, is the site of the Ream estate, where "Count" Anastase Andreivitch Vonsiatsky, ex-Czarist officer and agent of the Japanese High Command, made his headquarters.

A tall powerfully built man with a sullen, handsome face and dark short-cropped hair, the bogus young "Count" Vonsiatsky made a deep impression on the rich middle-aged divorcée, Mrs. Stephens, née Marion Ream, when she met him in Paris in 1921. Mrs. Marion Buckingham Ream Stephens had inherited one-seventh of the $40,000,000 Ream fortune in Chicago. She helped the attractive penniless Russian emigré to come to the United States, and she married him shortly afterwards. At the time Vonsiatsky was twenty-three and she was forty-five.

There were many things about his past which the "Count" must have concealed from his bride. He would hardly have told her that his diary contained a record of kidnappings and torture-killings in which he had participated in Russia. . . .

After the dissolution of the Czarist armies, Vonsiatsky and several other ex-Czarist officers had organized a gang in the Crimea which specialized in kidnapping Russian citizens, holding them for ransom and torturing them to death if the money was not forthcoming. Vonsiatsky, who has never been very discreet, recorded the kidnappings in gruesome detail in his diary. The victims were divided into two categories: those with "caviar" and those without "caviar." In the language of the kidnappers, "caviar" meant money.

A description in Vonsiatsky's diary of one torture-killing in which he participated concludes with this bloodcurdling passage: "Both bullets hit the head, and the skull burst into pieces. 'Hell!' swore Bicho [one of Vonsiatsky's band]. 'Look!' Pieces of brain-matter had splattered over the chest and sleeves of his raincoat. 'The hell with him, let's go!' " In another case, Vonsiatsky related how a victim was tortured by having a bayonet stuck into his thigh. "Blood gushed in a fountain," reports the diary, ". . . the bayonet penetrated deeper and deeper, the tortured one shrieked with his last strength." The man's agony, however, was not sufficient to satisfy Vonsiatsky and his friends. "At once, needles one after another were stuck under the man's fingernails. He emitted a few more terrible cries and lost consciousness. . . . Half-dead, he was dragged into the park, to the sea."

This was the "Count" Anastase Vonsiatsky who in the early 1920's became an American citizen and took up residence at his wife's estate in Thompson, Connecticut. His wife's millions inspired grandiose dreams in the head of the former Czarist officer. He had visions of returning to his native land as a leader of a whole world anti-Soviet movement.

Vonsiatsky began spending his wife's money on preparations for the great day when he would launch his "Holy Crusade" against Bolshevism. He traveled extensively, not only in North and South America, but also in Europe and Asia, recruiting White Russian emigrés in all parts of the world for his "Crusade."

In August 1933, Vonsiatsky founded the "Russian National Fascist Revolutionary Party," with its headquarters at the Ream estate, himself as Leader, and Hitler's swastika as the official emblem. Branch offices of the new fascist organization were established in New York City, San Francisco, Los Angeles, in São Paulo, Brazil, and in Harbin, Manchukuo. Behind its "anti-Bolshevik" facade, Vonsiatsky's Party was soon actively conspiring with the German American Bund and other Axis agencies to bring about a fascist coup in the United States.

At the same time, working closely with the Japanese and German Governments, Vonsiatsky financed the smuggling of saboteurs and spies into Soviet Russia. The February 1934 issue of *The Fascist,* official organ of the Russian Fascist Party, published at Thompson, Connecticut, proudly reported these accomplishments of Vonsiatsky's agents in the Soviet Union:

> ... the Fascist Trio No. A-5 caused the crash of a military train. According to information received here, about 100 people were killed.
>
> In the Starobink district, thanks to the work of the "brothers" the sowing campaign was completely sabotaged. Several Communists in charge of the sowing mysteriously disappeared.

In April 1934, *The Fascist* carried this item:

> The editorial office wishes to announce that it is in receipt of

1,500 zlotys to be delivered to Boris Koverda when he is discharged from prison. The money is a present from Mr. Vonsiatsky.

Boris Koverda was then serving a prison term in Poland for having murdered in Warsaw the Soviet Ambassador to Poland.

At his American headquarters in Thompson, Connecticut, Vonsiatsky set up a private arsenal of rifles, machine guns, tear gas grenades and other military equipment. Scores of uniformed swastika-wearing young men were soon receiving military training on Vonsiatsky's grounds. The Ream estate was guarded night and day by huge, savage dogs.

The Russian fascist leader was in constant communication with such Americans as William Dudley Pelley, chief of the Silver Shirts; Robert Edward Edmondson, key anti-Semitic pamphleteer; and Henry Allen, head of the American White Guard, ex-convict, and collaborator with the Nazi-inspired Gold Shirts of Mexico. When Father Charles E. Coughlin began to assume prominence as a pro-Axis propagandist in Royal Oak, Michigan, Vonsiatsky immediately got in touch with him and material from Coughlin's *Social Justice* was republished in *The Fascist*.

Fritz Kuhn, Gustav Elmer, James Wheeler-Hill, and other leaders of the German American Bund spent week-ends at Vonsiatsky's estate. Occasionally, wearing his own smart uniform with its swastika band done in Czarist colors, Vonsiatsky addressed large meetings of Bund Storm Troopers at Camp Nordland, in New Jersey.

When the Hitler-instigated Franco revolt broke out in Spain, Vonsiatsky helped finance the running of arms to the fascist forces.

Scarcely a week passed without important Japanese, German or Italian functionaries visiting Thompson, Connecticut.

Sitting in comfortable chairs within Vonsiatsky's luxuriously
furnished house or outside on the spacious lawn, they discussed with the White Russian Fuehrer ways and means of
expediting the victory of World Fascism and, particularly,
of bringing about a fascist coup in the United States. Periodically, after such discussions, Vonsiatsky would leave Thompson on mysterious missions that took him to Central and
South America, to Asia, to Hawaii, and to Alaska. His trips
to Berlin, Rome and Tokyo became increasingly frequent.
His last visit to Tokyo was in 1941; he returned to the United
States shortly before the Japanese attacked Pearl Harbor.

As the Nazis had directed and financed the fascist White
Russian movement in Europe, the Japanese at an early date
had taken it over in Asia. White Russians living in Japanese
territory were organized into a fully equipped fascist army
some 150,000 strong. At its head was the burly saboteur-spy
Lieutenant-General Gregory Semenoff, an ex-Czarist officer
and self-proclaimed "Ataman" (Cossack chieftain). The Japanese pretended for many years that they had no connection
with Semenoff's army, but one week before Pearl Harbor
they dropped this subterfuge and officially incorporated
Semenoff's forces into the Japanese Army under the command
of Major Batase.

From the outset, Tokyo was interested in the fascist White
Russian movement in the United States, and particularly in
Vonsiatsky's Party. In May 1934, Vonsiatsky went to Tokyo
to confer with the Japanese militarists regarding the fascist
White Russian movement in America and in the Far East.
From Tokyo, Vonsiatsky traveled to Dairen, Manchukuo,
one of the Far Eastern centers of fascist White Russian operations. There he received a letter from Konstantin Rodzaevsky,
head of the Russian Fascist Union in Harbin, Manchukuo,
telling him of the elaborate preparations which "Ataman"
Semenoff had made to receive him. In the letter Rodzaevsky

informed Vonsiatsky that through Semenoff's efforts—

> The authorities in Dairen have received orders to issue a visa to you, and also to issue a special document for traveling to any part of Manchukuo without a visa. . . .
> To assist you a responsible member of the Japanese Gendarmerie will accompany you.
> The entire line of the Dairen-Harbin railroad will be placed under a special guard during your transit.
> The police department, as well as the Gendarme Corps, will take special measures for your safety.
> Finally, in Singzin, you are to be waited on by representatives of the general staff of the Kwantung army for very special and extremely important, absolutely secret, negotiations.

Vonsiatsky was informed that his itinerary included a two-day stay at Singzin, where General Semenoff would meet him. "You are to devote those two days to a detailed conversation with Semenoff, and subsequently you are to work out a secret plan together with the staff of the Kwantung army," Rodzaevsky wrote. The letter concluded: *"I beg you to burn this letter immediately. . . .* With Fascist Greetings, [Signed] R. V. Rodzaevsky, General Secretary of Russian Fascist Union."

Vonsiatsky, however, did not burn the letter. His vanity was so great that he found it impossible to destroy any letter, newspaper clipping or article in which his name was mentioned. He placed the incriminating document in his files. . . .

From Japan, Vonsiatsky proceeded in 1934 to Germany. In Berlin, he conferred with Alfred Rosenberg, Dr. Goebbels, and representatives of the Military Intelligence of the German High Command. He then returned to the United States, where he applied himself with renewed energy to promoting Fascism in America.

Предсѣдателю ЦІКа ВНП   А. А. Вонсяцкому,

Ꙗꙮꙿꙗꙅꙇ ꙃꙗꙇꙃꙅꙗꙃꙇ

Слава Россіи,

Дорогой Соратникъ!

Привѣтствуя Ваше и Д. I. Кунле прибытіе в Дайренъ,
спѣшу сообщить Вамъ нѣкоторыя новости и высказать
нѣкоторыя соображенія, с которыми Вы навѣрное согла-
ситесь.

Пріѣхав в Дайренъ, я убѣдился, что слова Атамана Се-
менова в телеграммѣ, которую он прислал Вамъ до моего
пріѣзда в Токіо, - имѣютъ весьма солидныя под собою ос-
нованія. Оказалось, что Атаман Семеновъ имѣетъ гораздо
большія связи с японскими военными сферами, которымъ
будетъ принадлежать рѣшающая роль в предстоящихъ собы-
тіяхъ, чѣмъ можно было предполагать. В частности- Атаман Семеновъ добился:

а/того, что Правительство Маньчжу Ди-го официаль-
но-разрѣшило Вамъ въѣзд в Маньчжу-Ди-го, о чем токійс-
кое представительство было поставлено в извѣстность
/Вы, к сожалѣнію, в это время уже уѣхали/,

б/того, что дайренское представительство Маньчжу-
Ди го получило распоряженіе немедленно дать Вамъ ви-
зу, больше того - выдать особое свидѣтельство для путе-
ствія в любыхъ районахъ Маньчжу-Ди го без всякихъ виз,

в/того, что чиновник Маньчжу-Ди го в Дайренѣ дол-
жен будетъ привести Вамъ неоффиціальныя извиненія,

.... что для содѣйствія Вамъ прикоман.......
.... и японско ....

.... к а у .... д у.
.... тѣм не причина .... льно достичь соглашенія с Атама-
....., чтобы он вошел в организуемую нами Всероссійскую Фашистскую
Партію со всѣми своими казачьими организаціями и взял бы на
себя руководство будущей фашистской Арміей.

В бытность мою в Дайренѣ, мы обсудили с Атаманомъ текст осо-
баго акта, которым он и изглашаемыя ими организаціи ин-корпори-
вуются в создаваемую нами В.Ф.П. Инициалами Этот текст в двухъ
варіантахъ Вы можете получить у Атамана и у Б.П.Замкова. Само
собою разумѣется, что это первоначальный проект, подлежащій уточненію и
детализаціи, а равнымъ образомъ тѣмъ измѣненіямъ, которые Вы найдете
нужнымъ.

Настоящее письмо передаст Вамъ помощник начальника дальневос-
сточнаго сектора и член Верховнаго Совѣта Р.Ф.П. С.И.Доловъ, вы-
полнявшій в дни моего и Ч.А.Ватковскаго отсутствія из Харбина
функціи Замѣстителя Генеральнаго секретаря. Думается, что .....
.... отвѣтственнымъ работамъ, им выполненная, позволит отнестись Вамъ к не-
му с полнымъ и всестороннимъ довѣріемъ Данное письмо прошу Вас
немедленно сжечь.

Слава Россіи

С фашистскимъ привѣтомъ

ГЕНЕРАЛЬНЫЙ СЕКРЕТАРЬ Р.Ф.П.

/К. В. Родзаевскій/

The letter from Konstantin Rodzaevsky, head of the Russian Fascist Union in Harbin,
Manchukuo, to Anastase Vonsiatsky, head of the Russian National Fascist Revolutionary Party of Thompson, Connecticut. Written in 1934, the letter outlines plans
for secret discussions between Vonsiatsky and Japanese military officials. Translated,
the full letter reads as follows:

GLORY TO RUSSIA

Dear Soldier:

We greet you and Kunle [one of Vonsiatsky's U. S. lieutenants] on your arrival to Dairen. I wish to inform you of a few developments, and express certain possibilities with which you will undoubtedly agree.

Upon my arrival in Dairen, I was assured that the commitments made by Ataman Semenoff, in his telegram sent to you prior to my arrival to Tokyo, have a solid basis. It is evident that Ataman Semenoff has a great many more connections with Japanese military authorities who are destined to play an even more important role in the coming developments than I anticipated. Confidentially, it was through Ataman Semenoff that

(a) The Government of Manchukuo officially permitted you to enter Manchukuo; subsequently, the government in Tokyo was advised accordingly.

(b) The authorities in Dairen have received orders to issue a visa to you, and also to issue a special document for traveling to any part of Manchukuo without a visa.

(c) An official of the government of Manchukuo will arrive in Dairen, and offer you an official apology.

(d) To assist you, a responsible member of the Japanese Gendarmerie will accompany you.

(e) The entire line of the Dairen-Harbin railroad will be placed under a special guard during your transit.

(f) The police department, as well as the Gendarme Corps, will take special measures for your safety.

(g) Finally, in Singzin, you are to be waited on by representatives of the general staff of the Kwantung army for very special and extremely important, absolutely secret, negotiations.

As you see, Ataman Semenoff has accomplished a great deal. For some unknown reason, you did not reply to his telegram, sent to you from Dairen on April 12th. In the interests of our cause, say that you did not receive his telegram or that your reply did not reach its destination.

At any rate, in view of considerations enumerated above, you cannot go to Harbin directly, for that would be interpreted as ignoring General Semenoff. Therefore, I beg you, as a friend, to talk to General Semenoff prior to your departure, and then proceed to Singzin where you will stay two days. General Semenoff will immediately arrive there by plane and I will subsequently join you if necessary. You are to devote those two days to a detailed conversation with Semenoff and, subsequently, you are to work out a secret plan together with the staff of the Kwantung army. Then, on Wednesday, you are to arrive in Harbin.

In view of all the circumstances so closely connected with events which we anticipate, and realizing the tremendous significance of the conferences to be attended by you, we have decided to give you a grand reception at the railroad station, as well as at the Russian Club on Wednesday.

For these very reasons, it is desirable that you should reach an agreement with

Ataman Semenoff whereby he is to join the Russian Fascist Union with all his Cossack organizations and to assume the leadership of the future Fascist army.

While visiting Dairen, we discussed with Semenoff the text of a special act of incorporating his organization with the whole Russian Fascist party. Two copies of this act are now in possession of Ataman Semenoff. It is understood that it is subject to revision, correction, and detailed rewriting, subject to your approval.

This letter will be delivered to you by assistant leader of the Far Eastern section, and a member of the Supreme Council, S. E. Doloff. In my absence from Harbin, he functions as acting General Secretary. He carries out his important work very diligently, and I recommend that you trust him and depend on him. *I beg you to burn this letter immediately.*

Hail Russia.

With Fascist Greetings,
General Secretary of Russian Fascist Union.
K. V. Rodzaevsky

Shortly before Japan attacked the United States, a clandestine meeting was held in a room at the Hotel Bismarck in Chicago. Present at the meeting were G. Wilhelm Kunze, then head of the German American Bund; Otto Willumeit, head of the Chicago division of the Bund; Father Aleksi Pelypenko, a Ukrainian priest; and "Count" Anastase Vonsiatsky. Future plans for espionage-sabotage activity in America were discussed. Kunze stressed the growing difficulties of getting funds from abroad. He asked Vonsiatsky to help finance the work of Nazi agents in the United States. Vonsiatsky handed the Bund leader $2,800 in cash, as a down payment. More would be forthcoming, he said, on one condition. The condition was that Berlin "guarantee" him a high post in Russia when the Nazi armies had "crushed" the Soviet Union.

Not long after this meeting, Vonsiatsky sent Aleksi Pelypenko to Washington to report to the Japanese Military Attaché. The Ukrainian priest was given the calling card of a Japanese general as a means of identifying himself as Vonsiatsky's representative. When Pelypenko made his report to the Japanese Military Attaché, he was given a message to bring back to Vonsiatsky: the Russian fascist leader was to get in touch immediately with his contacts in Alaska and to accumulate all the latest available data on that section of the United States. Alaska, the Japanese Military Attaché implied, was soon to figure prominently in Tokyo's war plans.

But something happened in the case of Pelypenko that Vonsiatsky and the Japanese had not reckoned on. The Ukrainian priest reported to the FBI all he knew about Vonsiatsky. . . .

An interesting anecdote Aleksi Pelypenko told Federal agents concerned Fiodore Wozniak, "The Firebug" of World War I notoriety.

One evening, in the summer of 1941, the priest was sitting in his room at the Hotel Bristol in New York City when the telephone rang. He was told by the desk clerk that a man who would not give his name wished to see him. Pelypenko asked the clerk to send him up. A few minutes later, a man entered Pelypenko's room and introduced himself as Fiodore Wozniak.

Although the Ukrainian priest had never met Wozniak before, he knew his name. "The Firebug's" fame as a saboteur had traveled far. Pelypenko asked Wozniak what he wanted.

"I hear you stand well with Berlin," said Wozniak. "My money is running low. I want work, big work. I want to do a job for the Germans like the one I did in the last war."

Pelypenko told Wozniak that he had no connection with Berlin. "The Firebug" shrugged his shoulders disappointedly, mumbled a few words, and left. Pelypenko later told a friend that he knew Wozniak was associated with a number of Nazi-Ukrainian agents.

If Wozniak wanted more sabotage work, surely he had means of getting it from his Nazi-Ukrainian friends. . . .

CHAPTER FIVE

BOMBERS AND KILLERS

I. *The Fifth Column Without a Country*

In 1938 a sensational series of kidnappings occurred in New York City. A number of well-to-do persons were seized by a mysterious gang which blindfolded them, gagged them, and took them by car to a secret hideout in the city. Ransoms ranging from $100,000 to $200,000 were demanded. In certain cases the kidnapped victims were tortured to make them write pleading notes to their relatives and friends. One of the victims, Norman Miller, who had been forced to pay $15,000 ransom, remembered that while he had been held captive he had heard church bells ringing and the sound of billiard balls clicking. He also recalled the number of steps down which he had been led, blindfolded, by his kidnappers. These clues helped the police to locate the Ukrainian National Home, "a mutual benefit society" at 217-19 East 6th Street, New York City, as the place that fitted Miller's description.

On November 2, 1938, the police raided the Ukrainian National Home. In the basement they found a torture chamber, its walls pitted with bullet holes. They also found a German-made machine gun and other weapons. The police dug up the basement floor and came upon human bones. One of the kidnapped men, Arthur Fried of White Plains, had died under the torture. His body had been stuffed in the heating furnace, and the bones later hidden under the basement floor.

The four gangsters who made up the kidnapping gang were arrested. Two of them were sentenced to life-imprisonment.

The other two, Demetrius Gula and Joseph Sacoda, were convicted of murder and executed in the electric chair at Sing Sing.

One highly significant fact not mentioned at the trial was that Gula and Sacoda were both members of a Berlin-directed Ukrainian terrorist organization known as the ODWU. At the time no one thought of connecting these brutal kidnappers with the Nazi espionage-sabotage machine in the United States. . . .

The Berlin-directed ODWU again hovered just behind the headlines when, early in 1941, a Ukrainian-American captain in the United States Army was courtmartialed and deprived of his commission for betraying confidential information to a foreign agent. This captain was the leader of an ODWU unit in Pennsylvania. The foreign agent in the case had been Omelian Senyk-Gribiwisky, a Ukrainian terrorist who had come from Berlin in 1931 to found the ODWU in the United States. . . .

Another hint of the inner nature of the ODWU came on July 13, 1940, when the New York police arrested a Ukrainian-American named William Piznak on charges of violating the Sullivan Law. In a basement storeroom of Piznak's residence at 225 East 95th Street, detectives of the New York sabotage squad found a veritable arsenal which included two machine guns, tear gas grenades, rifles, sets of brass knuckles, a trench knife and 1,112 rifle cartridges of assorted calibers.

William Piznak's brother, Michael Piznak, is the attorney of the Ukrainian Nationalist Association, an old Ukrainian-American society which the ODWU has sought to infiltrate and dominate. Until shortly before the police raid, the two Piznak brothers lived together in the house which contained the basement arsenal. The usually cautious attorney, Michael Piznak, revealed his own political proclivities at a Ukrainian meeting in Belvedere Park, New York, on July 1, 1938, when he declared: "Now Hitler calls the youth to organize. Now, also, Mussolini calls the youth to organize. And now, we, the Ukrainian Nationalists, too, must call the youth to organize!"

In August 1940, the Hetman, another Berlin-directed Ukrainian organization, staged a public Storm Troop demonstration in Chicago. The "Order of the Day," issued by the Chicago Hetman "District Command," called upon "the uniformed Male Youth Hundreds" to appear *"armed with rifles"* . . .

There are close to one million Ukrainian-Americans in the United States. The overwhelming majority of them are pro-democratic; but a Naziphile minority make up the ODWU and the Hetman, two of the most dangerous espionage-sabotage organizations in the world.*

The ODWU operates under the supervision of Colonel Walther Nicolai's *Section IIIB*, German Military Intelligence.

The Hetman operates under the supervision of Alfred Rosenberg's *Aussenpolitisches Amt*, Foreign Political Office of the Nazi party.

The ODWU is more powerful than the Hetman and, if possible, more violent. Both organizations have built their cells in American industrial centers. Their agents work in munitions plants, mines, steel foundries, aircraft factories, shipyards, freightyards and docks. A number of them have gained access to the United States Army.

Both the ODWU and the Hetman are international organizations with branches throughout Europe, Asia and North and South America. Their activities include spying, sabotaging, spreading pro-Axis propaganda and, not infrequently, committing assassinations. The United States leaders of the

---

* It should be kept in mind that the Nazi-Ukrainian movement discussed in this section of the book by no means represents the Ukrainian people or any large part of the Ukrainian-American community. The vast majority of Ukrainian-Americans have carried on a bitter struggle against the ODWU and the Hetman.

ODWU and Hetman have been in regular communication with German, Japanese and Italian agents, and with spies in South and Central America. In the spring of 1941, one of the confidential ODWU bulletins emanating from Berlin triumphantly described the sinking of several British ships sabotaged by ODWU members in Argentina and Brazil. . . .

It is remarkable that in all the literature dealing with the world-wide machinations of the Axis, practically no mention has been made of this most important auxiliary of the international Nazi espionage and sabotage machine: the fascist Ukrainian fifth column. Among fifth columns, it is unique in that the only land in which it cannot function is its native land. Its activities in the Ukraine were brought to an abrupt halt in 1938 when the Soviet authorities rounded up and executed its chief ring-leaders there. In almost every other country in the world, and particularly in the United States, this criminal and ruthless fifth column is still at work.

Just how Hitler got hold of these terrorists among the Ukrainians and converted a section of them into the Ukrainian-American fifth column makes a story of international treachery and violence unparalleled in all the weird annals of the underworld of political crime. . . .

II. *Theories and Practices*

A familiar sight in Berlin in recent years was a little old man with a scrubby white beard who usually wandered about in oversize plus-fours. The Nazis called him "Professor of the Ukraine." His name was Dr. Paul Rohrbach. Like his closest friend, the Nazi philosopher Dr. Alfred Rosenberg, Rohrbach was a Baltic German who contributed some important "theories" to the Nazi Party.

Rohrbach was still a young scholar when he evolved the theory that the Ukrainians are a Germanic-type people and should therefore come under German rule. To win the support of the Ukrainians, then subjects of the Russian Czar, the young Germanophile scholar wrote innumerable propaganda works urging the establishment of an "Independent Ukraine." The idea appealed strongly to Kaiser Wilhelm who had his Imperial eye on Ukrainian wheat and oil.

In 1918, after the Treaty of Brest-Litovsk, the Kaiser established an "Independent Ukraine" under German "protection." Rohrbach was dispatched to Kiev to act as personal adviser to Field Marshal Hermann von Eichhorn, commander of the German forces in the Ukraine. A Quisling Ukrainian government was set up, headed by a hitherto unrenowned Russian cavalryman named General Pavel Petrovitch Skoropadski. The General, who did not know one word of Ukrainian, received the title of The Hetman (Head Man) of the Ukraine, and a cabinet was formed around him composed of various Russian and Ukrainian adventurers chiefly distinguished for their murderous records as terrorists and anti-Semitic pogromists.

But Rohrbach's triumph was shortlived. The newly-formed Red Army, together with the forerunners of today's doughty guerrilla bands, decimated the Kaiser's armies of occupation and drove them out of the Ukraine. Rohrbach hastily packed his books and returned to Berlin along with General Skoropadski and his cutthroat cabinet. Field Marshal von Eichhorn, less fortunate, was buried in the Ukraine, after he had been shot by a Ukrainian guerrilla.

Back in Berlin, Rohrbach and his friends became the protegés of the German High Command which, by the early 1920's, was already plotting with the Nazi Party to overthrow the Weimar Republic and make a second bid for world conquest. Captain Franz von Papen joined the growing circle of

Rohrbach's admirers, and the concept of an "Independent Ukraine" appealed as strongly to Adolf Hitler as it had formerly done to the Kaiser. The "Hetman Organization" was placed under the personal supervision of Dr. Alfred Rosenberg, the chief Nazi advocate of Eastward expansion. General Skoropadski, who could still barely stutter in Ukrainian, retained his title as The Hetman of the Ukraine and leader of the Hetman Organization. . . .

At this point, Colonel Nicolai of the Intelligence Service of the High Command took a hand in the Ukrainian game. For various reasons, Nicolai felt that General Skoropadski was not the man to head the Ukrainian fifth column. While Nicolai did not interfere in any way with Alfred Rosenberg's organization of the Hetman apparatus, he went on to organize an international Ukrainian apparatus of his own. From the start, Nicolai had his eye on the large Ukrainian community in the United States.

The man chosen by Nicolai to head this international fifth column was Colonel Eugene Konovaletz, who had served with the Kaiser's armies of occupation in the Ukraine. Konovaletz was a tall, blondish man with gray, watery eyes, a military bearing, and a passion for jewels. He had earned himself considerable notoriety in the Ukraine as a rapist and killer. When he left with the Germans in 1919, he brought out with him two large trunks loaded with looted gold, silver and jewels. Hitler met him in 1922 and took an immediate liking to him.

By 1930, Konovaletz was known to the intelligence bureaus of the world's powers as one of Germany's leading espionage agents. He was also working for the Japanese General Staff. His various "missions" took him to every corner of the European continent, to Asia, and to North and South America.

The international organization of spies and saboteurs which Konovaletz set up under the supervision of the Intelligence Department of the German War Office went by the name of

Ukrajinska Organizace Nacionalistov (Organization of Ukrainian Nationalists), commonly referred to as the OUN.

Wherever there were Ukrainian communities—in Soviet Russia, France, Rumania, Czechoslovakia, Poland, South America, Canada, the United States—Colonel Konovaletz's emissaries traveled at the expense of the German Government and established OUN cells.

Special schools for OUN members were opened in Germany where the students were carefully trained in the arts of espionage, sabotage and assassination. The first of these schools was founded by the German War Office in Danzig around 1928. German Intelligence officers acted as instructors. The OUN students were taught the various methods of stealing military secrets, making bombs, blowing up factories and carrying out political murders. Courses in regular German army training were also part of the curriculum.

OUN graduates from this Danzig school destroyed scores of factories and farms by sabotage fires and explosions in Poland during the years 1928-31. They also assassinated a number of prominent Polish politicians before the Polish authorities finally arrested several OUN terrorists and imprisoned or executed them. The remaining OUN members were temporarily withdrawn from Poland and were put to work, with other of Konovaletz's followers, in the Nazi Party in Germany.

When Hitler came to power, a central academy for the OUN was founded in Berlin. The Nazis spared no expense in building this academy and supplying it with expert instructors and scientific equipment. The academy's address is 75 Mecklenburgische Strasse, Berlin. Its title is "School for Espionage, Sabotage and Terrorism."

The OUN received its first major setback in 1938 when the Soviet Government smashed its entire underground organization in the Ukraine. That same year, Adolf Hitler and Colonel

Nicolai reached an agreement that Colonel Konovaletz, the head of the OUN, was rather too well acquainted with the secrets of the German Government, and that his international influence had reached a point where it might prove difficult to control. They therefore arranged for a special present to be delivered to Konovaletz in Rotterdam, where he was attending a convention of Ukrainian "nationalists." One of Konovaletz's own aides, who was a trusted Gestapo man, handed him the present outside the convention hall, telling him that it was a personal gift. When the Colonel opened the small package, the bomb exploded and tore him to bits. He became the martyr of the Ukrainian "nationalist" movement, and high Nazis have since remarked, not without sincerity, that Colonel Konovaletz has proved even more valuable to them dead than alive.

After the removal of Colonel Konovaletz, the work of organizing the OUN on an international scale went forward at an accelerated pace.

III. *Salesman of Terror*

For the important task of organizing the Nazi-Ukrainian network in the United States, Nicolai selected Colonel Konovaletz's right-hand man, the most talented saboteur and ruthless killer in the OUN. His name was Omelian Senyk-Gribiwisky. Feared by even his closest intimates, this slim, gentle-mannered, Russian priest's son had been linked, directly or indirectly, with almost every major assassination which had taken place in Poland during the early post-war years. The OUN later sent Senyk-Gribiwisky on special errands of murder, sabotage or intrigue as far afield as Canada, South Africa, South America, Italy and Japan. His compatriots gave him a nickname which, freely translated, means "Salesman of Terror."

This was the man who arrived in the United States in 1931 to organize the ODWU—the Organization for the Rebirth of the Ukraine — which was to serve as the American counterpart of Berlin's OUN.

Two years later, with the Nazis in power, and unlimited funds at his disposal, the "Salesman of Terror" returned to the United States to develop the ODWU and spread its sinister branches across the forty-eight states.

With German money, Senyk-Gribiwisky financed scores of ODWU "front" organizations which mushroomed under his expert guidance in the industrial cities where Ukrainian-Americans lived. The ODWU fronts appeared in all sorts of guises. Some were supposed to be doing "Ukrainian Red Cross" work. Others were "insurance companies," "sports clubs," "chemical firms" and "film companies." They all had one thing in common: they were headed by pro-Nazi Ukrainian-Americans, who were to serve as propagandists, spies, and, when the right time came, as saboteurs for the Third Reich. In many cases Ukrainian-American members of ODWU-controlled organizations were unaware that they were being used by the Nazis.

For those of his United States agents who were unable to attend the German espionage-sabotage schools, Senyk-Gribiwisky drew up a special memorandum of instructions which could be used by them as a textbook. A copy of this extraordinary document has come into the possession of the authors, and the portions of it quoted here are translated and published for the first time.

"Methods of espionage," begins the document, "depend on the domain in which the given agent of espionage is active. . . ." Various methods of spying to be employed by ODWU agents in the United States are then listed. Senyk-Gribiwisky discusses "buying persons in the opposite camp who are in the possession of valuable information," "diplomatic espionage,"

"press espionage," and "espionage proper." He instructs his
followers in the art of "worming into various circles of the
community under observation" and in the "recruiting of informers." The document goes on:

> The agent works underground and, every minute, he must be
> prepared to be unmasked. He must therefore know how to
> behave in order not to attract attention; he must know how
> to make notes and how to transmit the latter; how to meet
> and get in touch with other agents. . . .

Most essential of all, according to Senyk-Gribiwisky's instructions, is the art of "camouflage":

> . . . the agent must adopt some kind of profession or occupa-
> tion and actually practise this profession or occupation. He
> must therefore be some kind of a specialist. Finally, an agent
> usually works in one given domain. If his work is to be useful,
> he is to be a specialist in that domain, too.

The "Salesman of Terror" instructed his ODWU agents
in the United States to start building private arsenals. In
Pittsburgh, Chicago, Detroit and other American cities, he
organized armed detachments of ODWU "sharp-shooters"
and established several camps where ODWU recruits received
military training. He also arranged for the distribution among
ODWU units of certain confidential booklets which had been
prepared in Berlin. The titles of a few of these booklets were:
*Conspiracy Methods, The Ukrainian Military Organization,
Chemical and Bacteriological Warfare, Guerrilla Warfare
Technique, Aviation* and *The Technical and Auxiliary
Troops.*

In May 1934, Senyk-Gribiwisky contrived to found the
"Ukrainian Aviation School" at Montgomery, New York.
ODWU units throughout the country received this

"SPECIAL NOTICE TO ALL UKRAINIANS":

> All Ukrainians residing in the United States and Canada and who possess knowledge of, or experience in, aeronautics, engineering (any branch), military science, wireless and telegraph communication are requested to register their names and addresses with the Ukrainian Aviation School.

The "Aviation School" was an ideal front for the training of spies and saboteurs. After receiving instruction at this school, ODWU agents could then apply for special jobs in United States aircraft plants or aeronautical stations, where the opportunities for sabotage are plentiful.

A financial supporter of this ODWU Aviation School was Demetrius Gula, the New York murderer-kidnapper who was subsequently executed at Sing Sing for his crimes.

The chief "flying instructor" at the school was "an American engineer," Burton H. Gilligan, who was intimately associated with the German American Bund. Just before he joined the school, Gilligan had returned from a visit to Nazi Germany.

Another "prominent American" who took an active part in the Aviation School was the Ukrainian-American captain who in 1941 was to lose his United States Army commission for supplying the ODWU leader, Senyk-Gribiwisky, with confidential information concerning the United States armed forces.

By January 1935, Senyk-Gribiwisky reported to his superiors in Berlin that more than one hundred ODWU units were operating in the United States, and that there was not an important industrial center without its active cell of Nazi-Ukrainians. Posing as workers, insurance agents, salesmen, priests, journalists, the ODWU agents worked their way into key positions in the mass Ukrainian-American organizations.

As part of the ODWU network, a number of "photographic" and "film" companies were set up. The most important of these was the Avramenko Film Company, headed by Vassil Avramenko, who worked with the powerful ODWU unit in Pittsburgh. Avramenko's partner in the enterprise was named Kalina Lissiuk.

The authors of this book have secured an affidavit from a Ukrainian-American who for a time served as a photographer for Avramenko and Lissiuk. His statement, which has been turned over to the Federal authorities, tells how during the years 1934-40 these fascist Ukrainians took numerous pictures of American industrial cities, military highways, bridges, airfields, rivers, railroads and factories. The signer of the affidavit (who for obvious reasons wishes his name to be withheld) records specifically that the ODWU agents photographed: factories in Pittsburgh, Scranton, Allentown and Bethlehem; industrial sections of Detroit; the International Bridge connecting Detroit and Windsor, Canada; factory towns in New Jersey; aircraft plants in California; and the Mexican-United States border. The affidavit relates the following incident:

> I was told that I might go to Czechoslovakia with Mr. Lissiuk for the purpose of taking pictures of Czechoslovakian military activities. This was shortly after the Munich Peace Pact, but before Germany occupied that country. The understanding was that this film would be turned over to Avramenko. However, I did not go and Lissiuk's son took my place. He was shot by the Czechoslovakian authorities. . . . Lissiuk stayed in America a few months and then returned to Europe where he visited Berlin. Just what his purpose was I do not know. From what I hear I believe he returned to America in the early part of 1940. I do know that he came back with more films, but I do not know the subject matter of these films.

Occasionally, Senyk-Gribiwisky's spies and saboteurs got out of hand and started rackets of their own. When the Gula-

I first met Avramenko in 1935. He asked me to go to work for him in the spring of 1935. I left Chicago and came East in accordance with his request. One of my first jobs was to photograph the Pulaski Highway leading to the U. S. Route #1, which in turn led to the Newark Airport.

I then made many photographs of folk dances and parades of various towns in which Ukrainians lived.

In the fall of 1936, Avramenko decided to go into motion picture filming, instead of still photography. I made several pictures of entertainment value; that is to say, I assisted in the making of them. In his studio at 747 Broadway and at 69 Hope Avenue, Passaic, New Jersey, I went through thousands of feet of film in the dark-room, which film was owned by Avramenko. The vast majority of the film devoted itself to pictures of industrial sites and centers of the United States. Those sites which I remember, and can now mention by name, are as follows: Pictures taken from a height of Pittsburgh, with its steel mills, rivers, and transportation facilities reaching the various factories; pictures taken from a height of Scranton showing the rivers used for transportation, the coal supply centers, and the larger steel producing mills; Allentown and Bethlehem, with pictures taken from a height of a large steel company, which name I don't recall; pictures of Detroit, which were not taken from a height, showing various parts of the city, however, I do not remember the exact subject matter;

I left his employ late in 1936 and returned upon his request in the spring of 1938. Avramenko then had a location near Newton, New Jersey. I ~~assisted in the~~ During that year I worked on amusement pictures, but in the summer of 1939, I was asked to go to Detroit and take some film of the city for him. Among the requests for pictures, he asked that I try to obtain a picture of the International Bridge, which connects Detroit to Windsor, Canada. (I think the name is the Ambassador Bridge.) Avramenko wanted me to get this picture from some height. For some reason which I cannot explain, I felt the taking of this picture would not be used for proper purposes, and consequently did not take it.

When I returned to New York, Avramenko was highly incensed over my failure to follow his instructions. He then wanted to send me to Pittsburgh for further motion-picture film sites of the city, which I refused, and subsequently left his employ.

I might add this in conclusion --- during 1937 and 1938 Avramenko made innumerable trips to Canada, visiting the territory from Montreal to Vancouver. He told me that it was for the purpose of raising money for his films. I was puzzled by that answer, inasmuch as he pretended to be working for Ukrainians, and I knew that very few Ukrainians resided in that territory.

I recall one other incident that night have some bearing: I was told that I might go to Czechoslovakia with Mr. Lissiuk for the purpose of taking pictures of Czechoslovakian military activities. This was shortly after the Munich Peace Pact, but before Germany occupied that country. The understanding was that the film would be turned over to Avramenko. However, I did not go and Lissiuk's son went in my place. He was shot by the Czechoslovakian authorities while in the process of taking these pictures and killed. Lissiuk escaped and is now back in America. He brought back with him those films which they were able to take until the fatal incident of his son and turned them over to Avramenko.

Lissiuk stayed in America a few months and then returned to Europe where he visited in Berlin. Just what his purpose was, I do not know. From what I hear, I believe he returned to America in the early part of 1940, I do know that he came back with more films, but I do not know the subject matter of these films.

I make these statements for the simple reason that, if there was any ulterior purpose in the taking of these films, it is my intention that the authorities should be made aware of it. I am an American citizen, proud of my country and resent being used as a tool, if that is the case, by any person or individual whose interests are inimical to America. I make these statements voluntarily and am in sound condition, mentally and physically. I am receiving no consideration for it and do it as my duty as an American.

An affidavit concerning ...

Sacoda ODWU kidnapping and murder gang was rounded up in New York City in 1938, Senyk-Gribiwisky was fearful that the incident might lead to the uncovering of the whole ODWU network. The "Salesman of Terror" hurried to Europe. However, he was soon back in the United States to give last-minute instructions to ODWU agents before the outbreak of war. Before long, he again left for Europe, this time to take his place with Adolf Hitler's armies marching into the Soviet Ukraine.

As a reward for his many services to Nazi Germany, Senyk-Gribiwisky was to receive a high government position in the Nazi-occupied Ukraine. Instead of that, in the fall of 1941, a bullet from a Soviet Ukrainian guerrilla brought the career of the "Salesman of Terror" to a sudden close. Newspaper communiques reported that the name of the Soviet guerrilla was Kosius and that Senyk-Gribiwisky had been killed "while traveling with the German Army of invasion. . . ."

On the last evening he spent in the United States before leaving for Germany, Senyk-Gribiwisky visited an office at 83 Grand Street, Jersey City, New Jersey. He went there to pick up confidential mail which he was to carry to Europe, and to leave final orders for ODWU work in the United States.

Eighty-three Grand Street, Jersey City, is the headquarters of the powerful Ukrainian Nationalist Association and of its official publication, *Svoboda,* which is edited by Luke Myshuha, otherwise known as the "Big Mouse."

There are some facts worth knowing about the "Big Mouse."

IV. *The "Big Mouse"*

Luke Myshuha (in Ukrainian the name "Myshuha" means "Big Mouse," hence the nickname) is a tall, thin, fifty-five-year-old Ukrainian-born American with sharp, birdlike features, a narrow forehead, and a tight mouth that habitually twists in a caustic smile. The "Big Mouse" likes to dress well and to eat at expensive restaurants. Of a somewhat hysterical disposition, his mood is usually one of intense elation or abject depression. He is inordinately vain, conceited and ambitious.

Back in World War I, Myshuha was a petty officer in the Imperial Austrian Army. He served with the Kaiser's forces in the Ukraine, where his knowledge of the language made him useful to the Germans. He came to the United States in 1921 and soon got a job on the staff of the newspaper, *Svoboda*, organ of the Ukrainian Nationalist Association, a fraternal benefit society with some 40,000 members.

In 1933, when the Nazis took over in Germany and started their organization of the ODWU in America, Myshuha became the editor of *Svoboda*. He was already in touch with Colonel Nicolai's agents who were seeking to place their co-workers in strategic positions in the Ukrainian-American community. As the Nazi influence in the powerful Ukrainian Nationalist Association was still small at that time, it took some typical scheming on the part of the "Big Mouse" to get himself elected editor of *Svoboda*.

Shortly before the Association convention at which the *Svoboda* editor was to be elected, Myshuha went to Washington, D. C. He contrived to see the chief White House usher, Ike Hoover. He presented the chief usher with a package of Ukrainian Easter eggs. On emerging from the White House, Myshuha spread the word that he had been received by "Hoover," omitting the first name, and thus creating the impression that Herbert Hoover, then President of the United States, had accorded him an interview. ODWU agents at the Association convention talked about the great "honor" that had befallen their candidate, Luke Myshuha. Greatly impressed, the convention delegates elected him editor of

Svoboda. The "Big Mouse" has held his editorial office ever since.

With Myshuha at its head, *Svoboda* was converted into an organ of Axis propaganda and a medium for conveying instructions to ODWU spies. The *Svoboda* offices at 83 Grand Street, Jersey City, became a clearing house for espionage directives coming in from Berlin, Tokyo and Rome. For many years, these directives have been regularly reaching the *Svoboda* offices by mail from Spanish and South American "drops," or through the special "couriers" of the Axis spy systems. Liaison officers from Germany and Japan made their headquarters at 83 Grand Street when they visited the United States. Senyk-Gribiwisky's mail was always sent to this address. Here certain Axis agents paid their last calls before sailing for Europe, and from here they were accompanied to the pier where last confidential words were exchanged to remain as sealed secrets until "couriers" arrived with further orders.

Before the outbreak of the Second World War, the "Big

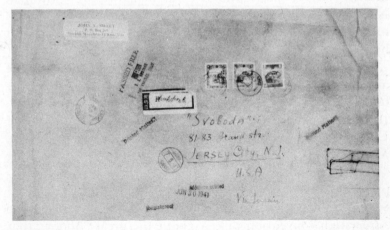

This envelope contained certain documents which were sent from Axis territory in Asia to Luke Myshuha's *Svoboda* offices in Jersey City, N. J. Myshuha's offices served as a clearing house for confidential directives from Berlin, Rome, and Tokyo.

Mouse" made numerous trips to Europe. From London, on October 28, 1938, he mailed home a dispatch to his associates in the United States which informed them that he had "just sent off two long telegrams to Ribbentrop and Ciano," the Foreign Minister of Nazi Germany and the Foreign Minister of Fascist Italy.

"In two hours I am leaving for Paris," wrote Myshuha in the same letter, "where I'll stop over for a day and whence I'll proceed to Vienna, that is, to the spot, or, rather, nearer to the spot where the Power resides. . . ." The "Power," of course, was Nazi Germany.

When Myshuha showed up in Vienna, he was welcomed by high Nazi officials, and the Nazi Propaganda Ministry invited him to deliver a special propaganda address over the controlled German radio. Myshuha spoke for the Nazis as requested.

The "Big Mouse" returned to the United States that year aboard the Nazi liner, S. S. *Bremen*. He was full of confidence. "For no price must we let ourselves be intimidated," he told a Nazi-Ukrainian gathering in New York, urging his associates in America to carry on boldly with their pro-Axis propaganda and other activities. ". . . We are not afraid when someone tries to frighten us because we support the terrorists, because in this country it is allowed to do even this, especially when it is done so manifestly and openly as we are doing it."

When the war broke out in Europe in 1939, Myshuha received word that he was no longer to communicate directly with Berlin. His chief contact in the future was to be a Nazi-Ukrainian agent in Rome, Italy, named Eugene Onatsky. This agent wrote to Myshuha on October 10, 1939, discussing the work in America and mentioning certain directives already sent to Myshuha "which contain a request that you defend Germany." These directives, added the Rome agent, "have been sent to you direct by the Propaganda Division of the German Ministry."

The Nazi conquest of Poland was a great event for Luke Myshuha and his friends in the United States. The conquest opened up a number of new "jobs" for the fascist Ukrainians. The Nazis were in need of hirelings to act for them as informers, terrorists and hangmen against the conquered but still insurgent Polish people. Some of Myshuha's friends in America hastily left for Germany. One of them was "General" Kurmanovitch, a Ukrainian emissary from Berlin who had been visiting in the United States. Shortly afterwards the Rome agent Onatsky reported to Myshuha: "General Kurmanovitch is now Military Commander of the Grodno District, with the rank of Lieutenant-Colonel. . . ."

The Rome agent assured Myshuha that all Nazi-Ukrainians could "get administrative posts—without the slightest difficulty—under the Germans in Western Galicia, seeing that the Germans do not trust the Poles and the Poles themselves are loath to accept such appointments."

Meanwhile the work in America went on. *Svoboda,* with its circulation of 40,000, continued to spread pro-Axis propaganda in American cities. But the "Big Mouse" did not stop at propaganda.

The United States was launching its gigantic defense program, and sterner measures were being called for by Berlin.

On February 1 and again on February 3, 1941, Myshuha printed in his newspaper detailed instructions on the manufacture of homemade bombs and explosives suitable for sabotage purposes. Here is an excerpt from these instructions printed in *Svoboda* just nine months before Pearl Harbor:

> An ordinary cotton out of which, for instance, our shirts are made can be changed into a "firing cotton" if you add to it the already mentioned "nitrate mixture": with this admixture the cotton changes its chemical composition and becomes explosive. The collodion cotton is one of the varieties of the "firing cotton". . .

At the time these instructions appeared in *Svoboda,* the authors of this book telephoned Luke Myshuha at his New Jersey offices.

"Why are you printing instructions on bomb-making?" we asked him.

There was a long pause at the other end of the wire. Then, in a very heavy accent, the editor of *Svoboda* replied, "We print them in the interest of science."

"Are you running a correspondence school in bomb-making?" we asked.

"Yes," said Luke Myshuha.

The "Salesman of Terror" had departed, but the "Big Mouse" was carrying on.

CHAPTER SIX

HOW MANY WERE SABOTAGED?

I. *What About the Normandie?*

It was the afternoon of February 9, 1942. The great liner *Normandie* was lying at her pier in the North River, near the foot of West 49th Street, New York City. Her name altered to S.S. *Lafayette,* she had been converted into an auxiliary vessel for the United States Navy. The final changes were being made on the giant ship. Many of the new crew were already aboard, waiting to take her out of the harbor. She was scheduled to sail in five days. . . .

At 2:30 P.M., the cry of "Fire!" suddenly rang out.

A pile of kapok life-preservers in the ship's main lounge was ablaze. Men rushed to extinguish the flames. They could not get the fire under control. It was a windy day. Driven by the currents of air, the flames began whirling rapidly through the corridors of the 83,400 ton ship. As the conflagration spread, furiously feeding on everything in its path, the ship-yard workers, crew members and Coast Guardsmen — some 3,000 in all — began swarming over the mountainous sides of the vessel, clambering down ropes and ladders to the safety of the docks.

Within an hour, the S.S. *Lafayette* was a blazing inferno. Great black waves of smoke poured from the ship and drifted over the city. The black clouds carried across town as far as Fifth Avenue and downtown as far as 18th Street. Fire engines and fire boats, which had rushed to the scene, hurled tons of water onto the flaming ship. The water seemed only to intensify the flames. An endless file of stretcher-bearers marched from the ship to waiting ambulances, carrying the burned and the injured.

All afternoon and evening the *Lafayette* burned. In the early hours of the morning, the enormous ship, weighted down by tons of water in her hold, with fires still burning in her superstructure, listed toward the water side of the pier, tilted to a 45-degree angle and slowly began to settle down on her side.

At a time when ships were desperately needed, the United States Navy had lost its largest auxiliary vessel.

One man was dead.

Over 250 sailors, workers, Coast Guardsmen and firemen were injured.

Two weeks of provisions for 2,000 men had been destroyed.

Thousands of working hours had been lost.

Millions of dollars of damage had been accomplished. . . .

Who was to blame?

On January 13, twenty-seven days before the burning of the *Normandie,* Attorney General Biddle revealed at a closed session of the House Appropriations Committee that he had recently received a memorandum from President Roosevelt urging him "to look into the situation of possible sabotage of vessels." The President of the United States had received word that vitally strategic docks in a number of key U. S. ports were being frequented by Axis agents. The President urged that immediate action be taken by the Department of Justice.

It was known that Nazi agents had for a long time been secretly watching the *Normandie.* Two weeks before France fell, on June 3, 1940, the German secret service had sent a coded short-wave radio message to Nazi spies in the United States. The message, which was flashed from Hamburg to the Nazi secret radio station at Centerport, Long Island, stated when deciphered: "Thanks for reports. Observe Normandie."

Following instructions, Nazi spies began to "observe" the *Normandie*. At regular intervals they reported to the Third Reich about the $60,000,000 luxury liner, which was to be converted for use by the U. S. Navy. The Nazi spy Kurt Frederick Ludwig wrote in invisible ink to his superiors in Germany on April 15, 1941: "At pier 88 north is still NORMANDIE."

Ludwig regularly visited the New York waterfront to examine the *Normandie*. An FBI Agent who was assigned to trail the Nazi spy, described one of Ludwig's trips to the waterfront in the following report:

> On June 18 [1941] he walked down 12th Avenue from 59th Street. He was watching the piers. When he came to the Normandie's pier at 50th Street he stopped for some time. He seemed to be examining it carefully. Then he walked on, looking back. At 42nd Street he took the Weehawken ferry, went on the upper deck and kept watching the Normandie.

This same agent of the FBI also reported that after Ludwig arrived in Weehawken he spent twenty minutes writing in a small black notebook.

Two months after the *Normandie* fire a House Naval Affairs subcommittee, which had been established to investigate the disaster, announced the results of its findings. Its report stated that "the cause and consequence of the fire are directly attributable to carelessness and lack of supervision." According to the subcommittee, the responsibility for the disaster lay with the Navy which "had accepted the vessel and 'full responsibility' therefore."

Five days after the House subcommittee's report, a Naval Court of Inquiry made public the results of an investigation it had conducted. The Naval Court charged that the Robbins Drydock and Repair Company, which had held the contract for converting the *Normandie* into a naval transport, was to be held fully responsible for the disaster. "Gross carelessness and utter violation of the rules of common sense" on the part of the Robbins Drydock and Repair Company, were reported to have been "the direct and sole cause" of the fire.

Shortly afterwards the Senate Naval Affairs Committee reported the findings of an investigation it had been carrying on. This report stated that it was "difficult to fix the blame on any one individual or group of individuals." However, the report declared that the New York Fire Department was responsible for the ship's capsizing because of "the undue amount of water placed on board by the New York City Fire Department in the act of extinguishing the fire."

Although all three contradictory reports refused to admit the possibility of sabotage, they brought to light a number of strange and interesting facts:

Four small fires had broken out aboard the ship during the week immediately preceeding the disastrous conflagration of February 9.

Only two water buckets were within reach when the fatal fire broke out and one of them was only half-filled.

The city fire-alarm system had been disconnected from the vessel twenty-two days before the fire broke out and the Coast Guard, which had not been advised of this fact, turned in a blind alarm at the time of the fire.

There were a number of alien employees aboard the ship and no detailed check had been made of their records.

It had been possible for individuals to board the ship without any credentials or identification other than a numbered badge indicating the name of the contractor or subcontractor by whom they were supposed to be employed.

The House Naval Affairs subcommittee bluntly stated, "Opportunities for sabotage or almost any subversive activity were . . . abundant on the *Normandie*."

There were some significant facts about the *Normandie* fire which went unmentioned in the various reports of the official investigatory bodies.

One of these was the story of Edmund Scott, a reporter on the New York newspaper *PM*. Shortly after Pearl Harbor, Scott had been assigned to investigate reports that the New York waterfront was wide open to sabotage. Disguising himself as a longshoreman, the newspaperman prowled up and down the docks "playing enemy agent." He secured a job on the *Normandie* and worked on the ship for two days.

"By the end of the first day," Scott later reported, "I knew: Where the *Normandie* was going after she left New York. How many guns she was going to mount. The thickness of the armor over her portholes. What type of service she was going into."

While on board the *Normandie*, the reporter found there were innumerable opportunities for setting fire to the ship. He wandered alone and unmolested among barrels and boxes packed with excelsior and other inflammable goods. On his second day aboard, he took off his coat, which might, as he said, "have been loaded with incendiary or explosive materials," and left it lying on some packing cases for a number of hours. "That same day," Scott related, "I locked myself in six different toilets . . . for 15 minutes each time. I could have had my pockets filled with incendiary pencils, and used them with devastating effect. I could have soaked the walls and floor with gasoline; it would have been simple to carry a small flask of it on my hip."

Several weeks before the *Normandie* fire, *PM* reported Scott's experiences to an official of the Anti-Sabotage Division of the United States Maritime Commission. According to *PM,* the official was not interested. On the day after the fire, *PM* published Scott's story. It had not been published before, the newspaper explained, because it was a "blueprint for sabotage" which "would tell any enemy agent . . . just how to go about setting the *Normandie* afire, just how easy it would be."

Another fact of interest not touched upon in the government reports on the fire concerned the Oceanic Service Corporation, which handled the hiring of a number of the workers and guards on the *Normandie.*

The man who had organized Oceanic Service Corporation and who for a time was its vice-president was William Drechsel. He had formerly been marine superintendent of the North German Lloyd Steamship Line. Drechsel admitted before the McCormack-Dickstein Committee in 1934 that he had supplied $125,000 bail for Nazi agents who had been arrested in the United States. In 1936, during the trial of eleven persons who had been charged with disorderly conduct for staging an anti-Nazi demonstration on the *Bremen,* Drechsel was asked by the defense counsel: "As a member of the Nazi Party, do you owe allegience to Adolf Hitler?" Drechsel's loud answer was: "Yes!"

Two weeks after the burning of the *Normandie,* Congressman Samuel Dickstein charged in a speech on the floor of the House of Representatives that Drechsel had placed Nazi guards aboard the great liner. Referring to Drechsel as "the nation's No. 1 Nazi spy," the Congressman declared: "He . . . organized the Oceanic Service Corporation and through that agency is supplying guards to ships, warehouses and piers in New York. He placed more than thirty Nazi agents on the *Normandie.* . . ."

Was the *Normandie* sabotaged?

The evidence shows that the Nazis were keeping the giant ship under close observation, that enemy agents had access to the ship, and that opportunities for sabotage were abundant.

Sabotage is sometimes very difficult to prove. It took over twenty years before Germany was finally saddled with the guilt of the Black Tom and Kingsland sabotage disasters of World War I. Although events move more rapidly nowadays, it seems that for some time to come the burning of the *Normandie* will remain one of the major mysteries of World War II.

II. *The Mystery of the Eight Ships*

Early in 1942, eight American merchant ships, bound for Soviet Russia and heavily loaded with war supplies vital to the Red Army, suffered strange and similar fates. Not one of the ships reached its destination. Three of them foundered on the high seas; four limped back into the ports from which they had set out; and one crippled ship was torpedoed as it struggled to return to port.

Thousands of tons of munitions, airplane parts, tanks, guns and other war materials went down with the ships that sank. Seventeen seamen lost their lives. Precious weeks of time were forfeited before the four vessels which had managed to return to port were able to set out again.

In each case, according to the men who sailed the ships, "shifting cargo" was to blame. . . .

On March 1, 1942, the S.S. *Independence Hall,* after having been loaded at Philadelphia with tanks, airplane parts and munitions, set sail for the Soviet Union. For six days the vessel proceeded on her course without mishap. On the evening of March 6, when the boat was within a couple of hundred miles of Halifax, Nova Scotia, she ran into a storm. Lashed on the deck were a number of 28-ton Army tanks and large trucks. As the seas rose, the deck cargo began to shift. It had been improperly secured. Several seamen went to fasten the cargo. One of them was immediately washed overboard by an immense wave. Another was smashed up against a tank and seriously injured. Tanks and trucks broke loose and began careening across the deck. Towering fifty-foot waves swept over the boat, hurling the cargo of steel giants from one side of the boat to the other. In the hold, great cases enclosing airplane parts and munitions also began shifting, pounding against the side plates of the boat. There was now nothing the seamen could do, except watch their vessel being gradually smashed to pieces by her own cargo. Hour after hour the immense weights lurched back and forth. As the gray wind-swept day of March 7 wore on toward noon, the ship's framework gave way under the terrific strain. Suddenly, with a splintering roar, the *Independence Hall* broke in two. All the lifeboats had been crushed into matchwood under the blows of the deck cargo and there seemed to be no escape for the crew. But the two parts of the ship kept afloat until they grounded on the rocks of nearby Sable Island — although not before nine more of the crew had been swept overboard and drowned. The entire cargo, of course, was lost. . . .

Two weeks before, the steamship *Collmar* had sailed from Philadelphia, bound for Archangel. She carried a cargo of heavy guns, high explosives and other lend-lease supplies for the Russians. Shortly after picking up her convoy at Halifax, she ran into a heavy sea. The deck cargo, which was composed of big guns, had been faultily secured. A number of guns broke loose and were washed overboard. The balance of the cargo also began shifting. Crippled by the shifting cargo, the *Collmar* was forced to slow up. Less than twenty-four hours out of Halifax, she dropped out of the convoy and hove to.

She began limping back to Halifax. Early in the morning, when the foundering *Collmar* was within fifteen miles of port, she was rocked by a tremendous explosion. She began sinking rapidly. As the men took to the lifeboats, they saw the Nazi submarine that had fired the torpedo. A few hours later, the *Collmar's* lifeboats were sighted by the British freighter *Empire Woodcock,* and the survivors were rescued. Seven seamen had been killed when the *Collmar* was torpedoed.

Shifting cargo likewise proved to be the nemesis of the *Dumboyne,* which set out from Boston carrying a heavy load of guns and other lend-lease supplies for Russia.

"We were two days out when we were hit by a heavy sea," Edmund Luik, ship's carpenter, stated later. "In looking over the deck cargo to see if everything was secure, I noticed that the cotter pins were out of the shackles on the deck cargo. Portholes were not watertight, steering rods were uncovered and should have been inspected before leaving port. When the guns were mounted on the brig, the weight was so terrific that the lower part of the section was too weak to hold them. As a result, the entire brig swayed 8½ inches from port to starboard."

Confirming Luik's statement, Bos'n Jack Kitsen reported: "We had a cargo of ten tanks, weighing 19 tons apiece. Six tanks were forward and four aft. They were held on deck by means of turnbuckles and heavy timbers. The cotter pins attached to the turnbuckles were not in place."

Almost wrecked by her shifting cargo, the *Dumboyne* had to return to Halifax, and from Halifax to Boston for repairs. The delivery of her cargo of vitally needed war supplies was delayed for many weeks.

The *West Jaffery,* which sailed from Boston loaded with airplane parts, tanks and other war materials for the Red Army, sank off Newfoundland after shifting cargo had rendered her unmanageable.

The *Effingham,* carrying similar supplies, was forced to return to port after five days because her cargo had shifted dangerously.

The *City of Flint* had to return to port for reloading after four days at sea.

The *Juan de Larranga* had to return after three days; the *Tinteagle,* after five.

If only one ship had sunk or been crippled as a result of shifting cargo, suspicions might not have been aroused. But eight ships, almost within eight weeks . . . that was a different matter. The National Maritime Union, a number of whose members had lost their lives on these vessels, undertook a careful investigation of the strange voyages of the eight merchant ships bound for Russia.

On March 26, 1942, Joseph Curran, president of the National Maritime Union, appeared before a special hearing in Washington of the House Committee on the Merchant Marine and Fisheries. He presented to the committee the findings of the investigation which had been conducted by his union. He began by pointing out that shifting cargo was a danger that for some time past had rarely been encountered by the seamen.

"For many years," Curran told the congressmen, "we, as seamen, have been sailing ships that carried deck loads, deck loads of cargo, sometimes as high as you could possibly get it on, and we never lost any of that cargo. It was properly lashed and secured to stay snug in the worst type of western ocean weather. In this particular case, since this war has begun, something has happened to each of these seven* ships, one after the other."

Mr. Curran then described how all the ships in question had either foundered or been forced into port because of the shifting of faultily secured cargo.

---
* There were later found to be eight ships involved.

"We have supporting affidavits of men who were on these ships," he continued, "and these ships were all loaded by a particular company, a stevedoring company, that there is a great deal of discussion about around in various circles, and I understand there is interest in the Department of Justice in it. I understand that the owner of that stevedoring company was supposed to have been interned in the last war as a dangerous alien. . . . We do not say anything about the company, but seven ships loaded by the same company, bound for the same destination, were lost right in succession, and certainly there is something wrong. . . ."

At the time of writing, the mystery of the eight ships remains officially unexplained.

III. *Facts and Figures*

The year was 1940.

On July 10, President Roosevelt submitted to the United States Congress a $4,800,000,000 defense program.

On August 28, the United States Senate passed the Selective Service Act.

On September 5, fifty American destroyers were exchanged with England for British bases in the western hemisphere.

September 12: A thunderous explosion shook New Jersey. The Hercules Powder Plant at Kenvil had exploded. Fifty-two men died. Fifty were seriously injured. The damage ran into millions of dollars.

On September 27, Germany, Italy and Japan signed a pact pledging joint action if one of them should be attacked by a country not yet in the war. The pact was admittedly aimed at the United States.

On November 5, Franklin D. Roosevelt was elected President of the United States for a third term.

On November 8, in a speech at Munich, Adolf Hitler said in tones half-sarcastic, half-threatening: "As far as American production figures are concerned, they cannot even be formulated in astronomical figures. In this field, therefore, I do not intend to be a competitor."

November 12: Tremendous explosions occurred within a space of twenty minutes in three war-production plants in New Jersey and Pennsylvania. At Woodbridge, New Jersey, two buildings of the United Railway and Signal Corporation were destroyed by explosions. The company was manufacturing torpedoes and signal flares. At Edinburg, Pennsylvania, the Burton Powder Works of American Cyanimid and Chemical Corporation blew up. At Allentown, Pennsylvania, an explosion wrecked the plant of the Trojan Powder Company. The disaster killed sixteen persons. Scores were injured. The blasts occurred in the morning at 8, 8:10, and 8:20. Commenting on them the following day, Secretary of War Henry L. Stimson said the clocklike regularity of the explosions "might suggest Teutonic efficiency."

Also on November 12: A huge crane mysteriously collapsed in a San Francisco shipyard. In Atlanta, Georgia, fire destroyed the Municipal Auditorium in which Army equipment valued at $1,000,000 was stored. All the equipment was lost. Damage to the building, which housed a National Guard Armory, was estimated at $250,000.

During 1941, according to figures published by the Hartford Fire Insurance Company, industrial disasters (fires, explosions, etc.) caused American production a loss of 1½ billion man-hours. Scores of working men and women died in these catastrophes. The production time lost could have given the United States: 15 battleships, 5,000 heavy bombers, 65,000 light tanks.

Here are some of the mysterious accidents and disasters that occurred in 1941:

January 10: The British freighter *Black Heron* burned at Pier 8 in Brooklyn. The damage was estimated at $50,000 to $100,000. Three Douglas bombers were lashed to the dock at the time the fire started.

January 20: A mysterious fire broke out between two wings of the Navy Department building in Washington, D. C.

January 22: Storage shack in Philadelphia Navy Yard damaged by fire.

January 26: Administration Building of the naval operating base at Norfolk, Virginia, burned down. The fire destroyed communications office, telephone exchange, post office and disbursements office. Damage estimated at $275,000.

February 9: A fire broke out at the Frankford Arsenal at Philadelphia.

(February 24: Three boxes of dynamite, 50 feet of fuse and 5 boxes of blasting caps were stolen from the Farmerell Coal Company, Blakely, Pennsylvania.)

February 27: An explosion at the American Powder Company plant at Acton, Massachusetts. One man killed and one critically injured.

March 9: Second fire within a month at the Frankford Arsenal at Philadelphia, wrecking the interior of a powder mixing building.

March 16: The Cleveland to Pittsburgh train on the Pennsylvania R.R. line was wrecked near Baden, Pennsylvania. Five persons killed and 121 injured. The wreck was caused by "malicious tampering with the track."

March 24: Army barracks under construction at Ft. McDowell, Angel Island, San Francisco Bay, destroyed by fire of "undetermined origin."

(April 9: Dynamite sticks found at several plants in New York

State. One at the Auburn plant of the International Harvester Company, which was manufacturing Army combat truck parts. Six sticks of dynamite found at Ilion, in a coal car being unloaded at the plant. Authorities said that several similar discoveries had been made at Rochester and Amsterdam.)

April 28: Explosion on the French freighter *Angouleme,* docked in New Orleans. One man killed, one injured.

April 28: Fire broke out in the Navy Department powder plant at Indian Head, Maryland. There was $150,000 worth of damage.

May 15: Three major fires damaged piers and shipyards in Philadelphia, Baltimore and San Pedro.

The Philadelphia fire destroyed 22,000,000 feet of lumber consigned to defense industries, swept three blocks of homes and factories and destroyed a building of the Cramp shipyards, which had a $120,000,000 contract with the Navy. Total damage estimated at $5,000,000. An official said the fire apparently started in five places at once, about 5:00 A.M.

The Baltimore fire destroyed the steamer *Tolchester,* damaged a sister ship *Southport,* burned down a part of the Tolchester Line's pier, and ruined two of the Chesapeake Line's piers.

The San Pedro fire destroyed four blocks of pier sheds, as well as five small vessels and Harbor Department offices, which housed valuable records of the Army Engineer's office and the Weather Bureau.

May 27: Fire broke out at the Jersey City pier of the Greenville Terminal of the Pennsylvania R.R. This pier stands near the famed Black Tom Terminal. Thirty freight cars burned. Damage was estimated at $100,000. No defense materials were destroyed, but nearby were freight cars filled with crated artillery and bombing planes.

May 31: Fire swept the Jersey City waterfront. Damage to stockyards and warehouses estimated at $25,000,000. The fire destroyed 300,000 bushels of wheat, hay and grain; half of a six-story warehouse; 1,300 feet of cattle pens; 18 freight cars; a tugboat; 3 barges; 442 steers; 1,265 sheep; 414 calves.

June 8: Fire destroyed two of Clyde-Mallory Line's terminals at Jacksonville, Florida, as well as part of a ship which was at the dock. Damage estimated at $800,000.

June 24: Series of explosions at the Mare Island Navy Yard, Vallejo, California, blew out transformers and caused a blackout. All work on warships halted for 12 hours.

(July 22: The Senate passed a bill authorizing an annual expenditure of $1,000,000 to establish a police force to protect shore establishments. The Senate Naval Affairs Committee introduced confidential naval information to show that there had been widespread sabotage and attempted sabotage at Mare Island on the Pacific Coast, and at Norfolk, Boston, Indian Head, Maryland, and Philadelphia.)

August 7: At the Standard Naphthalene plant, Kearney, New Jersey, which was working on government contracts, a pipe mysteriously broke which was pumping liquid chlorine into the plant from a tank car on the siding. Fumes spread over three square miles. Fifty persons were affected and 33 were taken to the hospital. Operations were seriously delayed.

August 8: The oil tanker *Transiter,* carrying 15,000 barrels of gasoline, exploded in the River Rouge near Detroit.

August 13: Fire broke out at the Fairlawn, New Jersey, plant of the Wright Aeronautical Corporation.

August 13: Fire broke out at the Clark Township, New Jersey, plant of the Lewis Asphalt Engineering Corporation, which was producing national defense material. Six buildings were destroyed. The loss was estimated at $50,000.

August 14: Explosion at the $13,000,000 naval airbase under construction at Japonski Island, Alaska. Five men were killed.

August 18: Fire destroyed the freighter *Panuco,* at Pier 27 in Brooklyn, New York. Three other piers and 18 lighters were damaged. Total damage estimated at $1,000,000.

August 23: There were a series of explosions at the Socony Vacuum Oil Company, of Paulsboro, New Jersey.

August 27: A bomb exploded and destroyed the roof of the Community Hall at Dannebrog, Nebraska, where 150 persons were attending an American Legion ceremony in honor of draftees.

September 10: The Swedish freighter *Eknaren* was damaged by fire at Pier 16 in Brooklyn, New York.

September 11: The New York Central R. R. pier at 62nd Street and the North River partly destroyed by fire. Damage estimated at $25,000.

September 24: Fire destroyed the New England Steel Ship pier of the New Haven R. R., as well as the freighter *Virginia*. Loss estimated at $200,000.

September 25: The Norfolk and Western R. R. grain elevator at Norfolk, Virginia, was destroyed, and along with it 100,000 bushels of wheat. Loss estimated at $200,000.

September 29: Fire destroyed part of an 800,000 lb. cargo of cork from the boat *Jane Ann,* docked at Pier 27, East River, New York.

October 11: Fire destroyed three units of the Firestone Rubber and Latex Corporation, at Fall River, Massachusetts, which was producing gas masks, army belts and machine gun clips.

October 12: Second explosion within two months at the $13,000,000 naval base at Japonski Island.

October 16: An explosion destroyed the production division of the National Magnesium Corporation at Newark, New Jersey.

October 24: Two tankers burned at Robbins Drydocks, Brooklyn, New York.

November 6: Explosion at the Carbide & Carbon Chemical Corporation plant at South Charleston, West Virginia. Two persons killed, five seriously injured.

(November 16: 250 lbs. of dynamite were stolen from the Lepre Quarry at South Orange, New Jersey.)

November 17: Fire destroyed $1,000,000 worth of blue prints and machinery at the Andale Company, Lansdale, Pennsylvania, manufacturers of machinery turning out power plant equipment for the Navy.

December 12: Explosion at the $60,000,000 ordnance plant at Burlington, Iowa.

December 20: Fire broke out in the Steel & Alloy Tank Company plant in Newark, New Jersey. Damage estimated at $100,000. Precision tools and hundreds of X-ray plates destroyed. Work halted on $500,000 defense contract.

December 24: Explosion in the main building of the Browntown Silica Company, Browntown, Wisconsin. Damage estimated at $150,000.

In the spring of 1942 a series of forest fires broke out in North Carolina, New Jersey, Rhode Island and Connecticut. All of the fires had certain mysterious features in common.

In western North Carolina, forest fires started on April 19 and lasted for more than a week, destroying hundreds of thousands of dollars worth of valuable timber. New fires were constantly breaking out while fire-fighters tried to suppress the flames. District Ranger J. B. Fortin of Brevard, North Carolina, described how on April 20, about midnight, 21 new blazes started on Sunburst Mountain. He said the fires were set by one or more persons, and that officials were seeking the "phantom firebug" or saboteurs.

During the same week raging fires swept through the woodlands of New Jersey. More than 5,000 acres of forest land were destroyed. One hundred and sixty-eight different fires were reported burning in one area. A crew of 2,500 men — including hundreds of soldiers, fire service wardens and volunteers — was involved in fighting the fires. Much of the wood burned was pine and cedar which is in heavy demand for war use. District Fire Warden John Wiley of Wayside, New Jersey, said that the fire in his area was "without a doubt" touched off. "It is the third fire we have had in this vicinity the last two weeks and each one came when the wind was blowing toward the Army encampment," the Fire Warden declared.

On the last day of April, forest fires broke out in a dozen different places in a fifty mile area in Rhode Island. Governor J. Howard McGrath said the fires were the worst in the history of the State. He proclaimed martial law in three towns and in sections of three others. A fire-fighting force of more than 3,000 soldiers, sailors, and fire service wardens sought to bring the flames under control. James R. Simmons, district supervisor of the Department of Agriculture Forest Service, commented on the suspicious origin of some fifteen small fires discovered in an area including lumber yards where 1,750,000 feet of lumber intended for defense production were stored. "It seems strange to me," said Simmons, "that fifteen fires should suddenly spring up where the United States Government has so much lumber stored."

On the same day that the Rhode Island fires started, two big forest fires broke out in Connecticut near the town of Sterling.

And near Keene, New Hampshire, state police reported finding a small balloon to which was fastened a paper bag containing a candle that had burned out. In World War I, the Germans called this sabotage device the "Zepplinite". . . .

During the early months of 1942, forest fires were not the only means by which vital war materials were being destroyed. These are some of the other catastrophes which were occurring:

January 1: Fire on the freighter *Pocone,* docked at Brooklyn, New York. 40,000 bags of castor beans, 30,000 bags of coffee and a large number of bales of cotton were destroyed.

January 8: Fire at Pier 83, North River, New York City, destroyed pier, two buildings, and 3,000 bags of copra and other freight.

January 14: Fire destroyed Texas Company pier and warehouse at Claymont, Delaware. Both pier and warehouse border on compact defense industry area. Damage estimated at $250,000.

January 25: Fire destroyed Army Administration Building at Voorheesville, New York.

January 30: Fire destroyed 150 bales of cotton on American Export S. S. Line pier at Jersey City, New Jersey.

January 30: Fire in building under construction at Springfield, Massachusetts. Damage estimated at $100,000. Officials say expansion of manufacture of Garand rifles may be delayed three months.

February 13: Explosion wrecked Navy TNT house at Southeast Washington. Three persons killed, four injured.

February 22: Fire at Ford Motor Company, aircraft plant in Dearborn, Michigan.

February 23: Fire destroyed large quantities of lumber at J. Cohen & Bros., New York City, a concern supplying lumber to Army camps.

And here is a list of headlines from the month of March, 1942:

SEVEN KILLED IN BLAST IN ORDNANCE PLANT—
15 Others Are Injured As An Explosion Rocks Factory in Iowa When Shifts Change   (New York *Times,* March 5)

SEVEN FIREMEN INJURED IN HUGE WOOL FIRE—
1,500,000 Pounds Wool Destroyed
                              (Boston *Evening American,* March 6)

TWO DEAD, THIRTEEN HURT IN OIL BARGE EXPLOSION   (Houston, Texas· *Post,* March 7)

FOUR DIE IN BLAST OF MUNITIONS TRUCK—4 Die and 100 Injured   (New York *Times,* March 8)

PHILADELPHIA PROBES THIRD SHIP FIRE IN FOUR DAYS   (New York *Journal-American,* March 9)

CUT CABLES OF SOUTHERN CALIFORNIA TELEPHONE COMPANY STARTS SABOTAGE INQUIRY
                       (Los Angeles *Times,* March 11)

U. S. PROBES SABOTAGE IN PARACHUTE SILK FIRE AT SAN DIEGO   (Los Angeles *Examiner,* March 12)

GYPSUM COMPANY PLANT SWEPT BY FIRE
                 (Niagara Falls, N. Y., *Gazette,* March 13)

FIRE AT GETTYSBURG DESTROYS PLANT OF CENTRAL CHEMICAL CORPORATION
                       (Washington *Star,* March 14)

FLAMES SWEEP WAREHOUSE USED BY ARMY—Adjoining War Plant Was Badly Damaged—Official Declares Blaze Was "Not Accidental"
                 (San Francisco *Examiner,* March 16)

TWO DIE, FIVE HURT IN BLAST AT WELLAND CHEMICAL COMPANY PLANT
                 (Buffalo *Courier Express,* March 17)

FIRE SWEEPS WAR PLANT—Sabotage Inquiry Started Into Sculler Safety Corp. Blaze
                       (New York *Times,* March 21)

BRITISH SHIP DAMAGED BY FIRE AT NEW YORK
                       (Washington *Star,* March 23)

HELD IN ARMS PLANT FIRE—New Haven Watchman Seized in Inquiry Into High Standard Manufacturing Corporation Blaze   (New York *Times,* March 24)

DOCK SABOTAGE EFFORT TOLD BY COMMANDER C. H. ABEL, CAPTAIN OF THE PORT
                 (Baltimore *Evening Sun,* March 24)

ORIGIN OF FIRE AT AIR BASE TO BE PROBED BY ARMY OFFICIALS (Greenville, S. C., *News*, March 24)

BLAST WRECKS MANUFACTURING PLANT IN WALLINGFORD (New Haven, Conn., *Register,* March 26)

31 KILLED IN EASTON, PA. QUARRY EXPLOSION— A Mystery, Sabotage Clue Sought by FBI
(Washington *Times-Herald,* March 27)

REMINGTON ARMS CO. PLANT SHAKEN BY EXPLO- SION (Sheboygan, Wisc., *Press,* March 28)

48 INJURED IN REMINGTON ARMS BLAST—SIX MISSING (New York *Herald-Tribune,* March 29)

3 KILLED IN UNEXCELLED FIREWORKS CO. BLAST— 4 More Badly Burned (New York *Times,* March 29)

SABOTEURS FIRE TWO CALIFORNIA RAILROAD SPANS (New York *Herald-Tribune,* March 30)

TWENTY HURT IN 3 BLASTS AT TISI OIL STORAGE PLANT (New York *Herald-Tribune,* March 31)

FIRE DESTROYS CORTLAND BOAT FACTORY— Thompson Plant Was Preparing to Take War Contract
(New York *Herald-Tribune,* March 31)

EXPERTS SUSPECT SABOTAGE IN LEHIGH PORT- LAND CEMENT CO. BLAST
(Washington *Star,* March 31)

CHAPTER SEVEN

COUNTER-SABOTAGE

The three chief agencies for combatting enemy espionage-sabotage activities in the United States are the Federal Bureau of Investigation, G2 (Military Intelligence) and Naval Intelligence. On September 6, 1939, President Roosevelt issued a directive placing the FBI in charge of all investigations of espionage and sabotage in the United States, and requesting all local law enforcement officials to cooperate with J. Edgar Hoover's department in this work. That same month a General Intelligence Division was established in Washington under the direction of the FBI. Even before the President's directive placing the FBI in supreme charge, members of G2 and Naval Intelligence had been receiving part of their training at FBI schools, and the FBI had been working closely with the Army and Navy Intelligence Divisions.

Soon after the outbreak of war in Europe, the FBI took steps to protect American defense industries. The Bureau drew up a confidential booklet "incorporating the basic principles of protection against espionage and sabotage," which was distributed to reliable plant officials, law-enforcement officers, and representatives of public utilities, railroads, airlines and steamship companies. FBI agents in the field divisions summoned for special conferences the heads of corporations engaged in defense production, and outlined to them steps that should be taken to ensure protection for the products they were manufacturing under Army and Navy contracts. The Bureau also arranged to survey defense plants to see that the necessary protective measures were taken.

FBI agents were soon instructing local law-enforcement

officials in scientific methods of combatting espionage and sabotage. A number of cities set up special branches in their police departments to act as "anti-sabotage units" to cooperate with Hoover's men.

In the summer of 1941, the Federal Bureau of Investigation, after many months of careful preparation, rounded up members of two large Nazi espionage-sabotage rings in the New York area. One was the ring headed by the veteran saboteur-spy, Frederick Joubert Duquesne, an agent of Colonel Nicolai. The other ring was headed by Kurt Frederick Ludwig, an agent of Heinrich Himmler. There were forty-nine men and women agents caught by the FBI in this major round-up.

Another important Axis espionage-sabotage ring was smashed by the FBI in June 1942, when Anastase Vonsiatsky was arrested after a raid on his Thompson, Connecticut, headquarters. As a result of FBI findings, Vonsiatsky was charged with violating the Espionage Act and divulging United States military information to the German and Japanese Governments, "particularly information relating to the numbers, personnel, disposition, equipment, arms and morale of the Army; the location, size, capacity and other features of the United States fleet; the location, size, equipment and other features of military establishments, naval establishments, airports, aircraft, shipping and other establishments . . . essential to the national defense of the United States."

Indicted with Vonsiatsky as co-conspirators were Gerhardt Wilhelm Kunze, former Fuehrer of the German American Bund, who had escaped to Mexico a short time before and was subsequently arrested there and turned over to the United States authorities; Dr. Otto Willumeit of Chicago, former leader of the Chicago unit of the German American Bund; Reverend Kurt E. Molzahn, pastor of a Philadelphia Lutheran church, who was charged with serving as a go-between for the spy ring; and Dr. Wolfgang Ebell, a physician of El Paso, Texas, whose home was used as headquarters for German and Japanese agents. All of the accused pleaded guilty with the exception of Molzahn, who contested the charges against himself.

The growing power of America's counter-sabotage forces was dramatically made clear to the public on June 28, 1942, when the FBI announced the capture of eight Nazi saboteurs who had been landed by German submarines in Florida and Long Island. Four of the saboteurs had been landed during the night of June 13, 1942, at Amagansett Beach, Long Island. The other four had been landed six days later at Ponte Vedra Beach in Florida.

The eight saboteurs carried $174,000 in United States currency for bribery and for paying off their accomplices in the United States. Each man had been trained at a special sabotage school near Berlin; each had been chosen for his familiarity with the American language; and each had lived in the United States. Two were American citizens, and most of them had been members of the German American Bund.

They had come equipped with all the latest devices for sabotage: high-explosive bombs disguised as pieces of coal and wooden blocks, special timing devices, fuses of all sorts, blocks of TNT carefully packed in excelsior, rolls of electric cable, and a number of small incendiary bombs disguised as fountain pens and pencils. They had even been supplied by the German Intelligence with forged Selective Service and Social Security cards.

The eight saboteurs were: George John Dasch, alias Davis, who came to the United States from Germany in 1922, married an American citizen, and returned to Germany in 1941; Robert Quirin, alias Richard Quintas, who came to the United States from Germany in 1927, worked as a mechanic in this country, and returned to Germany in 1939; Werner Thiel, alias John Thomas, who came to the United States shortly after World War I, worked in Detroit automobile plants, and returned to Germany in 1939; Heinrich Harm Heinck, alias Henry Kanor, who entered the United States illegally in 1936, worked as a waiter in New York City, and returned to Germany in 1939; Ernest Peter Burger, alias Peter Burger, who came to the United States in 1927, became an American citizen, worked as a machinist in Milwaukee and Detroit, joined the Michigan National Guard, and returned to Germany in 1933; Herman Neubauer, alias Herman Nicholas, who came to the United States in 1931, worked in Hartford and Chicago hotels, married an American citizen, and returned to Germany in 1940; Edward John Kerling, alias Edward Kelly, who came to the United States in 1929, was employed by a New Jersey oil company, and returned to Germany in 1936; and Herbert Haupt, who came to the United States in 1922, became an American citizen, worked in an optical plant in Chicago, and returned to Germany in 1941.

The saboteurs carried with them detailed instructions for an extensive sabotage campaign in the United States. The campaign was to include:

> destruction of hydro-electric plants at Niagara Falls, New York, and of three plants of the Aluminum Company of America located at Massena, New York, E. St. Louis, Illinois, and at Alcoa, Tennessee;
>
> crippling of a cryolite plant at Philadelphia which produces materials essential for the production of aluminum;
>
> blowing up of Hell Gate Bridge over the East River in New York;
>
> destruction of the Pennsylvania Railroad Terminal at Newark, New Jersey, through which flow great quantities of war products and raw materials going into the nation's war effort;
>
> sabotage of New York City's reservoirs concentrated in Westchester County;

destruction of the canal and lock system at Cincinnati, Ohio, and St. Louis, Missouri;

destruction of the "horseshoe" curve of the Pennsylvania railroad at Altoona, to paralyze Pennsylvania's anthracite coal industry by wrecking rail transportation.

The scope of these plans, found in documentary form by the FBI on the captured men, indicated that the eight saboteurs had been sent into the United States to supervise the activities of a large and well-organized Nazi sabotage ring which was already in existence in this country.*

Immediately following America's entry into the war, the FBI began making raids in every part of the country on the homes and hideouts of enemy suspects. As a result of these raids, the FBI seized large supplies of explosives, incendiary materials, arms, short-wave radio equipment and other materials stored for purposes of sabotage and espionage. FBI agents undertook investigations on a nation-wide scale of Axis suspects working in the war industries.

Cooperating with the FBI and Military and Naval Intelligence, major United States defense plants organized anti-sabotage units and detailed trained guards to watch over all phases of production. Shortly after Pearl Harbor, General Motors Corporation, for example, doubled its guard force as a precaution against spies and saboteurs. The guards were placed on twenty-four hour duty in and around all of the company's ninety plants. All lunch boxes and packages were carefully inspected. Extra spotlights and alarm systems were installed. Under the direction of the trained guards, production workers were organized into special fire-brigades equipped to fight all forms of incendiary sabotage.

---

* On August 8, 1942, six of the Nazi saboteurs were executed at Washington, D. C. Ernest Peter Burger received a life sentence. George John Dasch was sentenced to thirty years in prison.

"We know that saboteurs will be quick to take advantage of any letting down of our guard," a departmental head of a large United States defense plant said, explaining his company's counter-sabotage policy. "We would rather have people on edge and alert to every little thing than have them take the view that they need not bother reporting something to us because it probably will not prove important."

American labor unions drew up practical plans for combatting sabotage in the various defense industries. The National Maritime Union held a conference in April 1942, "for the purpose of perfecting joint anti-sabotage committees on board all vessels." On the West Coast, Harry Bridges, president of the International Longshoremen's and Warehousemen's Union, proposed and, jointly with the Pacific Coast Maritime Industry Board, put into effect a "Plan For Maximum Production in Maritime Transport of War Materials and Supplies." This plan included a provision for "properly guarding terminals, docks, ships and cargoes against acts of sabotage and pilfering; improper or unsafe stowage of cargoes; fire hazards, such as smoking on ships and docks; and for detection and exposure of any fifth column elements."

The Railroad Brotherhoods, the United Automobile, Aircraft and Agricultural Implement Workers, and other large unions took steps to guard against sabotage.

Credit must be given to the American press for the superb job it has done in warning against the lack of vigilance at certain industrial plants and the consequent glaring opportunities for sabotage. The New York City newspaper *PM* assigned special reporters to visit docks, freight yards, and various plants manufacturing vital war materials for the Army and Navy. The reporters found that they were able to gain access to these strategic centers and to wander through them "with complete freedom and without identification of any kind." Reporters from the Cleveland *Plain Dealer* carried on the same type of investigation and exposed an equally dangerous situation in their area. Alert newspapers throughout the country vigorously campaigned against this sort of negligence and the "business-as-usual" attitude it evidenced.

It was clear from these newspaper investigations that in spite of the efforts of government agencies, management, and labor, alarming opportunities for sabotage still prevailed.

On March 30, 1942, C. W. Pierce, executive of the National Bureau for Industrial Protection, was quoted in the New York *Journal of Commerce* as warning:

> Let no one make the mistake of planning our war production in terms of appropriated billions which presupposes uninterrupted continuance of our facilities. Results in finished guns, ships, and equipment, must be counted only after they have rolled off the assembly lines and are delivered for actual service. Equipment cannot roll from a plant wrecked by fire or sabotage. Ships cannot be launched from yards laid waste by explosions or other disasters.

Despite all the measures taken, serious shortcomings clearly still exist in United States counter-sabotage preparations. How can these shortcomings be overcome?

The House Naval Affairs subcommittee which investigated the inexcusable *Normandie* disaster has recommended:

> The entire waterfront should be designated as a restricted area. Such sections of the waterfront that load and discharge war supplies should be declared a prohibited zone. . . . No one should be granted access to any prohibited zone unless they have a Coast Guard identification card, and such identification card shall bear an approval stamp of the Federal Bureau of Investigation.

As this book is written, the House subcommittee's recommendation to guard our vulnerable piers and ships from enemy saboteurs has yet to be put into effect.

Another important measure that might well be adopted is this:

The Joint Management-Labor Committees, which were set up at the request of War Production Chief Donald Nelson, could undertake a nationwide campaign to enlist all war-workers in the fight against sabotage. These committees could draw upon the knowledge and experience of 11,000,000 men and women in factories, railroads, warehouses, docks and shipyards, who are intimate with every detail of the United States production machine, and who could make valuable recommendations for the safeguarding of war machinery and war products. An army of 11,000,000 vigilant American workers could be mobilized to guard against Axis sabotage.

PART II

PSYCHOLOGICAL SABOTAGE

A DEFINITION

Fires, explosions, poisons and machine wrecking are not the only devices of Axis sabotage. The fascist powers have developed another and even more deadly method of crippling their enemies. This is *psychological sabotage.*

Psychological sabotage is the systematic undermining of morale, the warping of public opinion, the fomenting of doubt and indecision, the stirring up of dissension and disunity. It seeks to take advantage of legitimate differences of opinion, to intensify those differences, and thus frequently to make sincere and unsuspecting persons the unconscious instruments of psychological sabotage. It is a secret war directed against the mind and spirit of the people.

Here is how Dr. Ewald Banse, the foremost Nazi "strategist of terror," has defined this unique form of Axis sabotage:

> Applied psychology as a weapon of war means propaganda intended to influence the mental attitudes of nations toward war. It is essential to attack the enemy nation in its weak spots (and what nation has not its weak spots?), to undermine and break down its resistance, and to convince it that it is being deceived, misled and brought to destruction by its own government. Thus the people will lose confidence in the justice of its cause so that the political opposition in those nations (and what nation is without one?) will raise its head and become a more powerful trouble-maker. The enemy nation's originally solid, powerful and well-knit fabric must be gradually disintegrated, broken down, rotted, so that it falls apart like a fungus treaded upon in a forest.

Disruptive propaganda, malicious rumors and lies, artificially created opposition movements, deliberate exploitation of genuine opposition movements, bribery, corruption and intimidation — these are the weapons of the Axis psychological saboteurs. They operate in every field of national life. In business and politics, in the factories, on the farms and in the armed forces, they spread the germs of confusion and demoralization. It is their job to soften up the people, and to make them easy prey for the panzer divisions and the Gestapo hangmen. They are the advance guard of the Axis.

In the United States, the psychological saboteurs have had five major objectives:

1) to disrupt and disunite the American people by the stirring up of race hatred and by similar divisive techniques;

2) to undermine the confidence of the American people in their own form of government and in the Administration of President Roosevelt;

3) to isolate the United States and prevent it from joining any anti-Axis alliance and from aiding those nations attacked by the Axis aggressors;

4) to prevent the United States from being adequately prepared for the Second World War;

5) to build an American fascist party which would act as a fifth column ally to the Axis attack from without.

CHAPTER EIGHT

THE SECRET OFFENSIVE

I. *Hitler's Year*

The summit of the career of Adolf Hitler was reached in the year 1940. From the bleak Norwegian north to the warm sands of Southern France, his power straddled the European continent. Within an incredibly short time, one nation after another had crumpled before the Nazi assault. Too late a shocked world became aware of the insidious weapon which had made inevitable the sudden collapse of Hitler's opponents at the first blow of his mechanized armies.

In each country that he attacked, Hitler had previously organized his fifth column of psychological saboteurs to undermine morale and spread doubt, treachery and confusion. While Hitler prepared for war, his agents in Holland, Norway, Poland and France were crying "Peace!" While Nazi industry produced immense quantities of arms, Der Fuehrer's agents in other countries campaigned against rearmament. Hitler involved all sorts of people in his campaign of psychological sabotage. Premiers and diplomats, professors and businessmen, journalists, labor leaders and politicians — some wittingly and some unwittingly — spread Hitler's poison in their own lands. In many instances those who were innocently involved were just as useful to the Axis as the Quislings, for, though blind to the threatened dangers, they were sincere in their own motives and were therefore more easily able to convince others.

American eyes were on Europe in 1940, watching with

horror the havoc being wrought by Hitler's panzer divisions and fifth columns. To Americans, reading the terrible headlines of that year, the events in Europe had the quality of a nightmare.

It seemed impossible that these things could ever happen over here. Yet they *were* happening over here. Hitler's psychological saboteurs were busy here, too. . . .

Two months after France fell, on the afternoon of August 26, 1940, the late Senator Ernest Lundeen of Minnesota telephoned his secretary from the Senate floor to say that he was expecting a "visitor" at his office at 2:30 P.M. Rather to the surprise of his secretary, the Senator did not name this visitor. That same afternoon the anonymous visitor presented himself and was promptly shown into the private office of Senator Lundeen, who had already returned from the Senate floor and was awaiting him.

The man whom the late Senator Lundeen received in his private office, and whom he had hesitated to name on the telephone, was one of the leading Nazi agents in the United States. The Senator's visitor was George Sylvester Viereck, "the head and brains of an insidious propaganda machine, engaged in sabotaging the President's efforts to arouse the American people to their danger. . . ."*

Emerging from the Senator's office that afternoon, Viereck approached Miss Elizabeth Tomai, the Senator's secretary, and asked her to telephone the office of Representative Hamilton Fish and leave a message for the Congressman. The message was that he, Viereck, would be "a little late" for his 3:15 appointment with Representative Fish. Viereck then turned to another one of the girls in the office and asked her to deliver

---

* Viereck was thus characterized by William Power Maloney, Special Assistant to the Attorney General, on October 10, 1941.

a large envelope to the office of Senator Rush D. Holt of West Virginia. . . .

*   *   *   *   *

But in order to understand how George Sylvester Viereck, a paid Axis agent, came to be welcomed into the private offices of United States Senators and Representatives, one must first trace the devious ramifications of the vast and sinister conspiracy worked out in Berlin, Rome and Tokyo to weaken American defenses and undermine American morale. One must first unravel the whole tangled story of Axis psychological sabotage directed against the United States.

II. *Unser Amerika*

As soon as he took power in Germany, Adolf Hitler launched his secret war against the United States. At first Der Fuehrer was obsessed with the idea of "Germanizing" America. The United States Government was to be overthrown and a German-American *Gauleiter* appointed to rule over America.

According to Dr. Colin Ross, the Nazi ideologist of the "Germanization" program, and author of the book *Unser Amerika* (Our America), there were 30,000,000 persons in the United States with German blood in their veins. These millions constituted a vast reservoir of "Aryan manpower," ready to be mobilized by the Nazis and welded into a German army on American soil. "I firmly believe," wrote Dr. Ross, "in America's German hour." The Germanic legions in this country, if properly organized, could soon bring about a successful Nazi *putsch*. America "by any and all means" was to be converted into "Unser Amerika."

Dr. Joseph Paul Goebbels supported Ross's theory, publicly declaring, "Nothing will be easier than to produce a bloody revolution in North America. . . . No other country has so many social and racial tensions. We shall be able to play on many strings there."

The practical Nazi experts in the field of psychological sabotage — Rudolf Hess, Colonel Nicolai and other leaders of German psychological intelligence — recognized from the start that these over-enthusiastic dreams of a German Revolution in America were not to be taken too seriously. Hess and Nicolai foresaw the inevitable shortcomings of a purely German fifth column in the United States. They were in complete agreement with William Dudley Pelley, the ambitious U. S. Silver Shirt chief, who as early as June 22, 1933, wrote in a letter to a Nazi agent then active in New York:

> The adroit thing to do is to let a spontaneous American movement be born here that has exactly similar principles and precepts to Hitler's, that shall be American in character and personnel, and that shall work shoulder to shoulder with German aims and purposes. . . .

Nevertheless, Hess and Nicolai did not overlook the possibilities of a Nazified German-American bloc. They knew that such a bloc could play a vital role in their campaign of psychological sabotage. Consequently, they utilized scores of agents in the United States, such as Heinz Spanknoebel, Walter Kappe, Rheinhold Barth, Fritz Gissibl and Fritz Kuhn, to act as missionaries to the German-Americans, to spread disruptive propaganda and to carry out general fifth column assignments.

Within a year after the destruction of German democracy, every section of the United States had its quota of Nazi-dominated German-American rifle clubs, "cultural" and "fraternal" organizations. Nazi *Frauenschaften* (women's auxiliaries) and *Jugendschaften* (youth movements) were set up, the latter for indoctrinating American children of German descent with race hatred and with contempt for democracy.

After 1933 the Nazi-controlled German-American organizations functioning on American soil included:

League of the Friends of New Germany (Predecessor of German American Bund)
A. V. Jugendschaft (Hitler Youth)
Bund der Deutschen Maedchen (League of German Girls)
Ordnungsdienst (Order Service — Storm Troops)
Kyffhaeuser Bund (German Veterans League)
Stahlhelm (Steel Helmets)
Deutscher Konsum-Verband (German-American Business League)
German Legion
German Edda Kultur League
Deutsch Amerikanischer Wirtschafts-Ausschuss (German-American Economy League)
League of German-American Waiters
Hindenburg Youth Association
Homeland Regional Groups
Deutschamerikanische Berufsgemeinschaft (German-American Vocational League)
Deutscher Bund
Deutschamerikanischer Siedlungsbund (German-American Settlement League)
Heimatbund (Fatherland League)
Deutscher Kriegerbund von Nord-Amerika (German Soldiers League of North America)

The job of supervising these organizations in America was turned over to Ernst Wilhelm Bohle, a young widely- traveled mild-appearing Nazi, who had been born of German parents in Bradford, England, and educated in South Africa and Germany. Bohle was made head of the *Auslands-Organization*

(Foreign Division of the Nazi Party) in 1934; he was also appointed to the position of Gauleiter of the *Gau Ausland* (District of Germans Abroad)

Operating from his headquarters at Tiergartenstrasse 4 in Berlin, Bohle vigorously applied himself to the task of Nazifying all persons of German descent who lived outside the Third Reich. He told the 1935 Nuremberg Congress of the Nazi Party, "Just now we are in the midst of our fight for the creation of a Nazi Germany abroad." At the Congress of Germans Living Abroad, held at Stuttgart in the summer of 1937, he fervently declared, "We only know the concept of the complete German who as a citizen of his country is always and everywhere a German and nothing but a German. This makes him a Nazi." A favorite phrase with Bohle is: "Blood is stronger than passports."

This little-known man of Nazi politics laid the groundwork for the "Germanization" of Austria, Czechoslovakia and Memel. Under his guidance, veritable armies of Nazi provocateurs stirred up violence, spread anti-Semitic propaganda and fomented dissension throughout Europe, South America and the United States. Bohle accumulated extensive files bulging with the names, life-histories and political beliefs of persons of German blood living in foreign lands. In securing this information, Bohle had the close cooperation of the Nazi Propaganda Ministry, the Gestapo and the Military Intelligence. In 1937, members of Bohle's *Auslands-Organization* were said to total 3,000,000. According to the Swiss newspaper *Berner Tagwacht,* Bohle had 548 groups in 45 foreign countries working under him. Directing these groups were 25,000 propaganda agents and 2,500 special Gestapo men. For his work in 1937, the master psychological saboteur Bohle spent close to $100,000,000. In 1938 and 1939 this expenditure was considerably increased.

Assisting Bohle in organizing campaigns of psychological

sabotage in foreign countries was another agency of the Third Reich — the Psychological Laboratory. This Laboratory opened quarters at Lehrterstrasse 58, Berlin, in 1929, under the supervision of Colonel (later General) Hans von Voss, commander of the German Army's Division of Psychology. The Laboratory was originally formed to assist the Reichswehr in preparing psychological aptitude-tests and for the general psychological study of military operations. After Hitler came to power, the Laboratory acquired two new special divisions. These divisions, which operated under Colonel Nicolai and Colonel Dr. Albrecht Blau, were devoted to the prosecution of psychological offensives. The Laboratory placed its findings and its trained saboteurs at the disposal of Bohle and the German Military Intelligence. It also gave advice on matters of psychological strategy to various subsidiary Nazi bureaus particularly interested in the United States These bureaus, whose chief function was to seek out grievances in America, and to exploit them, included:

German Academy, Munich
Bureau Ribbentrop, Berlin
Institute of Political Geography, Castle Kroessinsee
German Academic Exchange Service, Berlin
Institute of American Research, Wuerzburg
Ibero-American Research Institute, Bonn
Ibero-American Institute, Hamburg
America Institute, Berlin

The Psychological Laboratory conducted exhaustive researches into "American national psychology." The Laboratory assigned specially trained psychological observers (or spies) to study every phase of American life from the characters of prominent citizens to the morale in the CCC camps, and to make detailed reports to Berlin on all of these subjects.

The Laboratory was primarily interested in locating America's *Stoerungskern* (trouble-center), which by means of skillful propaganda might be further aggravated for subversive ends. As a result of its investigations, the Laboratory decided that this *Stoerungskern,* this nucleus of irritation in America, was antagonism to the New Deal and, specifically, the hostility which Roosevelt's Administration had aroused among a number of American conservatives. The Nazi psychologists hoped to foster and intensify this opposition, to direct it into subversive channels, and thus to utilize it as an Axis weapon against the United States.

In 1935 Bohle and Rudolf Hess, Hitler's deputy, issued orders to Nazi agents in the United States that they were to concentrate on fomenting antagonism to the Roosevelt Administration and to spread the propaganda that the Government of the United States had fallen into the hands of "Jews" and "Communists." An "American citizens' group" was to carry out these orders and to give leadership to the Nazi fifth column. It was called the German American Bund.

In March 1936, Fritz Kuhn, then a chemist at the Ford Motor Company in Detroit, and former Gauleiter of the *Gau Mittelwest* (Midwest District) , was chosen to head the new organization. From the Nazi point of view, Kuhn's background equipped him ideally for the job. In Bavaria, in 1919, he had been a member of the notorious Epp Brigade which specialized in the murder and terrorization of democratic Germans. In 1921 he had been convicted of petty theft and sentenced to four months in jail.

Kuhn announced to the American public that the German American Bund was to be a "100% American and Christian organization." The American public was unimpressed. While the Bund recruited several thousand pro-Nazi German-Americans, it failed to build a mass fifth column in the United States. Its career was marked by a series of unsavory misadventures, which culminated in the imprisonment of Fritz Kuhn for having embezzled Bund funds. Bohle angrily referred to Kuhn's organization as the "Blunderbund."

It became increasingly clear to the Nazi psychologists that the only way to foment real trouble in America was through an organization of truly American aspect. The Nazis were constantly on the lookout for a native fifth column that might rally large numbers of Americans to its ranks.

During the years 1933-39 scores of American fascist organizations mushroomed in the United States. Calling themselves Crusaders for Americanism, American Guards, Silver Shirters, Christian Fronters, and other such pseudo-patriotic or pseudo-religious names, these native fascists spread propaganda blaming all social and economic evils on "the Jews" and asserted that the New Deal was a "Jewish-Communist" plot to rob Americans of their independence. The extent of the Nazi effort in this field is indicated by the fact that whereas in 1932 there were a mere handful of anti-democratic organizations active in the United States, by 1939 more than 750 of these organizations had been formed.

From the outset the Nazis emphasized the desirability of dividing Americans by setting Gentile against Jew. "It's child's play to make good anti-Semites of the Americans," Werner Haag, second-in-command of the Friends of New Germany, reported to his Berlin superiors in a letter written on September 23, 1933.

Native American demagogues saw the invaluable role that Jew-baiting might play. On March 3, 1934, a pamphleteer named Edward H. Hunter of Boston sent a confidential message to Friends of New Germany, then the foremost Nazi organization in the United States, which was headed by Fritz Gissibl, a German agent who subsequently returned to the Third Reich and became a high official in the Nazi Government. Hunter wrote:

German American Bund

ADDRESS: GERMAN AMERICAN BUND, P. O. BOX 1, STATION "K", NEW YORK, N. Y.

DISTRICT: ....
SECTION: ....
UNIT: ....
ADDRESS: ....

Application for
Membership

*) Payable when applying
Initiation Fee $1.00
Monthly Dues $0.75
Voluntary Donation $0.50 up
Newspaper-Subscription $3.00 per
year (if desired)

I hereby apply for admission to membership in the „German American Bund". The purposes and aims of the Bund are known to me, and I obligate myself to support them to the best of my ability. I recognize the leadership principle, in accordance to which the Bund is being directed. I am of Aryan descent, free from Jewish or colored blood.
Please write distinctly.

Full Name: .... Occupation: ....

Exact Address: .... Telephone: ....

Born: .... Place of Birth: .... Single/Married/Widowed: ....
    Day   Month   Year

First Papers. No.: .... What Court and when obtained: ....

Final Papers. No.: .... What Court and when obtained: ....
....

When and where immigrated: .... Passport No.: ....

Two References: (1) ....

    (2) ....

To what Organizations do you belong? ....

Only U. S. Citizens are eligible for office. First Papers suffice for Membership in "Prospective Citizens' League".

Date: ....

Paid Dues
Initiation Fee .... $:	
Monthly Dues .... $:	
Vol. Donation .... $:	

Applicant's Personal Signature

Unit Leader

Please do not use this space
No. ....

Crusaders for Americanism, Inc.

Application for Membership

*) Payable when applying
Initiation Fee $1.00
Monthly Dues $0.50

I hereby apply for admission to membership in the CRUSADERS FOR AMERICANISM, Inc. The purposes and aims of the organization are known to me, and I obligate myself to support them to the best of my ability. I am of Aryan descent, free from Jewish or colored blood.

Full Name: .... Occupation: ....

Exact Address: .... Telephone: ....

Born: .... Place of Birth: .... Single/Married/Widowed: ....
    Day   Month   Year

First Papers. No.: .... What Court and when obtained: ....

Final Papers No.: .... What Court and when obtained: ....

When and where immigrated: .... Passport No.: ....

Two References: (1) ....

    (2) ....

To what Organizations do you belong? ....

Only U. S. Citizens are eligible for office. First Papers suffice for Membership in "Prospective Citizens' League".

Date: ....

Paid Dues
Initiation Fee .... $:	
Monthly Contribution .. $:	
Vol. Donation .... $:	

Applicant's Personal Signature

Unit Leader

Please do not use this space
No. ....

The almost identical text and format of these application blanks reveal the intimate relationship which existed between the German American Bund and the so-called Crusaders for Americanism, one of the many "American" organizations set up by Nazi agents in the United States.

Protestant War Veterans
OF THE
United States
Incorporated
UNDER AN ACT OF CONGRESS
FOR THE DISTRICT OF COLUMBIA

ADDRESS ALL COMMUNICATIONS
TO THE ORGANIZATION

OFFICE OF CHAIRMAN
National Executive Committee
EDWARD JAMES SMYTHE

149 VERMILYEA AVENUE
NEW YORK CITY

July 28th-1939.

Terramare Office.
Kronenstraße I.
Berlin. Germany.

Gentlemen;-

Many thanks for the books on Hitler and the New
Germany, they are already out in circulation, I gave
them away at meetings I was addressing on the subject
of keeping American out of another alliance with Great
Britian and France and going to war against Germany.

If you writers and neaspaper people over there in
Germany only knew how hungry the American people were
for the real news from your Country, you would see that
this was supplied them...and I dont mean German-Americans.

The American people know that the press over here i
is JEW controlled and that they are being fed a lot of
lies, but they dont know how or where to get the truth, I
feel that it is your duty over there to get it over to
them here.

I am leading the fight against Roosevelt and his
gang of JEW Communists, and I will keep fighting them until I drive them out of office 1940. then I feel that
under a Republican Administration new and more friendly
relations will be created with Germany. that is the wishes
of the American Christian people as a whole. I wish that
you could convey this to your people through your press.

Americans love the German people, they are our best
Citizens, and the most law abiding, that is a matter of fact
and public record....while on the other hand...the Jews
lead in all fields of criminal activity. Arson. Rape. Dope
peddling. Fake Bankruptcy. Political bribery and corruption.
smuggling and White Slavery...they stand indicted as our
worst Citizens. if they are really Citizens at all.

Send me any other literature that you have on hand.

Cordially Yours.   Edward James. Smythe.

COMMUNISM WILL NOT BE TOLERATED

Letter from Edward James Smythe, head of the pro-Nazi, so-called "Protestant War Veterans," to a German propaganda agency. As this book goes to press, Smythe is a fugitive from American justice, being sought by agents of the FBI.

U. Bodung-Verlag

Erfurt (Germany), May 25th, 1939
Daberstedterstraße 4

" Amityville, Long Island
    U.S.A.

   We thank you for your letter of May 11th and the enclosed stamps.

   Under separate cover you will receive an other package
with different interesting literature. Moreover you should try
to get some enlightening American news and papers, as "Social
Justice" by Father Coughlin, "Defender" by Rev.Winrod, Kansas,
and the English paper "Action" by the British Union, London.

   Books you should read are:

 "Bombshell Against Christianity" by Eli Ravage   10 cts

 "The Hidden Hand of Judah" by N.Markoff and

         C.B.Jood ....   15 cts

 "The Jewish World Conspiracy" by Dr.Hemmeister..   45 cts

These books you can obtain at this office at the named price.

   We enjoy reading that your discussion group is progress-
ing very nicely and hope that our literature will help you for
further understanding of the Jewish danger.

   Hoping to hear from you soon again,

            Yours very truly

             Schirmer
           American Section.

A communication dated May 25, 1939, from the American Section of *Welt-Dienst* (World Service), an official Nazi anti-Semitic propaganda agency, to a correspondent in the United States. Note that the Nazi agency recommends Father Charles E. Coughlin's *Social Justice* of Detroit, Michigan, and Reverend Gerald B. Winrod's *Defender* of Wichita, Kansas.

Several times I have conferred with Dr. Tippelskirch [the Nazi Consul in Boston] and at one time suggested that if he could secure the financial backing from Germany, I could start a real campaign along lines that will be very effective. All that is necessary . . . is to organize the many thousands of persons who are victims of Judaism and I am ready to do that at any time.

Keeping the American psychological saboteurs constantly supplied with anti-Semitic propaganda and with other disruptive material were two official German organizations: *Welt-Dienst* (World-Service), which had its headquarters at Daberstedterstrasse 4, Erfurt, Germany; and *Deutscher Fichte-Bund* (German Fighters Society), located in Hamburg, Germany. From these two sources emanated vast numbers of anti-democratic pamphlets and bulletins containing propaganda devised to incite race hatred. This propaganda material, which for the convenience of its recipients throughout the world was printed in a dozen languages, reached the United States public through such homespun publications as Father Charles E. Coughlin's *Social Justice* of Royal Oak, Michigan; William Dudley Pelley's *Liberator* of Asheville, North Carolina; Reverend Gerald Winrod's *Defender* of Wichita, Kansas; William Kullgren's *Beacon Light* of Atascadero, California; and many other pro-Axis, anti-Semitic newspapers, magazines and newsletters.

That this anti-Semitic propaganda was making headway in America was revealed as early as 1936 when the Senate Black Committee, investigating lobbying activities, uncovered the subversive work of an organization called the Sentinels of the Republic. This organization had managed to raise $168,000 from prominent Americans for the purpose of combatting the "Jewish threat" of the New Deal. The Black Committee read into the record an exchange of letters between Alexander

Deutscher Fichte-Bund e.V.
Union für Weltwahrheit

Bankkonten: Reichsbank Hamburg
Bank der Deutschen Arbeit A.-G.
Postscheckkonto: Hamburg 1930
Telegramme: fichtebund, Hamburg

Briefanschrift:
Deutscher Fichte-Bund e.V.,
Hamburg 36

Ho/Kö.

Gegründet Januar 1914

Hauptsitz: Hamburg 36
Jungfernstieg 30, Hamburger Hof

12th April 1937.

Mr.
Donald Shea
National Org.
Ambassador Hotel
Washington D.C.
U.S.A.

Dear Mr. Shea,

       Thank you very much for your letter of the 26th ult.
and the interesting information about your hard work over there.
I am very interested in your fight and we all wish you the best
of luck and success. I am sure even America will awake to the
~~~~~ of ~~~~~~~~~~~ but still much ~~~~~~~~~ done ~~~~

       It was very kind of you to distribut our leaflets among
influential people and those who are ready to help us in our
struggle against the Jewish lies about Germany. We know about
the attacks of Mr. LaGuardia against the Leader and Germany but
they are not worth a reply. They just gave us a good laugh, that
is all. - I shall not forget to advise our friends in U.S.A.
to communicate with you because everybody ought to realize the
good work you are doing and to join your association. In the
next days I send you further material, but what about your address?
Shall I send all future packages to the Ambassador Hotel? Please
let me know about it. Do you get your parcels without duty expenses?

I hope you will reprint extracts of our informations if possible
and send us the voucher copies. Do you have any special wish
about literature?

       What do you think about the English RAK.?

       I also read the of you to the Editor and was , indeed
very pleased at your fair play between true Americans and Germans
and rest assured we shall always co-operate with you with the
greatest interest in order to serve our common cause for still
better friendship between America and Germany. Therefore we always highly appreciate hearing from you.

       Any further suggestions to make our work still more
effective are also greatly appreciated.

       When in Germany I sincerely hope you will look us up.

       With best regards

       Yours very truly

       Dir. of organization
       Th. Kessemeier.

       b.o.

P.S. Do you issue any paper or periodical? Perhaps you are ready
to mention our association, if it is possible. A small ad. would
be quite sufficient.

A communication dated April 12, 1937, from Deutscher Fichte-Bund, an official Nazi
anti-Semitic propaganda agency, to its American agent Donald Shea, head of the
National Gentile League of Washington, D. C. The communication thanks Shea for
distributing Nazi propaganda "among influential people".

Lincoln, a Boston investment banker who was president of the Sentinels, and one W. Cleveland Runyon of Plainfield, New Jersey. Runyon's first letter to Lincoln, dated March 4, 1936, complained about the "Jewish brigade Roosevelt took to Washington" and went on in language reminiscent of Adolf Hitler:

> The fight for Western Christian civilization can be won; but only if we recognize that the enemy is world-wide and that it is Jewish in origin. All we need here is money. . . . The time is getting short. Can you not do something?

To which the President of the Sentinels, Lincoln, replied:

> I am doing what I can as an officer of the Sentinels. I think, as you say, that the Jewish threat is a real one. My hope is in the election next autumn, and I believe that our real opportunity lies in accomplishing the defeat of Roosevelt.

Mr. Runyon then wrote back:

> The people are crying for leadership and not getting it. Our leaders are asleep. The Sentinels should really lead on the outstanding issue. The old-line Americans of $1,200 a year want a Hitler.

In a like vein, if in somewhat less restrained language, the ex-convict Henry Allen, head of California's American White Guard, wrote in a letter on July 31, 1937, "The American White Guard gives *solemn warning* to the international goulash of oriental scum which today permeates our Government in Washington — let those who dare, attempt to betray America, and there will be more Jew corpses cluttering up American gutters, than were ever found in the most ambitious of European pogroms."

The Silver L Battalion

DIVISION HEADQUARTERS
LOS ANGELES CALIFORNIA
October 4, 1936

General Nicholas Rodriguez,
El Paso, Texas.

Dear General Rodriguez:

Upon receipt of this letter

Will you kindly communicate with me and advise me whether it would be possible for you to come to Los Angeles in the near future to make an address to our organization here. We shall be glad to defray all expenses which will include aero-plan both ways if you desire it. We shall also offer you body guard for your protection if you deem it necessary. Your fight is our fight and it is our desire to have you come to Los Angeles especially to confer with us relative to matters of vital importance to us both. I would suggest that if you can arrange to come. that you telegraph me (charges collect) upon receipt of this letter so that I may make arrangements without delay.

Fraternally yours,

Henry Allen.

A/p

American White Guard

DIVISION HEADQUARTERS
Los Angeles, California
U.S.A.   July 31, 1937

Kansas City, Missouri.

Sir:

I have before me your letter of the 12th inst. You refer to a proclamation published by us. We have issued numerous proclamations and publications in all parts of the United States, therefore I hardly know which one you refer to. I shall be glad to comply with your request for which you have enclosed postage, if you will describe the particular proclamation you desire, provided it is not out of print.

... May I suggest, however, that ...

The American White Guard gives solemn warning to the international ghoulash of oriental scum which today permeates our Government in Washington.--Let those who dare, attempt to betray America, and there will be more Jew corpses cluttering up American gutters, than ever were found in the most ambitions of European pogroms. THAT SHALL BE OUR ANSWER to those who seek to bring our American Republic under the rule of the Kremlin.

I might suggest that the Pelley Publishers at Ashville N. C. publish the Jewish Protocols, and they also have much other valuable literature for sale. The magazine "New Liberation" is a magnificent publication of educational worth.

P. O. Box 2630.

Very truly yours,

Henry Allen.

A/p

Left: Letter from Henry Allen, when he was head of the Silver Legion Battalion, to General Nicholas Rodriguez, then head of the Nazi-directed Mexican Gold Shirts. *Right:* Letter from Henry Allen, head of the American Wh...

By 1937, considerable progress had been made by the Nazi psychological saboteurs in the spreading of anti-Semitic propaganda and in the forming of subversive nuclei in America. But the American fifth column still lacked two vital factors. One was a really popular American leader.

"That's what we lack," admitted Franklyn Thompson, editor of the New York pro-Nazi weekly *National American* and author of the book, *Jew Deal*. "We lack a Leader like Hitler!"

The other essential element still missing was a "spontaneous American movement" of mass proportions.

III. *The Search for a Leader*

The question of America loomed large on the agenda of the World Congress of Nazi propagandists held at Erfurt, Germany, in 1937-38. The Congress was called by Lieutenant-Colonel Ulrich Fleischhauer, head of the *Welt-Dienst*.

Among the Erfurt World Congress delegates, who came from 22 countries in all parts of the world, were three Americans: George E. Deatherage, leader of the American Nationalist Federation, who had adopted the swastika as his emblem; C. G. Campbell, an American anti-Semitic propagandist; and Ernest F. Elmhurst, whose real name was Fleischkopf, a Nazi agent active in New York City. Deatherage delivered a speech at the Erfurt Congress entitled, "Will America be the Jews' Waterloo?"*

The American delegates returned to the United States with some important new ideas. If there was to be a really effective fascist movement in America, it must have its base in the United States Army. There must be an "American Ludendorff" who would influence the Army men, command the re-

---

* In February 1942, George Deatherage was found to be holding an important war job as an engineer in charge of a $7,000,000 naval construction project at Norfolk, Virginia. Ten days later, the Navy ordered his employers to dismiss him as "undesirable."

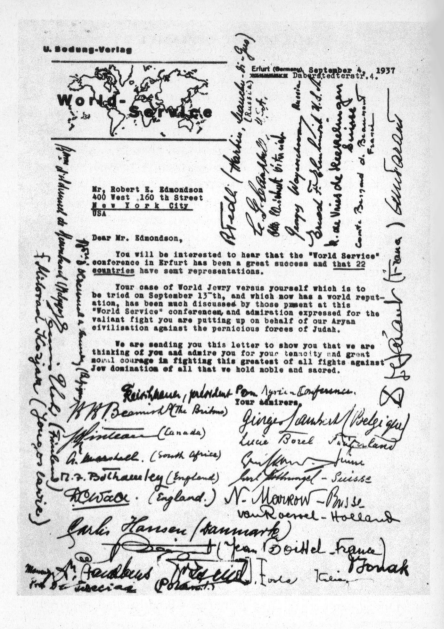

From the world congress of Nazi propagandists held at Erfurt, Germany, during 1937-38, this letter, signed by leading European and American anti-Semites was sent in September 1937, to Robert Edward Edmondson of New York City. Edmondson claims he has circulated over five million pieces of anti-Semitic propaganda in the United States.

spect of the nation, and at the same time provide a rallying point, just as General Ludendorff had done for Nazism in Germany, and as Marshal Pétain was later to do in France.

On November 15, 1938, George Deatherage wrote to one of his contacts in Kansas City: "We are delaying further reorganization in the hopes that we can get Gen. Geo. Van Horn Moseley, Hotel Biltmore, Atlanta, recently retired, to head up a national Christian organization that we can all back."

To another contact Deatherage wrote: "The organization must be built around a propaganda organization now that in a few hours can be turned into a militant fighting force. That is the idea of the boss also, but it must be kept on the Q.T. . . ."

General headquarters of the movement was established in the Biltmore Hotel in Atlanta, Georgia, and "feelers" went out to military men throughout the nation. Moseley was written up, flattered and heiled in Coughlin's *Social Justice*, Pelley's *Liberation*, the Bund's *Deutscher Weckruf und Beobachter*,* and in many other similar publications. Robert Edward Edmondson issued tens of thousands of leaflets headed, *"Hail Moseley!"*

Moseley later denied that he had any intention of heading an American Fascist Party. And, at any rate, it was soon clear that the aging Major-General had neither the personal magnetism nor the cunning needed to head and control such a mass movement.

The great search for the Leader went on.

One of the most promising candidates was Father Charles E. Coughlin, whose magazine *Social Justice* had in 1939 a circulation close to 1,000,000, and whose weekly radio program over 47 stations had a listening audience of approximately 4,000,000.

On September 25, 1936, Charles Coughlin had declared:

---

* The title of the official organ of the German American Bund was later changed to *The Free American and Deutscher Weckruf und Beobachter.*

A COALITION OF CHRISTIAN ANTI-COMMUNIST ORGANIZATIONS

AMERICAN NATIONALIST CONFEDERATION
BOSTON - NEW YORK - WASHINGTON - CHICAGO - HOUSTON
MIAMI - SAVANNAH - LOS ANGELES - SAN FRANCISCO

1007 W Peachtree Ave.
Atlanta
Ga.

Dec.5th.1938

~~Detroit~~
Detroit
Michigan.

Dear Sir;

    Gen.Geo.Van Horn Moseley,recently retired as head of the
3rd.Army,and formerly Asst.Chief of Staff,is about to start a new
national Christian Patriotic movement to run Un American influences
out of the nation.

    Will you not write him immediatly at the hotel Biltmore,
Atlanta,asking him to take this leadership,and offering your advise
and counsel? He will want to meet you a little later and arrange
for the co-operation of the organization that you represent.

    In my opinion,the General is the only man today whom we
can all follow,who is free of any political tieup,and who knows
what is wrong.

    I am taking the liberty of mentioning this to you,for
I know the interest of the Veterans of Foreign Wars in this subject
and that something must be done now-under national leadership.

    If you will give him your ideas on the matter,I know that
he will deeply appreciate it.

Yours very truly

Geo.E.Deatherage
National Commander.

GED/AET

Get In Touch With Your Local Christian Anti-Communist Patriotic Organizations

This is how George Deatherage, after returning from the world congress of Nazi
propagandists at Erfurt, Germany, tried to recruit followers for Major General
George Van Horn Moseley.

"When the ballot is useless, I shall have the courage to stand up and advocate the use of bullets."

That same year Dale Kramer, former secretary of the National Farm Holiday Association, recorded this interview with Coughlin:

"One thing is sure," Coughlin said in a soft, matter-of-fact voice. "Democracy is doomed. This is our last election."

"Is that so? What will happen?"

"It is Fascism or Communism. Take your choice."

"What road do you take, Father Coughlin?"

"I take the road to Fascism."

Coughlin's organization, the Christian Front, was formed in 1938. In May of that year, the radio priest urged his followers to form "platoons."

"Let your organization be composed of no more than twenty-five members," *Social Justice* ordered. "After a few contacts with these twenty-five persons you will observe that two of them may be capable of organizing twenty-five more. Invite these capable people to do that very thing."

The following month, *Social Justice* added: "When the proper moment arrives, and not before that time, Father Coughlin will assemble all those organizations whose leaders care to follow him."

By 1939 the Christian Front had assumed the proportions of a subversive army numbering some 200,000 members, many of whom were secretly drilling with rifles and other military equipment. Working closely with the German American Bund, the Christian Mobilizers, Silver Shirts and similar gangs, the Fronters made American cities the scenes of violent anti-Semitic agitation. Armed bands roamed the streets of New York City, indiscriminately insulting and attacking men and women. The same *Propagandamarsch* (terror parade) technique was practiced in Boston, Philadelphia, Cleveland, Akron and other cities. In these demonstrations, the Nazi cam-

paign of psychological sabotage reached a new peak in the
United States.

On January 13, 1940, the Federal Bureau of Investigation
arrested 17 members of the Christian Front. According to
J. Edgar Hoover, the Fronters planned "to knock off about
a dozen Congressmen," to assassinate prominent Americans
of Jewish extraction, and to seize Post Offices, the Customs
House, and armories in New York City. The FBI uncovered
a number of Christian Front arsenals containing bombs,
cordite, rifles, ammunition, powder and dynamite, including
arms which had been stolen from the arsenals of the National
Guard. The arrested Fronters hailed Coughlin as their Leader.

There followed one of the strangest trials in the history of
the American law courts. Although the defendants were
proven to have plotted violent acts, although they had been
caught redhanded with weapons and explosives in their possession, the followers of Coughlin were acquitted of the charge
of conspiring against the United States Government and were
set free. (One of them, exposed as a Nazi agent, had committed
suicide in his cell.) When the jury was chosen, none of its
members was asked whether or not he belonged to the
Christian Front or was a follower of Coughlin. The foreman
of the jury, a Mrs. Titus, turned out to be related to Father
Edward F. Brophy, ideological leader of the Eastern division
of the Christian Front and author of one of its chief propaganda works, an anti-Semitic tract entitled *The Christian
Front*.

Although the Christian Front trial ended as a personal
triumph for Coughlin, the radio priest was not destined to
become the Leader of the "spontaneous American movement." The character of his activities and his extreme anti-
Semitism were too obvious. His organization, while still large,
failed to grow into a real mass movement.

The Nazis continued their search for the right Leader.

"You know who might become the Fuehrer of ou
political party?" Hermann Schwarzmann, leader of the A.
toria, Long Island unit of the German American Bund had
told a Chicago newspaperman in 1937. "Lindbergh! Yes, that
is not so far-fetched as you might think. You know he would
carry the public with him very easily. The Americans like
him. . . . Yes, there are a lot of things being planned the public
knows nothing about as yet."*

IV. *The Plot Against the President*

One of the most cherished properties of Colonel Walther
Nicolai's Section IIIB is a "morgue" containing personality-
analyses of hundreds of leading statesmen throughout the
world. The purpose of these *character-dossiers,* which are prepared by the "characterological department" of the Berlin
Psychological Laboratory, under the supervision of Colonel
Dr. Albrecht Blau, is to enable the Nazi chiefs to evaluate
their leading opponents, to facilitate the selection of Quislings
and Lavals, and to provide the basis for buying or blackmail-
ing such personalities.

Colonel Blau regards characterological study as a vital part
of psychological sabotage, to be "pursued consciously in a
planned and organized effort." To collect the data for his
character-dossiers, he trains expert psychological observers,
or spies, who are sent abroad by the Nazi Government disguised as newspapermen, businessmen, tourists, etc.

For years prior to the invasion of France, Colonel Blau
kept French politicians under close observation. Blau's spies
knew more about Edouard Daladier's weaknesses than the
French Premier's own cabinet. They also knew all there was
to know about Neville Chamberlain and other statesmen who
might aid or menace the Axis cause.

---

*This statement was made in July 1937 to John C. Metcalfe, reporter for the
Chicago Daily Times and later a Federal agent.

No great psychological research was necessary to convince the Nazis that Franklin Delano Roosevelt could not be won over to their cause. Nevertheless, the Nazis did not neglect to keep the President under observation.

On his 1936 presidential election campaign trip to Lincoln, Nebraska, President Roosevelt was accompanied by one of Dr. Blau's ace "observers." His name was F. Schoenemann. He had been ordered by his superiors in Berlin to get as close as possible to President Roosevelt, to observe his character, and to report back his findings to Germany. In the guise of a foreign correspondent, Herr Schoenemann managed to get aboard the presidential train and to accompany President Roosevelt on his trip to Lincoln. At the conclusion of the trip, Schoenemann sent a detailed "character study" of Roosevelt to Berlin.

A. Halfeld, a personal emissary of Dr. Goebbels, active in Washington as late as 1941, was also assigned to study President Roosevelt's character. Every psychological characteristic, every habit and opinion of the President was subjected by Halfeld and Schoenemann to the most painstaking scrutiny. The information was then filed with the "characterology department" of the Berlin Psychological Laboratory to supplement and bring up to date the exhaustive study of President Roosevelt's character which the Laboratory had been preparing since 1933.

Schoenemann's report to Berlin summed up his observation of the President of the United States in these words:

> War [from Roosevelt's point of view] is identical with militarism which Americans abhor, but a war for peace, a war to end war, is not only permissible but even necessary. . . . The democratic ideology is the core of that crusading mood which led to American intervention under President Wilson. Under President Roosevelt, it again represents a danger of the first magnitude, threatening our [the Nazi] security and our future.

At an early date the Nazis undertook a campaign of psychological sabotage against President Roosevelt, with the object of discrediting him and undermining his influence with the American people. The Nazis unleashed an incessant stream of provocative rumors and poisonous slanders directed against the President's personal character and his political philosophy. No lie was too grandiose, no vilification too obscene, for the Axis psychological saboteurs.

The campaign reached a new height in 1939. Dr. Goebbels opened a new tactical attack on President Roosevelt with a series of virulent articles in the controlled Berlin press. The Nazi Propaganda Minister charged President Roosevelt with seeking to betray the American people into an unjust war against Germany, Italy and Japan. President Roosevelt's opposition to the Axis, asserted Dr. Goebbels, was inspired by "Jews and Communists." Goebbels' articles were headlined: "ROOSEVELT'S SHAMEFUL TREASON!" He called for the President's impeachment by the American people.

Taking their cue from Dr. Goebbels, the Nazis and their fifth column allies in the United States initiated a propaganda campaign branding President Roosevelt as a "traitor" and demanding his "impeachment." Lending a sinister undertone to this campaign was the continuous incitement to acts of violence against the President of the United States.

Ernst Goerner, a Nazi agent in Milwaukee, distributed thousands of leaflets charging the President with "treason" and urging American citizens to "GET YOUR ROPES AND ON TO WASHINGTON!" The pro-Nazi newspaper *Publicity* of Wichita, Kansas, headlined: "Save America by Impeachment Now!" *Social Justice* headlined: "IMPEACH ROOSEVELT!" Charles B. Hudson, fascist propagandist of Omaha, Nebraska, wrote in his newsletter *America In Danger!*: "IMPEACH FDR! . . . The NUdeal majority is the lowest, dirtiest bunch of scallawag lawyers that ever gathered under one roof.

SAVE AMERICA BY IMPEACHMENT NOW!

On top of all previous demands made upon Congress, President Roosevelt is now demanding that they revise the Neutrality Act to enable him to order the arming of merchant vessels who are entering war zones in an attempt to supply aid to Communistic Russia and Jew Controlled Great Britain.

If the Congress Your representatives Acquiesce to his demands then they are a bunch of spineless cowards and should be removed along with Roosevelt and the rest of his war-mongering Camarilla Government.

Every Patriotic, Christian American should write to their Congressmen and Senators DEMANDING that they IMMEDIATELY institute IMPEACHMENT PROCEEDINGS against ROOSEVELT and all of his WAR-MONGERING CAMARILLA GOVERNMENT.

There is no question as to what the intentions of Roosevelt and his Camarilla Government are if they can get the Neutrality Act revised or repealed their intentions and determinations are to throw our young American manhood into the BLOODY, JEW REVENGE WAR IN EUROPE In an attempt (See Page Two)

What Is An American? An American Is Any Man Who Considers America A "Melting-Pot" And Not A MILKING-POT!

PUBLICITY

"LET THE PEOPLE RULE" "DO RIGHT AND FEAR NO MAN"
"TRUTH LIGHT"
"Wichita" "Kansas"

VOLUME 11   PRICE FIVE CENTS   Wichita, Sedgwick County, Kansas, Thursday, October 16, 1941   PRICE FIVE CENTS   NUMBER 40

JURY COMPOSED OF AMERICAN PEOPLE REACH A VERDICT

Legion Members Sold Down River

Red Activities In Schools Exposed

Yonkers Chapter Pass Resolution On Impeachment

'Lindbergh Party' In 1944

It Works Both Ways

Hired Man Vs. Farmer

Page 2   PUBLICITY   Wichita, Kansas, October 16 1941

ROOSEVELT WILL DIE

OF DISAPPOINTMENT IF HE DOESN'T GET US INTO WAR WITH SOMEBODY! EVEN THAT WOULD BE BETTER THAN KILLING AND VIOLATING MILLIONS OF OUR BOYS AND GIRLS—SOUTHERN PROGRESS

Save America By Impeachment Now

The Peoples' Forum

Give up the liberty to know, to utter, and to argue freely according to conscience, above all liberties.—MILTON

The pro-Axis propaganda newspaper, *Publicity*, published in Wichita, Kansas, by E. J. Garner, picks up the Nazi-inspired cry of "Impeach Roosevelt," and none too subtly links this theme with the "death" of the President.

. . . I've hoped the American people would wake up and hang the whole gangster outfit." William Kullgren, fifth column leader of Atascadero, California, declared: "The reins of government have been seized by outlaws. . . . Therefore we must impeach Roosevelt and his henchmen!" Parker Sage's Detroit National Workers League stated in its *News Letter:* "The answer . . . should be the impeachment of our President. . . . The only method left us as free men is that of revolution." Silver Shirt chief Pelley headlined an article: "Four Million Militant Women Getting Congress Aid for Roosevelt Impeachment!" Francis P. Moran, Director of the Christian Front in Boston, released a mimeographed letter addressed to "Every Christian American" in which he declared: ". . . if Roosevelt were tried before a jury composed of real Americans he would be hanged by the neck and that is what he deserves!"

The campaign was not confined to Nazi propagandists. The "Impeach Roosevelt" slogan penetrated all sections of American society, and it was picked up and reëchoed by prominent appeasers and isolationists in all parts of the country, most of whom were doubtless unaware of its origin.

Former Governor Philip F. La Follette of Wisconsin told a wildly cheering America First rally at Indianapolis on November 9, 1941, that he would move to impeach President Roosevelt if he were in Congress. Former Governor William ("Alfalfa Bill") Murray of Oklahoma, speaking before an America First rally in Newark, New Jersey, on November 12, 1941, charged President Roosevelt with being a "dictator" and forecast another American Revolution "to return the country to the people." Representative Hamilton Fish demagogically cried to a New York America First audience on November 3, 1941: "We shall impeach every member of Congress and the President if they declare war without the Congress having voted for it." In the House of Representatives, Congressman Clare E. Hoffman of Michigan demanded the "im-

peachment" of President Roosevelt for leading the country
into war by "deception."

The cry "Impeach Roosevelt" continued to be heard even
after the United States entered the war.

V. *The Coming of the "Committees"*

On March 16, 1939, a self-styled "group of New York business and professional men" met in the Lexington Hotel in
New York City and founded the American Fellowship Forum.
The avowed purpose of the Forum was "to concentrate the attention of the American people on the solution of their domestic problems." Public meetings were to be held at which
topics of economic and social importance would be discussed.
Forum literature was to be sent to a mailing list of influential
people throughout the United States. A tall, well-groomed,
former Professor of German Literature at Columbia University, Dr. Friedrich Ernest Ferdinand Auhagen, was appointed
National Director of the Forum.

The American Fellowship Forum established its headquarters in New York City. Polite, expensively printed cards
announcing the founding of the Forum were mailed to prominent professional and business men. On April 19, 1939, the
first public meeting of the Forum was held in New York City
at the Hotel Capitol. The subject of the lecture delivered at
this meeting was "America and Germany — Contrasts Without Conflicts." The speaker was Lawrence Dennis, author of
the book, *The Coming American Fascism.*

In June, the Forum began circulating a magazine called
Today's Challenge. The first issue contained an article entitled "A New Europe," by Dr. Auhagen, who was the Editor
of the publication. Dr. Auhagen wrote, "The Munich Conference . . . represents the most hopeful beginning of the New
Europe which should have come twenty years ago."

The first issue of *Today's Challenge* also included contributions by Lawrence Dennis, Senator Ernest Lundeen, Repre-

sentative Hamilton Fish, William R. Castle, and Philip Johnson, the "foreign correspondent" of Father Charles E. Coughlin's *Social Justice*. The Associate Editor of Dr. Auhagen's magazine was George Sylvester Viereck.

Behind the American Fellowship Forum and its magazine, *Today's Challenge,* was a Nazi conspiracy to initiate a highly important campaign of psychological sabotage in the United States. German agents in America had been advised by Berlin that the Third Reich was about to move into Poland. War was imminent. The American Fellowship Forum had been created to spread Axis appeasement propaganda, to encourage isolationism, and to promote opposition to the defense preparations for which the President of the United States was then prophetically calling.

Dr. Friedrich Auhagen was a paid Nazi agent. A former Second Lieutenant in the Kaiser's army, he had come from Germany to America in 1923. After Hitler's seizure of power, he had entered the employ of the German Intelligence.

In Germany, Auhagen had received degrees in economics and mining engineering at the University of Göttingen and the Mining Academy at Clausthal. This training enabled him to secure various academic positions in well-known American colleges. These positions served the Nazi agent Auhagen as a convenient disguise.

After 1933, Auhagen made yearly trips to the Third Reich, where he conferred with high officials of the Nazi Party. He received regular sums of money from Dr. G. Kurt Johannsen, a Nazi paymaster in Hamburg, Germany.

Another source of Auhagen's funds was the German-American industrialist, Dr. Ferdinand A. Kertess, president of the Chemical Marketing Company of New York City*, and one of the incorporators of the American Fellowship Forum.

---

*In the summer of 1942, the Foreign Property Control Division of the U. S. Treasury Department took over the property of the Chemical Marketing Company.

TODAY'S
CHALLENGE

OFFICIAL ORGAN OF THE AMERICAN FELLOWSHIP FORUM

VOL. I - NO. 1   JUNE - JULY, 1939   PRICE 25c

The cover of the first issue of the magazine, *Today's Challenge,* edited by the Nazi agents Dr. Friedrich Auhagen and George Sylvester Viereck. Contributors to the first issue included: the late Senators William E. Borah and Ernest Lundeen; Representative Hamilton Fish; former Under-Secretary of State William R. Castle; Nazi agents Auhagen and Viereck; and Philip Johnson, "foreign correspondent" of Father Charles E. Coughlin's *Social Justice.*

According to information later made public by a congressional investigatory committee, Dr. Kertess himself was carrying on espionage work for the German Government by securing information regarding "convoy movements and shipping movements of British and French purchases" in the United States and turning this information over to the German Consulate in New York City, from where it was relayed to the German Naval Attaché in Washington, D. C.

Dr. Auhagen's psychological sabotage campaign was closely supervised by Gestapo agents in the United States. Auhagen conferred regularly with Friedhelm Draeger, a German Consul in New York City. Draeger was a United States Section Leader of Ernst Bohle's *Auslands-Organization* and was in charge of espionage-sabotage operations in the New York area. The conferences between Draeger and Auhagen took place at the latter's home at 90-50 53rd Avenue, Elmhurst, Long Island, as well as in the room that Auhagen had permanently reserved at the Hotel Royalton in New York City.

Auhagen also met frequently with Dr. Herbert Scholz, the suave Boston Consul, who was the key Gestapo agent on the East Coast. . . .*

With the outbreak of the war in Europe, a new phenomenon appeared on the American political scene. A series of "Committees," whose character and composition strangely resembled those of the American Fellowship Forum, sprang up overnight and began urging a hands-off policy towards the war in Europe. These "Committees" sought to take advantage of the traditional isolationism of certain sections of the United States public and to capture the following of the left-wing anti-war movement.

The American Fellowship Forum retired from the scene.

---

* On March 3, 1941, Dr. Friedrich Auhagen was arrested at the La Salle, Illinois, home of the German-American industrialist Edward H. Carus, who provided $5,000 bail for the Nazi agent. Previously, Auhagen had been prevented from boarding a ship bound for Japan. On July 12, 1941, Auhagen was sentenced to serve eight months to two years in prison for failure to register as an agent of the German Government.

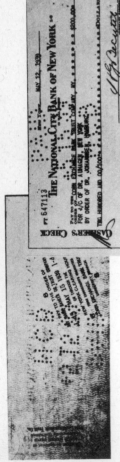

A check, deposit slip and foreign draft for sums received on various dates by Dr. Friedrich Auhagen. The funds came to Auhagen from Hamburg, Germany, and were deposited by him to his account at the Corn Exchange Bank Trust Company in New York City.

July 26, 1939.

Dr. F. Auhagen,
American Fellowship Forum,
11 West 42nd Street,
New York, N. Y.

Dear Fritz:

I enclose the second article. I have enclosed within penciled blocks a few sections which might be left out of the published piece if you find it necessary to shorten it.

I think it makes a good series. The third piece on the cures of the crisis will link the New Deal, Nazism and Fascism along with the British Re-over measures under the Tory Government and state the essential problems of work creation and relief which all these solutions have to meet. This, I think, is a swell attack on the problem for your purpose. It completely blanks the fire of the Government and Liberal crowd and it will even amuse and please the reactionaries more than it annoys them—to have the New Deal linked with Nazism. The big point is that it is foolish for a country running one type of unorthodox economy to damn Germany, Italy or any other country for running a similar type of unorthodoxy.

Sincerely,

Lawrence

Lawrence Dennis
40 Wall Street
New York

June 3, 1939.

Dear Auhagen:

I enclose the first of a series of three articles on the current economic-political situation. This one is entitled FULL RECOVERY OF STAGNATION? and states the problem in terms of the increase in unemployment and decrease in employment, the failure of full recovery and the persistence of stagnation—in a varying degree with the changes in the business cycle. The next article will discuss the causes of stagnation. The third the possible cures. I'll get these done in the course of the next two or three weeks. Meanwhile, you have the first, which is really complete in itself. Obviously, the nature of the current stagnation, its probable causes and possible cures cannot well be discussed in one article.

I also enclose my last two weekly letters. Why don't you subscribe?

Sincerely,

Lawrence

Let's have lunch after you have read this over.

Two letters from Lawrence Dennis, author of *The Coming American Fascism*, to the Nazi agent Dr. Friedrich Auhagen. Dennis discusses the contents of articles he is writing for Auhagen's propaganda publication, *Today's Challenge*. Both letters came from Auhagen's files.

There had already appeared certain far more effective and influential organizations headed by prominent American appeasers. Representative Hamilton Fish, who had written for Auhagen's *Today's Challenge,* led the "Committee" parade with his National Committee to Keep America Out of Foreign Wars. The Committee was set up just before Congressman Fish left on a visit to Nazi Germany in the fall of 1939. In Europe, immediately prior to the outbreak of the war, the Congressman met with Joachim von Ribbentrop, the Foreign Minister of the Third Reich; with Count Galeazzo Ciano, the Foreign Minister of Fascist Italy; and with other Axis leaders. Von Ribbentrop placed his private airplane at Fish's disposal, and the Congressman undertook a whirlwind campaign tour in Europe urging a second Munich. In Berlin, Fish told American newspapermen "Germany's claims are just."*

---

* This was not the first time Representative Hamilton Fish had been associated with the Nazis. As early as 1933 his name appeared as "sponsor" in an official Nazi propaganda book entitled *Communism in Germany* which was published in Germany and sent into the United States for distribution. The book, which was intended to show that the Nazis had saved Germany from the menace of Bolshevism, featured an introductory quotation from a speech by Adolf Hitler.

On October 2, 1938, Representative Hamilton Fish was the main speaker at a German Day celebration at Madison Square Garden in New York City. At this rally, the swastika was prominently displayed, and the audience sang the Nazi *Horst Wessel* and gave the Hitler salute.

When Nazi Germany published its *White Paper* in 1939, accusing the United States of making secret war alliances with Poland and France, Representative Fish sided with the Nazis and publicly declared, "I cannot conceive of the German Foreign Office fabricating or forging documents." Fish urged the "impeachment" of President Roosevelt on the basis of the Nazi accusations.

On October 31, 1940, Representative James P. McGranery of Pennsylvania incorporated in the Congressional Record a letter he had received from Michael A. Maloney, a distinguished lawyer in Philadelphia, recommending that the House of Representatives "investigate a rental of the property, 55 East 77th Street, New York City, to Johannes Borchers, consul general of Germany." The property in question belonged to Representative Hamilton Fish. Mr. Maloney's letter included this quotation from a Philadelphia newspaper:

> "Fish is reported to have begun renting the house to Germans about 1931, shortly before Hitler. The lease expired 2 years later, about the time Hitler came into power, and he renewed, reportedly with an increased rent. Two years ago, 1938, he is reported to have renewed the lease once again, this time with a substantial increase from the Nazis."

Representative Fish's association with the Nazi agent George Sylvester Viereck is discussed in Chapter Nine.

THE SECRET OFFENSIVE 165

The activity of Fish's Committee was greatly intensified after the Congressman returned from Europe. Early in 1940 the Committee began mailing out, under Fish's Congressional frank, tens of thousands of reprints of isolationist speeches and articles.

Another "peace" group which became active at this time was the Citizen's Keep America Out of War Committee, a Chicago organization headed by the well-known isolationist businessman Avery Brundage. In August 1940, this Committee invited Charles A. Lindbergh to Chicago to address a mass rally at Soldiers Field. Lindbergh accepted the invitation and spoke under the Committee's auspices. The Chicago rally was arranged in cooperation with a number of pro-Nazi German-American organizations grouped together in the *Einheitsfront* (United Front). While in Chicago, Lindbergh was a guest at the palatial home of Colonel Robert R. McCormick, publisher of the anti-Administration *Chicago Tribune*.

During this period, three other important Committees were formed in the nation's capital under the sponsorship of certain isolationist Senators and Representatives. These were the Islands for War Debts Committee, War Debts Defense Committee, and the Make Europe Pay War Debts Committee. All of them were soon using the Congressional franking privilege to deluge the country with isolationist propaganda.

On October 21, 1940, an attempt was made to unite all these Committees into a single powerful anti-Administration and isolationist bloc. At a Washington conference fifty representatives of various "peace" organizations formed the No Foreign Wars Committee. The main speaker at the Washington conference was Charles A. Lindbergh. Chosen to head the No Foreign Wars Committee was Verne Marshall, a Mid-Western isolationist newspaper publisher with a flair for promotional schemes.

Marshall's efforts to unite the whole isolationist movement under his No Foreign Wars Committee received financial

backing from William Rhodes Davis, a millionaire oil operator who had large investments in Germany. It was Davies
who claimed to have received a secret "Peace Offer" from
Field Marshal Hermann Goering in 1939 and to have handed
it over to Adolf Berle, Jr., Assistant Secretary of State. As
soon as Marshall's Committee was formed, Davis showed up
with an offer of $100,000 to finance a nationwide advertising
campaign.

The No Foreign Wars Committee had a brief, spectacular
career highlighted by hectic mass meetings, nationwide radio
hookups and barrages of printed propaganda — all devoted
to what Marshall called a "fight to the last ditch to foil the
interventionists, the rabble rousers, the deceptionists in their
high-financed campaign to start this country shooting."

Marshall's vociferous agitation became increasingly un-
guarded. This, coupled with Marshall's crude publicity-seek-
ing blunders, rapidly discredited the No Foreign Wars Committee in the eyes of the American public. The Committee's
backers dropped away. Some time before its final dissolution,
Charles A. Lindbergh, its chief spokesman, had tactfully withdrawn from the Committee.

A far more promising Committee had already shown up on
the American scene.

At Yale University, a wealthy young socialite named
R. Douglas Stuart, Jr., who was heir to the Quaker Oats for-
tune, had lined up a group of appeasement-minded classmates
and organized the first chapter of what was to become *the*
"anti-war" Committee in the United States.

At one of its earliest meetings, young Stuart's group at Yale
was told by the guest speaker, "We must make our peace with
the new powers in Europe." The speaker was Charles A.
Lindbergh.

On September 18, 1940, Stuart's group was formally incorporated in Chicago, Illinois, under the name of the America
First Committee.

CHAPTER NINE

"THE HEAD AND BRAINS"

I. *Courtroom Scene*

On the afternoon of February 19, 1942, in the crowded Federal District Court in Washington, D. C., a thin frightened little man with a faint mustache was on the witness stand.

"Do you know the defendant, George Sylvester Viereck?" the prosecuting attorney asked.

"I do."

"Do you see him in the court?"

The witness peered nervously through his large spectacles at the rows of upturned faces confronting him. He nodded timidly. He had found the Nazi agent. "I do."

"Tell the court and the jury the circumstances under which you met Mr. Viereck, and the date."

"It was in the first part of July 1940, and it was in the office of Congressman Fish."

"The circumstances?"

"He came from the private office of Congressman Fish, Mr. Fish brought him over to me. Mr. Fish said Mr. Viereck had some speeches to send out — of Senator Lundeen's. Mr. Fish told me to send them to the mailing list of the National Committee to Keep America Out of Foreign Wars."

"What else was said?"

"Mr. Fish left the room and Mr. Viereck asked me how large the list was. I told him it was 100,000 names. Mr. Viereck doubted we had 100,000 names. I showed him the list. He asked me for a copy. We had an extra copy and I gave him

167

one. He asked if there was any other list we could use and I told him of our Who's Who in America list."

"Did Viereck give you anything else?"

"He gave me a tip. He gave me two bills rolled up. When I looked at them later I found they were two $50 bills."

The pale badly scared witness was a clerk from the office of Hamilton Fish, Representative from the 26th Congressional District of New York. His name was George Hill.

Under ordinary circumstances, George Hill would have remained an insignificant figure in the politics of his country. Fate, however, involved him in a drama of international Axis intrigue. He became, as Prosecutor William P. Maloney declared at the trial of George Sylvester Viereck, "an important cog in the most vicious, the most effective propaganda machine that the world has ever seen — a machine so diabolically clever that it was able to reach in and use the halls of our own Congress to spread its lies and half truths to try to conquer and divide us as they did France and other conquered nations."

II. *"Equitable Remuneration"*

George Sylvester Viereck was born in Munich in 1884 and became an American citizen in 1901. He likes to boast that he is a descendant of the Hohenzollerns. Whether he is or not, he has long been in the employ of German Imperialism. Throughout the First World War, this thick-lipped, cynical, bespectacled intellectual energetically defended the Kaiser's Government and spread propaganda opposing the entry of the United States into the war on the side of the Allies.

According to evidence made public in 1918 by the United States Attorney General, Viereck received $100,000 from the Central Powers for his propaganda services during World War I. The money came to him through various paymasters connected with the von Papen sabotage ring. Among them were Dr. Constantin Dumba, Ambassador of Austria-Hungary and one of the first diplomats in World War I to be expelled from the United States; Dr. Carl A. Fuehr, a top financial agent in the Kaiser's propaganda machine; and Count Johann Heinrich von Bernstorff, the German Ambassador to Washington who supervised sabotage operations in America.

When Adolf Hitler came to power, Viereck began to work for the Nazis. As he had formerly extolled the Kaiser, he now sang the praise of Der Fuehrer. "I made it clear that I was an admirer of Hitler, that I was in sympathy with the New Germany," he later explained.

Again, he charged a good price. He admitted before a congressional committee in 1934 that he had been receiving $500 a month from Dr. Otto Kiep, the Nazi Consul General in New York, and another $1,750 a month from an American publicity firm which was under contract to the German Tourist Bureau.

By the time Hitler's legions were smashing their way through Poland in the autumn of 1939, Viereck — who shortly before had declared "the Rome-Berlin Axis is the backbone of world peace, and the steadfast determination of Hitler and Mussolini at Munich saved the peace of Europe and western civilization" — had added various new Nazi sources of income to his already well-fattened bankroll. One of these was the *Münchner Neueste Nachrichten,* a newspaper edited in Munich by Dr. Giselher Wirsing, an assistant of Dr. Goebbels. As "correspondent" for the *Nachrichten,* Viereck got $500 a month. He was getting still another $500 a month from the German Library of Information, the official Nazi propaganda agency located at 17 Battery Place, New York City, in rooms adjoining the office of the German Consulate General.

The German Library of Information maintained a speakers' bureau of pro-Axis orators and an elaborate library of Nazi-

Münchner Neueste Nachrichten   Munich,
Office of the Editor-in-Chief   Sendlingerstr. 80

C O N T R A C T

between the Chief Editorial Department of the
Münchner Neueste Nachrichten, Munich,

a n d

GEORGE SYLVESTER VIERECK,
305 Riverside Drive, New York.

the following Agreement has been concluded today:

1). Mr. Viereck assumes the representation of the Munchner
Neueste Nachrichten for the United States of North America.
He obligates himself in accordance with the general instructions of the Editor-in-Chief of the Munchner Neueste Nachrichten to furnish reports on the general situation, digests
of the press, etc. as well as material for publication at
regular intervals. Mr. Viereck will furnish at least once
a week the above mentioned digests from the press. He will
write, at least once a month, one article of a political or
economic nature, for publication in the Munchner Neueste
Nachrichten.

2). The Munchner Neueste Nachrichten compensate Mr. Viereck at
once with the sum of $2000. (read two thousand dollars) and
will attend to the transfer of this sum to New York. These
$2000. represent traveling expenses and salary for the months
of August and September, 1939. Beginning with October, 1939,
Mr. Viereck will receive a monthly compensation of $500. -
(read five hundred dollars) for the above mentioned services.

3). It is expressly understood by both contracting parties that
in case the transfer of dollars to the United States, owing
to the general condition of exchange, should not be possible,
either with beginning of October 1939, or at any later date,
this contract becomes null and void without further formality.

4). Special expenses for trips will be dealt with and regulated
in accordance with mutual agreement.

5). No more oral agreements beyond this contract exist between
the two parties and have no validity.

MUNICH, July 20, 1939.   (signed) Dr. G. Wirsing, Editor-in-Chief
                                  Munchner Neueste Nachrichten
(signed) George Sylvester Viereck

George Sylvester Viereck's personal translated copy of his contract with Dr. Joseph
Goebbels' assistant, Dr. G. Wirsing of the *Münchner Neueste Nachrichten*.

phile books, moving pictures, and phonograph records of Hitlerite speeches and songs. All of this material was placed at
the disposal of "sympathizers." Viereck edited the Library's
publication, a handsomely-printed weekly called *Facts in Review,* which was sent free and unsolicited to a large mailing list
of prominent Americans. *Facts in Review* described in glow-
ing if somewhat monotonous detail the miracles of progress
Der Fuehrer was supposed to be accomplishing in the Third
Reich.

Viereck, who described himself as "a poet, author and journalist," wrote several books, the best known of which is a novel
called *My First Two Thousand Years.* But above everything
else Viereck was a cold-blooded, hard-headed business man,
interested in collecting every last possible penny.

A typical example of Viereck's bargaining for Nazi cash was
the letter he wrote on January 25, 1941, to Dr. Matthias
Schmitz, a former professor at Smith College who had been
persuaded by the Nazis to take over the direction of the German Library of Information. Viereck began his letter by saying that it was "perfectly obvious" that he should be getting
"four or five times the salary" he was receiving from the Nazis,
and he carefully enumerated the reasons:

> When I was first associated with *Facts in Review,* its circula-
> tion did not exceed more than a few thousand copies, and
> you did not print more than four pages a week. Today the
> circulation is nearly 100,000 and you print 16 pages every
> week, not to speak of occasional extra numbers. . . .

Viereck went on to discuss the question of an "equitable"
fee:

> You asked me what I thought would be an equitable remuner-
> ation. After considerable thought, I reached the figure of
> $2,500 a month, which was the basis of our last conversation.

Owing to your absence I have not received the full salary for January to which I am entitled under our verbal agreement. I trust this matter, too, will be adjusted as soon as feasible.

Permit me to assure you that it is both a pleasure and an honor to work with you, a man who, like myself, has drawn his intellectual sustenance from German and American sources and who considers no task more sublime than to break down with the battering ram of truth the barriers of hate and misunderstanding which propaganda, abetted by malice and ignorance, attempts to rear between your country and my own, the United States.

Cordially yours,

(signed) George Sylvester Viereck.

Arrodi:

Dr. Matthias Schmitz

GEORGE SYLVESTER VIERECK
305 Riverside Drive
New York

CABLE ADDRESS
VIERECK - NEW YORK

TELEPHONE
ACademy 2-7030

January 25, 1941.

Dear Dr. Schmitz:

We agreed upon my new income in our last conversation, but your absence from town has delayed the execution of our agreement. It is perfectly obvious, as you yourself pointed out, that I am entitled to four or five times the salary I receive at present.

When I was first associated with Facts in Review, its circulation did not exceed a few thousand copies, and you did not print more than four pages a week. Today the circulation is nearly 100,000 and you print 16 pages every week, not to speak of occasional extra numbers. While undoubtedly the lion's share of this success is due to your own editorial guidance, I have some share in the success of the venture.

... together with ...

..., imposes new ...

You asked me what would be an equitable remuneration. After considerable thought, I reached the figure of $3,500. per month, which was the basis of our last conversation. American magazines never pay me less than $500. per article. I have in fact occasionally received considerably more. The work I do in revising and preparing material for Facts in Review is equal to at least four or five articles monthly. For the sum mentioned I shall continue my work for Facts in Review and act as your chief literary adviser on all books sponsored by the Library. It is not appreciably more than I receive at present, all things considered.

Extracts from a letter in which George Sylvester Viereck discussed business terms with his Nazi employer, Dr. Matthias Schmitz of the German Library of Information.

. . . For the sum mentioned I shall continue my work for *Facts in Review* and act as chief literary advisor on all books sponsored by the Library. It is not appreciably more than I receive at present, all things considered. . . .

Even when the United States Government, in June 1941, ordered the closing of the German Library of Information, the German Consulates and other United States agencies of the Third Reich, Viereck's income from Germany was not cut off. The Nazis had farsightedly set up various "American agencies" to carry on psychological sabotage activities in the United States, and Viereck had been chosen to supervise a number of these agencies.

In compliance with the 1939 Foreign Agent Registration Act, Viereck was registering at regular intervals with the State Department as a paid propaganda agent of the Government of the Third Reich. But there were a number of vital facts which he carefully neglected to mention in his registration papers. Some of these facts concerned Viereck's connections with certain United States Senators and Representatives, and some of them concerned his dealings with an organization known as Flanders Hall, Inc.

III. *From Scotch Plains to Capitol Hill*

In September 1939, the three sons of a certain Adolph Hauck rented a room above the Post Office of Scotch Plains, a little town in New Jersey. The Hauck brothers—Siegfried, Detlev, and Adolph, Jr.—had just incorporated a small publishing concern which they called Flanders Hall, Inc. Twenty-six year old Siegfried was named as President of the firm. Adolph, Jr. was Secretary and Treasurer. Adolph's twin brother, Detlev, was listed simply as "stockholder." The room they had rented over the Post Office was to serve as their office.

The Hauck brothers were known to have little money. Yet

REGISTRATION No. ___367___

DATE OF REGISTRATION ___MAR 17 1941___
(Not to be filled in by registrant)

UNITED STATES OF AMERICA
DEPARTMENT OF STATE

REGISTRATION STATEMENT

For persons required to register with the Secretary of State pursuant to section 2 of the Act, Public, No. 583, 75th Congress, 3d Session, approved on June 8, 1938, as amended by the Act, Public, No. 319, 76th Congress, 1st Session, approved August 7, 1939.

(NOTE.—ALL spaces must be filled in. Where space in the registration statement form does not permit full answers to questions, the information required may be set forth in supplementary papers incorporated by reference in the registration statement and submitted therewith. Supplementary documents and papers must be referred to in the principal statement in chronological or other appropriate order and be described in such manner that they can be easily identified.)

1. Name of registrant ___GEORGE SYLVESTER VIERECK,___

2. Status of registrant (individual, partnership, association, or corporation) ___Individual___

3. Principal business address ___305 Riverside Drive, New York City,___

5. Residence address, or addresses, if more than one ___305 Riverside Drive, New York City,___

7. Name of foreign principal, or principals, if more than one, for which registrant is acting as agent ___
___Dr. Giselher Wirsing and Verlag Knorr & Hirth___

8. Address, or addresses, if more than one, of foreign principal ___
___Dr. Giselher Wirsing c/o Muenchner Neueste Nachrichten, Muenchen, Germany.___

___Verlag Knorr & Hirth, Muenchen, Germany___

10. Nature of business of foreign principal, or principals ___
___Dr. Wirsing is a writer and Editor of the Muenchner Nueste Nachri___

11. Comprehensive statement of nature of business of registrant ___Author, Editor and Publicist___

Portion of Registration Statement filed by George Sylvester Viereck with the Department of State, describing various of his activities as a propaganda agent in the service of Nazi principals. There were a number of vital facts concerning his activities in the United States which Viereck deliberately omitted from this and similar Registration Statements.

shortly after the incorporation of Flanders Hall, Inc., they deposited $3,000 to a bank account which they had opened in the First State Bank of Scotch Plains. They soon opened a second account at the Scotch Plains branch of the Westfield Trust Company. . . .

Twenty-five years before, Adolph Hauck, Sr., the father of the three young men, had become friendly with a clever young journalist named George Sylvester Viereck. In 1915, Hauck and Viereck had served together on a committee "raising funds for German war orphans."

In the fall of 1939, Viereck and Hauck were again collaborating.

The unobtrusive middle-aged school teacher Adolph Hauck, who in 1939 was living in Scotch Plains, New Jersey, and teaching German at the nearby Plainsville High School, provided ideal camouflage for Viereck's illegal propaganda work. With the assistance of the teacher and his three sons, Viereck arranged for the incorporation of Flanders Hall, Inc. He provided the initial $3,000 to get it going.

Before the end of 1940, Viereck had turned over $22,500 to the Haucks.

Immediately after the incorporation of Flanders Hall, bales of books began arriving at the little office above the Scotch Plains Post Office. The books came from out of town. The Hauck brothers sorted them into smaller parcels and mailed them to all parts of the United States. Most of the books were paper-bound. Their prices ranged from 50 cents to $1.50, although many were distributed free. The books were violently anti-British, anti-Semitic and subtly pro-Axis.

By midsummer 1940, Flanders Hall, Inc., had published a dozen books.

The original texts for four of these books were secretly pro-

Left form:

UNITED STATES OF AMERICA
DEPARTMENT OF STATE

REGISTRATION No. 522

DATE OF REGISTRATION

APRIL 9 - 1941

(Not to be filled in by registrant)

REGISTRATION STATEMENT

For persons required to register with the Secretary of State pursuant to section 2 of the Act, Public, No. 583, 75th Congress, 3d Session, approved on June 8, 1938, as amended by the Act, Public, No. 319, 76th Congress, 1st Session, approved August 7, 1939.

(NOTE.—All spaces must be filled in. Where space in the registration statement form does not permit full answers to questions, the information required may be set forth in supplementary papers incorporated by reference in the registration statement and submitted therewith. Supplementary documents and papers must be referred to in the principal statement in chronological or other appropriate order and be described in such manner that they can be easily identified.)

1. Name of registrant FLANDERS HALL

2. Status of registrant (individual, partnership, association, or corporation) Corporation

3. Principal business address 1800 Front Street, Scotch Plains, New Jersey.

4. Other places of business in the United States or elsewhere Bank Building, Park Avenue, Scotch Plains, New Jersey.

6. If registrant is a partnership, names and addresses of partners; if a corporation or association, names and addresses of officers these: Sigfrid H. Hauck, President, 1973 Alina Street, Elizabeth, N. J; Mary K. Hauck, Vice Pres., 1973 Alina Street, Elizabeth, N. J; Adolf K. Hauck, Jr., Sec-Treas., 1800 Front Street, Scotch Plains, New Jersey; Registered agent upon whom process may be served, Adolf Hauck, Jr., 1800 Front Street, Scotch Plains, N. J.

BOO.010211 REGISTRATION   FLANDERS HALL/15

Right form:

7. Name of foreign principal, or principals, if more than one, for which registrant is acting as agent
   George Sylvester Viereck of 305 Riverside Drive, New York, N. Y., who is the agent for Dr. Giselher Wirsing of Munich, Germany, and who is also the agent for Verlag Knorr & Hirth, a publishing house located in Munich, Germany.

9. Nationality of foreign principal, or principals, if more than one
   George Sylvester Viereck is an American Citizen.
   Dr. Giselher Wirsing and the firm of Verlag Knorr & Hirth are German.

10. Nature of business of foreign principal, or principals On information and belief, Dr. Giselher Wirsing is an author and writer. The firm of Verlag Knorr & Hirth, on information and belief, is a publishing house.

11. Comprehensive statement of nature of business of registrant Publisher of books, pamphlets, manuscripts, also printing brokers.

Although Flanders Hall, Inc., was incorporated in September, 1939, it was not until April, 1941, that George Sylvester Viereck's association with the publishing house was revealed in this Registration Statement filed with the State Department. It was after Flanders Hall had registered that the publishing house brought out Congressman Stephen A. Day's book *We Must Save The Republic*. It was also after this registration that ex-Senator Rush D. Holt delivered his manuscript to Flanders Hall.

vided by *Deutsche Informationsstelle* (German Institute of Information) in Berlin.

One book, entitled *The 100 Families That Rule the Empire,* was written by none other than Dr. Goebbels' assistant, Dr. Giselher Wirsing, editor-in-chief of the *Münchner Neuste Nachrichten.* In the spring of 1941, Dr. Wirsing sent the text of this book to George Sylvester Viereck, and the sum of $10,000 was given to Viereck for "publishing costs, advertising, publicity, distribution, etc."

But not all the authors of Flanders Hall books worked in the official government bureaus of the Third Reich. Viereck saw to it that there were also American authors. They were prominent Americans, too.

There was, for instance, Senator Ernest Lundeen. On June 19, 1940, Lundeen had delivered on the floor of the Senate a lengthy speech attacking Lord Lothian, then British Ambassador to the United States. This speech was reprinted from the Congressional Record by Flanders Hall as a book entitled *Lord Lothian vs. Lord Lothian.*

The book was an immediate success with the fifth column in the United States. The *Deutscher Weckruf und Beobachter,* official newspaper of the German American Bund, devoted a large portion of the front page of its December 12, 1940, issue to praising the volume. Elizabeth Dilling, authoress of such Nazi-endorsed works as *The Red Network* and *Roosevelt's Red Record,* undertook a nationwide distribution of free copies, and the book was enthusiastically hawked at public meetings of the Christian Front and other pro-Axis organizations.

On its cover, the Flanders Hall book *Lord Lothian vs. Lord Lothian* carried the note, "Edited by James Burr Hamilton."

WE MUST
SAVE THE
REPUBLIC

A FLANDERS HALL
AMERICA
FIRST
BOOK

by

Stephen A. Day

Congressman at Large, State of Illinois

One Dollar

On the opposite page are two books published in the United States by Flanders Hall, the publishing concern which was secretly organized and financed by George Sylvester Viereck. Beside the two books are the official German propaganda pamphlets, of which the Flanders Hall books were almost word-for-word translations.

Reproduced immediately above is the book by Representative Stephen A. Day, which was also published by Flanders Hall.

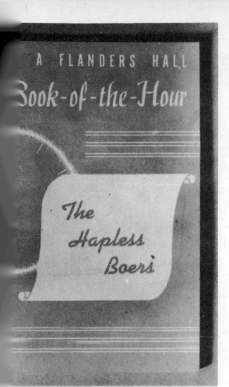

A FLANDERS HALL

Book-of-the-Hour

The Hapless Boers

STEFAN SCHROEDER

England und die Buren

60 Pfg.

A FLANDERS HALL

Book-of-the-Hour

Democracy on the Nile

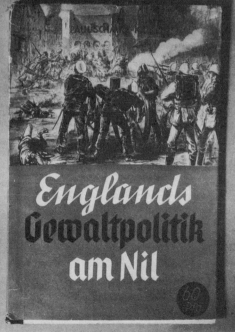

Englands Gewaltpolitik am Nil

The name was fictitious. "James Burr Hamilton" was actually George Sylvester Viereck.

Viereck had every right to edit this book. He himself had written the speech attacking Lord Lothian which Senator Lundeen had delivered in the Senate Chamber. For the most part, the speech was a compilation of material Viereck had acquired at the German Embassy in Washington.

There were other Congressmen who were used by the Nazi propaganda agency, Flanders Hall, Inc. One of them was Representative Stephen A. Day of Illinois. In the summer of 1941, Day turned over to the Hauck brothers a manuscript in which he savagely attacked the foreign and domestic policy of the Administration. The writing did not entirely satisfy Viereck and Siegfried Hauck. "Mr. Viereck and I looked it over and agreed that it needed touching up," Hauck later related. "I left the manuscript with Viereck who said it had to be revised." After the proper revisions, Congressman Day's manuscript was published by Flanders Hall under the title of *We Must Save the Republic.*

The Bund's *Deutscher Weckruf* published an ecstatic review of Day's book. The Board of Trade for German American Commerce distributed a large number of complimentary copies. The America First Committee energetically promoted the book at its public rallies and in its bulletins.*

Another politician who was in touch with Flanders Hall, Inc., was ex-Senator Rush D. Holt of West Virginia. One eve-

---

* Largely because of *We Must Save the Republic,* Representative Stephen A. Day was to become one of the outstanding heroes of the America First movement. On October 30, 1941, Day was introduced as a guest of honor at the important America First Madison Square rally which was addressed by Senator Wheeler, Charles Lindbergh and John Cudahy.

ning in May 1941, Siegfried Hauck and George Sylvester Viereck conferred with Holt at his house in Washington, D. C., regarding the possibility of writing a book for Flanders Hall. Holt reacted very favorably to the proposal. In fact, according to Siegfried Hauck, "He [Rush Holt] agreed to buy a certain number of the first book — $1,000 worth, I think it was."

Holt delivered to Hauck a manuscript entitled, *Who's Who Among the War Mongers*. Viereck made a few editorial changes, and the book was set up in type. For some reason, Holt's book was never published, but the manuscript went on an interesting journey. On July 29, 1941, Viereck mailed it from New York City in a large manila envelope addressed to "Senhor Hoyningero Hueneras—Rua Pau de Bandera 9—Lisbon, Portugal."

"Hoyningero Hueneras" was an alias for the German Ambassador to Portugal. Inside the envelope mailed to the Ambassador, Viereck had enclosed another smaller envelope with this address: "Dr. Hans Heinrich Dieckhoff—Berlin, W.—Wilhelmstrasse 75."

George Sylvester Viereck was sending Rush Holt's manuscript for filing in Berlin.

The envelope never reached its destination. It was intercepted at Bermuda by the British censors.

IV. *Viereck on the Hill*

In the spring of 1940 Viereck became very busy in Washington. Urgent business took the Nazi agent to the Capital at least once a week during the months of April, May and June. By August, in spite of the disagreeable heat, he had stepped up his visits to twice a week. Much as the fastidious propaganda ace would have preferred to remain in the comfort of his luxurious apartment at 305 Riverside Drive in New York City, his duty to Nazi Germany made imperative his keeping

FIRST CLASS MAIL

SENHOR HOTNINGERO HUENERAS,

Rua Pau de Bandera 9,

L I S B O N,

(Portugal)

Dr. Hans Heinrich Dieckhoff,

B E R L I N, W.

Wilhelmstrasse 75.

It was in the large envelope (*at top*) that George Sylvester Viereck mailed the manuscript of ex-Senator Rush D. Holt to a "maildrop" in Lisbon, for forwarding to Berlin. Enclosed in the large envelope was the smaller one, which was to carry the manuscript to its final destination.

in constant touch with Washington during this politically crucial period.

On July 10 President Roosevelt had submitted to Congress a $4,800,000,000 defense program. In August, United States Congressmen were debating whether or not the Selective Service Bill should be passed. It was Viereck's job to do everything possible to prevent the passage of these measures.

Invariably, when Viereck arrived in Washington during these hectic days, one of his first calls was at the office of his old friend, Senator Ernest Lundeen. This office had really become Viereck's Washington headquarters. Here he conducted most of his business. From here he got in touch by telephone with his intimates at the German Embassy and with the office of Congressman Hamilton Fish. Here also, Viereck wrote certain important speeches for Lundeen, which the Senator delivered on the floor of the Senate. One of these Viereck-Lundeen compositions was the speech which, when reprinted and mailed out under Lundeen's franking privilege, became known to tens of thousands of Americans under the title of "Six Men and the War." It was a tirade against United States preparedness efforts. Viereck worked particularly hard on this speech in order to catch the exact flavor of the Senator's oratorical style. "I've tried to phrase it in the language you would use," he told Lundeen, in the presence of one of the Senator's secretaries, Mrs. Phyllis Spielman, who later testified to this fact at the trial of Viereck.

Viereck felt so much at home in the Lundeen office that he made no attempt to conceal from the office staff the fact that he was writing the Senator's speeches and collaborating with Lundeen in various other ways. He would frequently dictate to one of Lundeen's secretaries the outline for a talk to be delivered by the Senator. On several occasions, as in his preparation of the speech "Lord Lothian vs. Lord Lothian," Viereck broke off dictation to telephone the German Embassy for background material and supplementary data. Within a short time after such calls were made, a messenger would arrive at Senator Lundeen's office with an envelope bearing the return address of Dr. Hans Thomsen, acting Ambassador from the Third Reich.

Viereck paid his last visit to Senator Lundeen's office on August 26, 1940. A couple of days after this visit, the Senator mailed to Viereck — for editing and revision — the manuscript of a speech entitled "German Contributions to American Life." Lundeen was to deliver this speech over the Labor Day holidays. The revised speech came back to Lundeen on the afternoon of August 31, the day on which the Senator was killed in an airplane crash at Lovettsville, Virginia. Senator Lundeen took the manuscript with him on his fatal airplane trip.

Viereck was a practical man. The contents of the speech he had prepared for Lundeen were not wasted. Shortly after the Senator's death, a speech with similar title and contents was delivered by Theodore H. Hoffmann, head of the Steuben Society. The Hoffmann speech was inserted in the Congressional Record, reprinted and mailed around the country postage free under the franking privilege of Senator Gerald P. Nye of North Dakota.

V. *The Franking Privilege*

It was George Sylvester Viereck who conceived how the congressional franking privilege* might be used as an effective instrument of psychological sabotage.

---

* The franking privilege was originally created to enable members of Congress to carry on free correspondence with their constituents. But there is no regulation which prevents a Congressman from turning over the use of his franked envelopes to anyone who wishes to send congressional material through the mails. All the Congressman has to do in such a case is sign a requisition before the Public Printer. The latter then delivers the specified amounts of franked material to the party named, who in turn may address and mail out this material without payment of postage.

Photograph of the late Senator Ernest Lundeen addressing a banquet held by the Board of Trade for German-American Commerce at New York's Hotel Waldorf-Astoria, March 20, 1940. Left to right are German Consul General Dr. Hans Borchers; Otto A. Stiefel; the Duke of Saxe-Coburg, international Nazi emissary; Dr. Roberg Reiner, president of the Board of Trade for German-American Commerce; the late U. S. Senator Ernest Lundeen; Lieut Gen. F. von Boetticher; former German Consul Heinrich Stahmer, and German Consul Friedhelm Draeger.

Viereck established in Washington an apparatus for placing pro-Axis propaganda in the Congressional Record, purchasing tens of thousands of reprints of this and other material, and mailing out these reprints on a nationwide scale, postage free, by using the franking privileges of various Congressmen, many of whom were doubtless unaware of the use to which their franked envelopes were being put.

The headquarters of Viereck's Washington propaganda machine was in Room 1424 in the House Office Building. Room 1424 was the office of Congressman Hamilton Fish of New York.*

George Hill, forty-five-year-old clerk in the office of Hamilton Fish, was in charge of Viereck's Washington propaganda mill. Hill first met Viereck early in July 1940, when Representative Fish introduced him to the Nazi agent. Hill was told that Viereck wanted to mail out some reprints of a speech which Lundeen had delivered on the floor of the Senate. The speech was called "Six Men and the War." As previously related, it had been written by Viereck himself.

Senator Lundeen's office did not have adequate facilities for sending out the number of reprints Viereck contemplated distributing. The mailing was therefore to be handled from Fish's office and the Congressman's private mailing lists were to be used.

Hill followed his instructions. It was quite a job, because the Viereck-Lundeen speech was sent to 125,000 persons. Hill had to hire a special crew of girls to handle the mailing.

---

* For some time Representative Fish has been friendly with George Sylvester Viereck. Fish considered the Nazi agent "a great publicist" and was not averse to collaborating with Viereck on political writings. On November 26, 1937, Viereck wrote to Charles Fulton Oursler, editor-in-chief of *Liberty Magazine*, suggesting an article on the need for "a war referendum." Viereck wrote that his collaborator on this article would be Representative Hamilton Fish, who—said the Nazi agent—would "be very glad to write an article with me on the necessity of a war referendum." Viereck explained that he had already discussed the matter at length with Congressman Fish.

From that time on, George Hill had two employers: Congressman Hamilton Fish and the Nazi agent George Sylvester Viereck.

"Viereck told me not to write him," Hill later testified in court. "He told me he would get in touch with me."

Viereck was cautious. As much as possible he avoided direct personal contact with Fish's assistant. He handled the necessary negotiations through Prescott Dennett, an isolationist publicist in Washington, D. C.

When Viereck needed an aide to set up a special propaganda "committee" in Washington, he chose this snappily-dressed, mustached publicist for the job.

With Viereck's expert advice and the Nazi funds he supplied, Dennett created this organization in the spring of 1940. Consisting of a few carefully-selected Senators and Representatives, most of whom did not know its source of financial backing, the organization operated under three different names: War Debts Defense Committee, Make Europe Pay War Debts Committee and Islands for War Debts Committee.

Senator Lundeen was named as Chairman of the group (which continued to operate long after his death). Honorary Chairman was Senator Robert R. Reynolds of North Carolina, the Chairman of the Senate Military Affairs Committee. Representative Martin L. Sweeney of Ohio acted as Vice-Chairman. Prescott Dennett was Secretary-Treasurer.

The headquarters of this organization, which came to be generally known as the Islands for War Debts Committee, was at the office of Dennett's Columbia Press Service at 1430 Rhode Island Avenue, Northwest, Washington, D. C.

"The objective of German propaganda was three-fold," Viereck explained when discussing his work in World War I in his book *Spreading the Germs of Hate*. "To strengthen and replenish Germany; to weaken and harass Germany's foes, and to keep America out of the war." This definition also sums up the propaganda aims of the Islands for War Debts Committee.

From his Riverside Drive apartment in New York, which was decorated with portraits of Adolf Hitler and Kaiser Wilhelm, Viereck directed the operations of the Washington committee.

Viereck carefully accumulated and sent to Dennett all propaganda items that might be useful: radio talks of America First leaders, extracts from anti-British books, isolationist and anti-Administration editorials, and abstracts of anti-Soviet articles. Viereck sometimes included his own writings. The material was relayed by Dennett to George Hill, who contrived to get it inserted into the Congressional Record.

Once the material had appeared in the Record, Hill, using his authority as Congressman Fish's clerk, ordered reprints by the tens of thousands. (He ordered reprints of all important isolationist speeches in Congress.) Dennett gave him the money to pay the Government Printing Office for these reprints.

Mail bags carrying tons of these reprints with franked envelopes were then delivered — on Hill's instructions — in United States Post Office trucks to the office of Dennett's Islands for War Debts Committee. Using the privilege of the congressional frank, Dennett mailed out the reprints to wherever he wanted them to go.

Thus the route which Viereck's material traveled was: from Viereck to Dennett to Hill to certain Congressmen and so into the Congressional Record. Finally, Viereck's material emerged bearing the Great Seal of the United States as a headpiece and with a Congressman's frank to take it through the mails postage-free to hundreds of thousands of American citizens.

VI. *Zero Hour*

By the summer of 1941 the Viereck-Dennett-Hill propaganda machine was working at high speed. Axis preparations
for the open military assault on the United States were already
under way, and Axis agents in this country were bending every
effort to sabotage defense legislation. Hectic scenes were taking
place in Prescott Dennett's offices at 1430 Rhode Island
Avenue Northwest. A constant stream of mail bags, crammed
with franked envelopes kept pouring in and out of the headquarters of the Islands for War Debts Committee. Often there
were as many as 30 mail bags piled in the basement below,
while upstairs in Dennett's main office eight girls were fever-
ishly addressing thousands of franked envelopes.

Between the months of March and September 1941, Congressman Fish's clerk George Hill received a total of $12,000
to cover the expenses of his activities for Viereck. During this
period George Hill bought more than half a million reprints
from the Congressional Record, the majority of them reprints of speeches by isolationist and anti-Administration
Congressmen, who—no matter how patriotic their motives may
have been—were thus creating propaganda material of use to
George Sylvester Viereck.

Here are some of the orders placed by Hill at the Government Printing Office for franked envelopes and reprints:

25,000 copies of Representative Hamilton Fish's speech on
"Power of Congress to Declare War," for which Hill paid
$86.20.

120,000 copies of Senator D. Worth Clark's speech, "England
Expects Every American To Do His Duty," for which Hill
paid $483. The Government Printing Office records show that
the use of Clark's frank was authorized by his "office."

66,000 copies of Representative Philip A. Bennett's speech,
"Congress Must Keep Faith With the Selectees," for which

Hill paid $213.84. The Government Printing Office records show that Bennett's son authorized the frank.

10,000 copies of Representative Martin L. Sweeney's speech, "Crosses in Flanders." The records show that the frank was authorized by Congressman Sweeney's "office."

25,000 copies of an item inserted by Representative Harold Knutson entitled "Mrs. Lundeen Answers Walter Winchell." The records show that Congressman Knutson authorized the use of his frank.

25,000 copies of anti-war speeches by Senator Gerald P. Nye and Representative Martin L. Sweeney. The records show that Miss Bates of Senator Nye's office authorized the frank.

66,000 copies of an insertion by Representative Bartel K. Jonkman, "Mrs. Roosevelt Mistaken." The records show that Mr. Pratt of Jonkman's office authorized the frank.

28,000 copies of anti-war material inserted by Representative Henry C. Dworshak. The records show that Representative Dworshak authorized the frank.

20,000 copies of two anti-war speeches by Senator Burton K. Wheeler and Representative Jeannette Rankin. The records show that Mr. Cooper of Senator Wheeler's office authorized the frank.

30,000 copies of an item inserted by Representative Clare E. Hoffman, "We Burned Our Fingers Once." The records show that Miss Boyer of Representative Hoffman's office authorized the frank.

Dennett prepared a mammoth mailing list of persons to whom the franked envelopes were to be sent. This list was a compilation of names and addresses secured from many sources. One list Dennett obtained had been compiled by the isolationist magazine, *Scribner's Commentator,* from names signed to letters addressed to Charles A. Lindbergh, Father Charles E. Coughlin, Senator Rush D. Holt, and other well-known isolationists. Another was Congressman Hamilton Fish's private mailing list, drawn up in connection with his National Committee to Keep America Out of Foreign Wars. A third was a mailing list compiled from fan mail received by Representative Martin L. Sweeney. Other lists came from Frank Burch, a Nazi agent in Akron, Ohio; from the Nazi agency, Flanders Hall, Inc.; and from the German Library of Information.

Pro-Axis organizations throughout the country also aided in the distribution of Dennett's propaganda material. Franked envelopes were handed out for addressing at the meetings of the Christian Front, the Christian Mobilizers, the American Destiny Party, the Silver Shirts, the National Gentile League, the Defenders, and other such groups.

Arthur Junga, chairman of New York Unit 55 of the Germanophile Steuben Society, sent out an announcement of a coming meeting of his organization, stating in part:

> At this meeting excerpts from the Congressional Record will be distributed to the members. These are in the form of a radio address delivered by our National Chairman over Station WHA, Madison, Wis., entitled "Americans of Germanic Extraction—Their Contributions to our Country and their Stand Today."
>
> These excerpts can be used to publicize our Society to great advantage. They can be sent to those of our race and others, to demonstrate in the first instance that our Society is doing something, and in the second instance, that those of our race have been an important part in the building of our country. (These excerpts are in franked envelopes, requiring no postage.)
>
> Come to the meeting and get a bunch of them to distribute among your friends.

A number of subversive pamphleteers, who distributed the congressional reprints in franked envelopes, often inserted

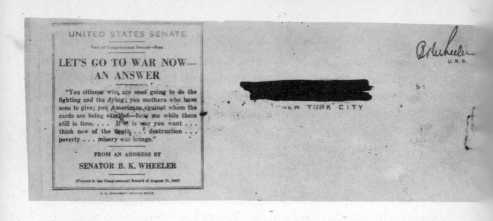

Envelopes mailed out by the Germanophile Steuben Society under the franking privileges of Senators Burton K. Wheeler and Gerald P. Nye. Note the identical addressing-plate code number (55) on both franked envelopes and on the Steuben Society's own wrapper.

into the envelopes violent anti-Semitic and Nazi propaganda which they were disseminating themselves. Franked envelopes of Congressman Hamilton Fish, for example, were used for the distribution of a William Dudley Pelley brochure advertising the *Protocols of Zion,* the notorious anti-Semitic forgeries.

Most important of all the distributing agencies used by Viereck's Washington apparatus was the America First Committee. Dennett transferred many of his mail bags filled with isolationist and appeasement propaganda to the America First Committee's Washington headquarters at 126 C Street, Northwest. Here franked envelopes were addressed and mailed out. Quantity lots were sent to America First Committee outlets for re-distribution in other areas. One of the chief individual re-distributors of this material was Ralph Townsend, a paid Japanese agent who was a leader of America First activity in San Francisco and who was subsequently sentenced to jail for failure to register as an agent of the Japanese Government.

Below is a list of the members of Congress whose franking privilege was used in this huge campaign of psychological sabotage. Beyond question, some of these Congressmen were totally unaware that their franking privilege was being used to further the schemes of the Axis, but the facts are a matter of public record.

Senators
D. Worth Clark
Rush D. Holt
E. C. Johnson
Gerald P. Nye
Robert R. Reynolds
Burton K. Wheeler
Representatives
Philip Bennett
Stephen Day
Henry Dworshak

NEW YORK
MAR 4
1941

CHURCH STREET
ANNEX

FIGHT FOR JEWDOM COMMITTEE
1270 Sixth Avenue
New York

Rescue the Republic!

¶ A collection of 39 speeches in defense of American liberty and institutions and against the despoilers of our Nation, by Hon. Jacob Thorkelson, Representative from Montana in the 76th Congress, revealing in trenchant, understandable language the conflict between New Deal objectives and the provisions of the Constitution for the welfare of the people and the safety of the Nation.

¶ Dr. Thorkelson is a man of parts, having been an aviator, longshoreman, ocean-going shipmaster and naval reserve officer, as well as physician and surgeon in the State of Montana for some 26 years before his election to the Congress of the United States, and withal demonstrates a keen knowledge of constitutional law.

¶ Since taking office he has proven himself to be one Member of Congress with the temerity and rugged patriotism to get up on his feet regardless of the consequences and fight for the restoration of constitutional government in this stricken Nation, against the ruthless cohorts of the sovieteers.

¶ This is a book that will give you a new conception of the Constitution for which our forefathers paid in blood and understanding effort, in order that the Nation might survive.

¶ Printed on substantial book paper, 463 pages, blue cloth binding.

Price $3.00 per copy, postpaid.

---o---

THE PELLEY PUBLISHERS

Box 2630   Asheville, N. C.

The
PROTOCOLS
of the Learned Elders of
ZION

A booklet of 72 pages comprising mainly twenty-four "Protocols" which purport to be the records of meetings of the Learned Elders of Zion and to reveal in more or less detail the plans of organized Jewry for the ultimate subjugation of the Gentile peoples of the world.
From Victor E. Marsden's translation of the document of Sergyei Nilus which was published in Russian in 1905 and a copy of which is extant in the British Museum.
In the face of the many statements and attacks impugning the authenticity of the Protocols, the conclusion reached by many serious investigators and observers that the Jewish plot against Christian civilization is real seems to be borne out by world events and developments of the past thirty years, to say nothing of the many confessions and braggings of representative Jews themselves.

25c each   Six for $1.00   100 for $12.50

PELLEY PUBLISHERS

Box 2630   Asheville, N. C.

LITERATURE ORDER BLANK

Date.., 1939

The Pelley Publishers,
    Box 2630, Asheville, N. C.

Enclosed please find $.............. in money order or currency, for which please ship the following literature:

.... Price $............
....
....
....
....
                    Total Remittance $.............

NAME ....
Street ....
City and State ....

This envelope franked by Representative Hamilton Fish was addressed to the "Fight for Jewdom Committee" and sent to the office of the Fight for Freedom Committee in New York City. The envelope when received by the Fight for Freedom Committee contained an anti-Administration speech by Congressman Fish and the brochure here reproduced advertising the notorious anti-Semitic forgeries *Protocols of Zion* and other literature published by the Silver Shirt chief, William Dudley Pelley.

Hamilton Fish
Clare E. Hoffman
Bartel Jonkman
Harold Knutson
James C. Oliver
Dewey Short
William Stratton
Martin L. Sweeney
Jacob Thorkelson
George Holden Tinkham
John M. Vorys

These members of Congress were the political heroes of the America First Committee.

The America First Committee offices in Washington, D. C., were raided by the United States Marshal in the fall of 1941, as this photograph shows. Government agents found at the America First Committee headquarters ten mailbags filled with congressional franked material which had

CHAPTER TEN

AMERICA FIRST!

The first thing I did was to hire a large hall and organize a meeting, at which well-known men thundered against the export of munitions. Messrs. Buchanan and Fowler, members of Congress; Mr. Hannis Taylor, the former American Ambassador in Madrid; Mr. Monnett, a former Attorney-General; together with a number of University professors, theologians and Labor leaders appeared and raised their voices. I sat unobtrusively in a corner and watched my plans fructifying. None of the speakers had the faintest suspicion that he was in the "service" of a German officer sitting among the audience. They knew the men who had asked them to speak, but had no idea that the strings were being pulled by somebody else.

> *Captain Franz von Rintelen, World War I*
> *saboteur in the United States, in his post-war*
> *confession, "The Dark Invader."*

I. *"New Leadership"*

In Philadelphia's large Arena auditorium, on the evening of May 29, 1941, sixteen thousand men and women attended a rally of the America First Committee to hear Charles A. Lindbergh denounce the President of the United States. On the speakers' platform, in addition to Lindbergh, were Senator David I. Walsh, Mrs. Burton K. Wheeler, Mrs. Bennett Champ Clark, Kathleen Norris, and Mrs. Anne Morrow Lindbergh. In box seats and in the reserved sections of the hall sat prominent Christian Fronters, German American Bund leaders, and local official representatives of the Third

197

Reich. The hall was packed with members of native fascist, anti-Semitic organizations. Thunderous applause and prolonged cheering greeted Charles A. Lindbergh as he rose to speak.

Branding the Defense Program of the Administration as a betrayal of the American people, Lindbergh called for the overthrow of the Administration and for "a new leadership."

"Our own President says that the safety of America lies in controlling the Cape Verde Islands off the coast of Africa," Lindbergh declared.

Instantly boos and catcalls rang out in the Arena.

Then Lindbergh added, "Even Hitler never made a statement like that!"

Cheers swept the auditorium.

Lindbergh went on, "They tell us it is undemocratic for us to question the type of leadership that has taken to defeat every nation in the world that followed it. . . . Their prophecies have been false, their policies have failed, and their promises have been worthless!

"I ask you, is our nation to follow them further?

"Is it not time for us to turn to new policies and to a new leadership?"

The response of the audience was hysterical. The frantic applause was interspersed here and there by shrill cries, "What are we waiting for?" "Impeach Roosevelt!" "Are we going to let the Jews run this country?" In their excitement, some members of the audience stood up and gave the Nazi salute.

"Most amazing of all," reported the Philadelphia *Daily News* on the following morning, "was the smile that spread over the face of United States Senator David I. Walsh of Massachusetts when the Arena rang and re-echoed with the booing of President Roosevelt. Instead of protesting, instead of resenting the disgraceful exhibition, Senator Walsh sat in his chair beaming on the half-frenzied crowd."

Observers said that the Arena meeting had the mood and character of the hate-crazed Hitlerite rallies in Germany which preceded the coming to power of the Nazis. . . .

The isolationist America First Committee, formed less than one year before by an ambitious young Yale law student, had somehow developed into the "spontaneous American movement" for which the Nazis had been searching and tirelessly working since 1933.

How had it happened?

II. *"Well-Known Men"*

Douglas Stuart, Jr., the twenty-four-year-old founder of the America First Committee, had first shown up on the political horizon at the 1940 Republican Party Convention in Philadelphia. Here young Stuart consorted with the disgruntled isolationist minority which was determined to oppose both the Republican and the Democratic presidential nominees in the forthcoming elections on the grounds that Wendell Willkie and Franklin D. Roosevelt were equally "interventionist." At Philadelphia Douglas Stuart got the idea of organizing these dissident elements on a national scale.

Charles A. Lindbergh had already shown interest in Stuart's Yale group which was originally called the Committee to Defend America First. On Lindbergh's advice, Stuart went to Chicago and saw General Robert E. Wood, chairman of the Board of Sears, Roebuck and Company. Stuart invited the prominent Chicagoan to become the leader of his projected national movement.

General Wood was strongly isolationist. He felt America had nothing to fear from Hitler. He had studied *Mein Kampf* and, according to *Time* magazine, had come to the conclusion: "Hitler . . . is mortal and he'll die some day. The way to tame a rebel is to make him rich, and then he becomes conservative and settles down." Wood was willing to hand Europe over to Hitler and, if necessary, all of South America "below the bulge." The notion of heading a national "anti-war" movement appealed to Wood. He agreed to accept the chairmanship of Stuart's organization, if and when the project materialized.

Stuart's next move took him to Washington, where he visited the palatial three-story, red-brick house of the wealthy ex-diplomat William R. Castle. The former Under-Secretary of State in the Hoover Administration was playing host that summer to leading American advocates of isolationism and appeasement. He was in close touch with former President Hoover, Senator Burton K. Wheeler, General Wood, Charles Lindbergh, Alice Roosevelt Longworth, and other anti-Administration bigwigs. At informal gatherings in the Castle home, the broad strategy and specific tactics of opposition to the President's foreign policy were discussed far into those hot July and August nights. Castle himself was strongly in favor of appeasing Japan and dropping all aid to China. He had written for Dr. Friedrich Auhagen's publication, *Today's Challenge,* and his views were being widely publicized in the official German and Japanese propaganda journals. The Castle *clique* was already, in fact, an American "Cliveden Set" almost identical in character and purpose to the Lady Astor-Nevile Henderson group which had so successfully promoted the Munich appeasement policy in Europe.

Castle was not immediately receptive to Stuart's project. The former diplomat preferred to work behind the scenes, quietly talking to and influencing Congressmen and businessmen. Young Stuart's idea of organizing a national movement struck Castle at first as being rather reckless and unnecessary. But with Lindbergh and General Wood enthusiastically supporting it, Castle was finally won over.

A number of other prominent public men, motivated by

antagonism to the Administration and its foreign policy, were soon lined up in the Lindbergh-Stuart camp.

Castle still urged "caution." He recalled the mistakes of the No Foreign Wars Committee under the impetuous leadership of Verne Marshall— "whom I like and respect" but who was rather too "violent on the subject of Jews and the New Deal." ("God knows," added William R. Castle, "I have no particular affection for such people, but I should much prefer to express it in private. . . .")*

After a series of conferences at General Wood's home, the America First Committee was launched on a national scale. William H. Regnery, a Chicago millionaire, and Clay Judson, a Chicago attorney for what Douglas Stuart described as "the smart money boys," were signatories of the incorporation papers, along with Stuart and General Wood. The original National Committee included Henry Ford, who had accepted a medal from Adolf Hitler, and Avery Brundage, who had been Chairman of the American Olympic Games Committee, when the games were held in Berlin in 1936. Charles A. Lindbergh, destined to be the Committee's number one hero and spokesman, was not named as a member of the original Committee.

National Offices for the America First Committee were set up on the eighteenth floor of the huge Chicago Board of Trade Building, and at once intense organizational activity began. A large scale advertising and promotional campaign was started to make America First known to the public.

Public attention was called to the new Committee by means of a series of full-page advertisements, which appeared in all the important newspapers, announcing the Committee's formation and its proclaimed objective of keeping America out of war. Mass rallies were staged in the major cities. Coast-to-

---

* Excerpts from a letter written by William R. Castle on December 28, 1940, to Merwin K. Hart of New York City.

coast radio hookups carried the "anti-war" message of America First into millions of homes. General Wood spoke, Lindbergh spoke, Senators Nye and Wheeler spoke. Anti-Administration and isolationist leaflets, pamphlets, bulletins, and form-letters poured from the Chicago headquarters. The Chicago office alone, according to its own published figures, printed and distributed during the first nine months of its existence:

373,150 copies of speeches
980,300 propaganda pamphlets and circulars
336,300 display pieces (buttons, posters and stickers)
405,200 letters to members and prospective members
599,000 mimeographed instructions and bulletins for members

America First Chapters, complete with funds and organizational apparatus, sprang up in every town and city. Speeches, public meetings, radio, newspaper editorials, posters, cartoons, magazines, pamphlets, books, advertisements, slogans, buttons, demonstrations, picket lines, street-corner agitators, and every other conceivable artifice of propaganda were used. By the start of 1941, young Stuart's idea had already materialized as a national organization which was rapidly on its way to becoming the most powerful pressure group in the United States. For eleven months thereafter, right up to the day the Japanese bombs fell on Pearl Harbor, the America First Committee blanketed the country with isolationist arguments aimed at building mass opposition to President Roosevelt's foreign policy, impeding defense legislation, and halting aid to Great Britain, China, the Soviet Union and other nations resisting Axis aggression.

The well-known men who made up the national leadership of the America First Committee had doubtlessly no intention of aiding the Axis at the expense of their own country. Yet,

however sincere their motives may have been, the fact is that
Nazi and Japanese agents made use of their Committee. Thus,
distinguished Americans who prided themselves on their commercial or political astuteness, actually became the dupes of
the enemies of the United States.

Here are a few typical public utterances of the America First
Committee at the height of its career:

> ... We have nothing to fear from competition with Hitler for
> markets outside this hemisphere and a Nazi-dominated Eu-
> rope. . . . we have nothing to fear from a Nazi European
> victory.
>> *"America First Bulletin," New York*
>> *Chapter, September 13, 1941.*

> Germany has a right to play with South America. If Germany
> wins, her wage scale and buying power will go up and she
> will buy more of our products, and if she loses, her wage scale
> will go down, which will mean more competition in the world
> markets, and less buying power to purchase goods in the
> American markets.
>> *Representative Hamilton Fish,*
>> *American First rally, Philadelphia, August 20, 1941*

> DID YOU KNOW that even if Nazi Germany conquers Com-
> munist Russia, the enlarged German economy may be weak-
> ened rather than strengthened?
>> *Bulletin prepared by America First Com-*
>> *mittee Research Bureau, Washington, D. C.*
>> *August 1, 1941.*

> German submarines are small. They were designed to operate
> close to their bases—within a few hundred miles of England.
> ... We are safe now and we are safe for years to come.
>> *Senator Burton K. Wheeler, America First*
>> *rally, Madison Square Garden, New York*
>> *City, May 23, 1941.*

The three most important groups which have been pressing this country toward war are the British, the Jewish and the Roosevelt Administration.

> *Charles A. Lindbergh, America First*
> *rally, Des Moines, September 11, 1941.*

President Roosevelt and his administration have never taken the American people into their confidence. They preach about preserving democracy and freedom abroad, while they practice dictatorship and subterfuge at home. . . . This war we are asked to enter would be the greatest and most devastating conflict in all history. And what have we to gain from either a material or an ideal standpoint? . . . There is no danger to this nation from without. Our only danger lies from within.

> *Charles A. Lindbergh, America First rally,*
> *Madison Square Garden, New York City,*
> *October 30, 1941.*

III. *The Fifth Column Moves In*

Although the America First Committee was not founded to help the Axis, Berlin from the outset saw in this organization an instrument for carrying on psychological sabotage in the United States on a hitherto undreamed of scale. While the American public was still reeling under the first barrage of America First propaganda, and wondering just what to make of it all, a voice from across the seas enthusiastically welcomed the Committee. Via shortwave radio to America on January 22, 1941, Dr. Joseph Paul Goebbels' Propaganda Ministry announced: "The America First Committee is truly American and truly patriotic!"

Members of the German American Bund began moving quietly, en masse, into the chapters of the America First Committee. By May 1, 1941, Bund leaders were openly writing in their official publication, *Deutscher Weckruf und Beobachter:* "Join the America First Committee and continue to bombard

The U.S.A. is NOT a "British" Nation!	# The Free American and ## Deutscher Weckruf und Beobachter	Keep the U.S.A. out of "Britain's" Wars!

No. 45. New York, N. Y., May 1, 1941 Price: 5c.

"We Cannot Win this War for England"

—Colonel Charles A. Lindbergh

say it is the Interventionists Who are Undermining the Principles of Democracy— More than 80% of the People Opposed to War

Canada Recruiting in New York in Violation of Federal Law

The Administration Drops the Mask

"Germany Must Perish"

A Book Review

BRITAIN'S BALKAN DEBACLE

PEOPLE BECOMING AROUSED

Hamilton Fish Hints at President's Impeachment — Senator Wheeler Will Crusade Against War — Senators Want Referendum on War by the Plain People.

"Into the War," says Sec'y Knox

"No," say the People

Hitler's Nine Peace Proposals

Join the America First Committee and continue to bombard your representatives in Congress with letters and telegrams of protest.

The Free American and Deutscher Weckruf und Beobachter, official organ of the German American Bund, headlined a quotation from Charles A. Lindbergh and instructed Bund members to join the America First Committee.

your representatives in Congress with letters and telegrams in protest against President Roosevelt's foreign policy."

The Silver Shirters climbed aboard the Committee bandwagon. "Slowly but inexorably the true leaders of a renovated and purged America are beginning to emerge," wrote the Silver Shirt chief, William Dudley Pelley. "Colonel Charles A. Lindbergh, Henry Ford, Major George Van Horn Moseley, and, last but by no means least, Senator Burton K. Wheeler of Montana, are stepping into the limelight of Roosevelt-Opposition, and receiving the plaudits of a hysterical multitude."

The Christian Fronters formed their cells within the America First Committee. To those of his Storm Troop followers who at first complained that the Committee lacked militancy, Father Coughlin declared in *Social Justice:* "Let all groups, as well as all individuals, who support the *America First Committee,* submerge, momentarily at least, their motivating objectives *to the one grand objective of keeping this country out of the war.* No other interest should engage our common mind."

The leaders of the America First Committee, while publicly repudiating the support of the German American Bund, did not reject Coughlin's Christian Front support. Chairman General Robert E. Wood himself wrote a letter, which was published in *Social Justice,* stating: "I have not rejected the Christian Social Justice movement. I welcome their support in our common objective — keeping this country out of war."

The Ku Klux Klan rallied behind the America First Committee. *The Fiery Cross,* the Klan's official publication, endorsed the America First program and declared in its issue of April 21, 1941: "The Klan's attitude toward the present world situation was aptly expressed recently by General Robert E. Wood, chairman of the board of Sears, Roebuck and Company, and chairman of the America First Committee."

Social Justice

Founded 1936   by Father Coughlin

Royal Oak, Michigan   July 28, 1941   10c

'America First' Committee Still Welcomes 'Coughlinites'

To the Editor:

When I heard that the America First Committee had denounced Father Coughlin and his followers, I immediately wrote a letter to Mrs. Burton K. Wheeler.

I wish that you would print this letter from Mrs. Wheeler in SOCIAL JUSTICE. She writes:

"My dear Mrs. B——: Your letter of May 7th has just reached me. I am afraid that you are a victim of newspaper propaganda, because there never has been any discrimination against Father Coughlin's followers or against any other religious body as far as America First is concerned.

"The thing that the war-mongers want, of course, is to stir up dissension among the anti-war people so that they will start fighting each other instead of fighting the war-mongers.

"I hope that we are not going to fall into that trap because nothing could be more disastrous. With kindest regards.

"Sincerely yours,
"Lulu Wheeler."

I am sure that there are a great many people who have dropped out of the America First Commit-

tee because they believed as I did.

—Mrs. R.A.B.

Woodside, N. Y.

Gen. Wood's Letter

To the Editor:

On Saturday the *Chicago Tribune* had an item in which the statement was made that Gen. Robert E. Wood had rejected the support of the Christian Social Justice movement from the America First Committee.

I wrote to Gen. Wood at once. I am sending the letter which he had sent to me. If you wish to use it in SOCIAL JUSTICE you may do so.

Gen. Wood's letter reads:

"Replying to your letter of July 5th, I have not rejected the Christian Social Justice movement. I welcome their support in our common objective — preventing this country from getting into the war.

"This whole report has come about through the magnifying of what was a very small incident which happened at a rally in Highland Park.

"Very truly yours,
"R. E. Wood."

Masthead and letter column from Father Charles E. Coughlin's *Social Justice* of July 28, 1941, with letters from Lula Wheeler (wife of Senator Burton K. Wheeler) and General Robert E. Wood, both welcoming Coughlin's followers into the ranks of the America First Committee.

Social Justice

Number 226

America First

WERE it not for the America First Committee, the message in favor of peace—messages delivered particularly by Senator Wheeler and Colonel Lindbergh—would not have been broadcast to war nation.

No other spontaneous organization in the entire history of this country has contributed such substantial and needed service during a crucial period.

From within, by individuals who joined the Committee for the one purpose of sowing seeds of discussion.

From without, by individuals and groups who are bent on hurdling the flesh and blood of America into a war designed in part to finish guard anything and those who control it; by those who have been reduced to near-slavery; and who more than God and the international bankers more than the poor, exploited, misguided Americans.

We rejoice that a most representative group of Protestant ministers in America openly campaigned for peace and for America first.

In the days of the aftermath, they will receive their reward, both from God and from the disillusioned, awakened American people.

We trust that Cardinal William O'Connell, the dean of the American Catholic hierarchy, has given the America First Committee his benediction—and this is a benediction that cannot be nullified by carping criticism emanating from other quarters.

From time to time, the America First Committee will make mistakes. It does not pretend to be a divinely guided institution.

But at all times the America First Committee is, in one respect, in our support, for America first, last and always.

Because the America First Committee is merely a human organization, it would be unfair for us to strain at the point of precision with indictment of its members and confine the cancel of pro-Britishism and pro-actions identified with opponent organization.

In this struggle on the part of the majority of unorganized and misrepresented Americans to keep this country

out of Europe's wars, the America First Committee must be prepared to suffer the stings and arrows identified with name-calling.

Honest men recognize that to be for America First—as opposed to being for Britain's Book of Englishism first—does not identify the members of the Committee as "pro-Nazi," or indicating "anti-Semite."

Although many Americans recognize that, though they lose all, it is their duty to continue not tampering clique and their satellites, lest the children of the next generation should think that all their forebears had deserted both them and the principles of Christian peace and nationality upon which was built the structure of our country.

It is labor unions, Catholic and Protestant, Socialist and nationalist, the sound citizen who is resolute to demand their God-given rights, a factor in this national ownership demanded by America First, Catholics and Protestants, Socialist and nationalist must stand side by side—without commission, lickspittles on one hand, to Catholics, on the other, pro-British, selfish wealth and mammon, from being disgusted and dissolved.

Let no group of Socialists, Catholics, Protestant, Germans, Irishmen entrust us to the *America First Committee* for the advancement of selfish aims.

Let all groups, as well as all individuals, who support the America First Committee, submerge, momentarily at least, their motivating identifies for the one grand objective of keeping this country out of war.

No other interest should engage our common mind.

No other interest will, even though, perchance, the chief spokesmen for the America First Committee—Senator Wheeler and Colonel Lindbergh—unintentionally and accidentally commit an error.

It is understandable why millions of our fellow citizens will not join the America First Committee. They are the silent individuals who are not addicted to joining any organization.

It is not understandable, however, why other individuals grudgingly are as supporters for the America First Committee, thereby letting themselves open to the illogical but invincible charge that they are supporters of some "British First Committee."

Read the Editorial in This Edition on Father Coughlin's Silver Jubilee

Father Charles E. Coughlin, in *Social Justice*, ordered his followers to give full support to the America First Committee.

Other subversive organizations which endorsed the America First Committee and participated in its activities included:

American Destiny Party
American Guards
American White Guards
Blackshirts and Italian Fascist Clubs
Christian Mobilizers
Ethiopian-Pacific League
Falangists
Gray Shirts
Kyffhaeuser Bund
National Copperheads
National Workers League
Patriots of the Republic
Save America First
Save Our America Clubs
Social Justice Clubs
White Russian Fascists

When Lindbergh, Senator David I. Walsh and John T. Flynn addressed a mass meeting of the America First Committee in Manhattan Center on April 23, 1941, the New York press reported that the audience was to an alarming extent made up of members of the Christian Front, the German American Bund, the Crusaders for Americanism, the Christian Mobilizers and other such organizations. Newspaper photographs showed among the crowd the faces of August Klapprott, New Jersey German American Bund leader; Edward James Smythe, who had recently negotiated joint activities between the Bund and the Ku Klux Klan; Lawrence Dennis, so-called ideologist of American Fascism; Daniel Horgan, organizer of Christian Mobilizer strong-arm squads; James Stewart, professional rabble-rouser for the Christian Mobilizers; and dozens of other people of the same sort.

The American Legion in California undertook an exhaustive investigation of Axis agents in the America First Committee. On October 10, 1941, the Legion issued a public report of its findings which stated:

> The American Legion Committee finds that in meetings of America First, processes are at work whereby a person attending merely to seek information, may unwittingly be transformed into a Nazi sympathizer, and even into a potential traitor to his country.
>
> This Committee further finds that the subversive infiltration into America First in California has not only confused the minds of the people it attracts, but also has poisoned the minds of persons of outstanding community reputation who have participated in its activities.

The report listed in careful detail the subversive groups and individuals active in Californian chapters of the America First Committee. Many of the persons named were members of the German American Bund. Until recently they had been openly parading in Storm Troop uniforms under the swastika flag. Now they were for "America First!"

The entire United States fifth column, organized during eight years of unremitting Axis efforts, had joined the America First movement.

They were all crying, "America First!"*

IV. *Leaders of America First*

The hero of the America First Committee was Charles A. Lindbergh, the famous aviator who had accepted a medal from Hitler. The heroine was Laura Ingalls, the famous aviatrix who turned out to be a paid Nazi agent.

---

*It is interesting to note that "Britain First" was the official slogan of the British Fascists led by Sir Oswald Mosley, who is now in jail in England, and that "Australia First" was the title of an Australian fascist organization which was disbanded by the Australian authorities in 1942.

Telephone 2-9186   Subscription $2.00

◄ VOICE OF THE INDEPENDENT PEOPLE ►

Subscribers In 44 States   **PUBLICITY**   5,000 Readers In Kansas

A Progressive Independent Paper
513 North Main Street

WICHITA, KANSAS

December 9--1940.

Edward James Smythe,
149 Vermilyea Avenue
New York City, New York
My Dear Smythe:--

     Received from you this a. m. three letters--one enclosing the folder of "The America First Committee--one with the copy for the column--the other letter and remittance from the German Railroads. Will write the American First Committee assuring them of our co-operation and will also write the German Railroads people and solicit some advertising from them.

     Let us hear from you as often as you can as to what you are accomplishing--we are running awfully close on finances here and need all the support that can possibly be had and need it now.

                       Very truly yours,

                   "PUBLICITY"

           By *J. F. Garner*
                        Associate Editor

A letter to the pro-Nazi propagandist Edward James Smythe from E. J. Garner, editor of *Publicity* of Wichita, Kansas. The German Railroads referred to was an official agency of the Third Reich, and served as a propaganda and espionage center in the United States.

Miss Ingalls, an eccentric thirty-eight-year-old socialite, dancer, actress and flyer, first made isolationist headlines on September 26, 1939, when she "bombed" the White House with anti-war leaflets. Shortly after the formation of the America First Committee, she became one of its most popular and most publicized speakers. She traveled from one end of the country to the other, tirelessly addressing scores of America First rallies, exhorting her listeners to fight the Roosevelt Administration and its "war program." She shared the same platform with Charles Lindbergh, Senator Gerald P. Nye, Senator David I. Walsh, Senator Burton K. Wheeler and other America First leaders, who no doubt were unaware that their fellow speaker was a Nazi agent.

Her speeches were noted for their vehemence. Addressing the Women United, unofficial women's auxiliary of the America First Committee, on November 11, 1941, she declared she was sick of democracy and went on to say, with her voice rising hysterically, "Women, the time has come to act. Don't fire until fired upon, but then get busy. This country is in the hands of alien forces, and you know what I mean. . . ."

From the beginning of her association with the America First Committee, Laura Ingalls was in the secret employ of the Third Reich. Her money and most of her instructions came from Baron Ulrich von Gienanth, head of the Gestapo in the United States, whose diplomatic title was Second Secretary of the Germany Embassy in Washington. She was also working with Hans Thomsen, the German Chargé d'Affaires, and Fritz Weidemann, German Consul in San Francisco. The Nazis bought her services comparatively cheaply, paying her only $300 a month. But then she had an additional income from the many speeches that she was making for the America First Committee.

The Nazis were well pleased with her work. Von Gienanth told one of his agents that he "couldn't withhold" his "joy"

(Above) A letter from Lula Wheeler, wife of Senator Burton K. Wheeler, to Thelma Herrick, head of Women United, an organization with which the Nazi agent Laura Ingalls worked closely.

Mrs. Wheeler was a member of the National Committee of the America First Committee. Her letter indicates that "spontaneous" isolationist demonstrations in Washington during the spring and summer of 1941 were organized by the America First Committee. Mrs. Wheeler's letter reads as follows:

"My dear Mrs. Herrick. Your letter to Sen. Wheeler today was read to me over the phone. /I think a pilgrimage to Washington is an excellent idea and hope that fully one thousand will come. /I would suggest that you go immediately from the station to the White House to call on the President. You probably better wire for an appointment in advance. /Some banners might be effective such as:—'No Convoys, No War' 'We Want No War and We Mean It' 'We don't like Hitler because he doesn't Keep his Word' 'Be sure you Keep your promises Mr. Roosevelt' etc. etc. /Then you might all go to the East steps of the Capitol (about 2 p.m.) where some Senators (whom you would write in advance of your coming) would speak to you and pictures be taken. /Then you could spend the balance of the day calling on your own Congressman and Senators. /These are just suggestions of course and Mrs. Taft, Mrs. Bennett Clark and I and Mrs. Cecil Bray of the Mediation Comm. will do what we can to help make your visit a profitable one. /Sincerely yours, /Lula Wheeler /May 10th /3757 Jocelyn St., /Washington, D. C. /Will you write or wire the exact time of your arrival."

(Below) Original draft of Thelma Herrick's telegram replying to Mrs. Wheeler. It reads:

"Would you Mr. Clark and Mrs. Tafte [?] get in touch with our Vice President Mrs. Owen Neil Brown at the Washington Hotel. She is arriving there at 2 o'clock today and is going directly to Senator Reynolds office. I have wired Senators Bird and Fish to get a room for us to assemble in and meet our Senators and Congressmen. Looking forward to seeing you on Wednesday. /Thelma Herrick."

when he heard how overflow crowds had cheered Miss Ingalls at an America First rally in New York. This agent wrote in a letter to Laura Ingalls that von Gienanth had added: "It's just what we (the King and Mama) did in the early days." In the code employed in this correspondence, "King" meant Hitler and "Mama" was von Gienanth. The "early days" referred to the early struggles of the Nazi Party in Germany.

On another occasion Laura Ingalls proposed to von Gienanth after the fall of France that she make a solo "peace flight" to Europe to promote a second Munich. The Gestapo chief told Miss Ingalls: "The best thing you can do for our cause is to continue to promote the America First Committee."

Miss Ingalls prepared for her America First speeches by studying propaganda material recommended by the Nazis. She read Hitler's *Mein Kampf* with great care, underlining many passages in red ink; and her large briefcases were invariably crammed with anti-Semitic pamphlets, copies of *Scribner's Commentator,* and miscellaneous literature provided by the German Library of Information.

She was quite convinced that Nazi Germany would be victorious. "Mr. Hitler will take care of that situation when he has won the war," she said, referring to the "lousy democracy" in the United States.

"Some day I will shout my triumph to a great leader and a great people . . . ," she wrote in April 1941 to Dr. Hans Thomsen, "I have a telegram already written 'sieg heil' to send you . . . Heil Hitler!"

In another letter, addressed to Catherine Curtis, head of a number of women's "peace" organizations, Miss Ingalls summed up her attitude toward the war in these words: "I have always known that the best way to keep the United States out of war was to pray for or aid a swift German victory. . . . Visit me in my little chalet near Berchtesgaden."

On December 11, 1941, the day that Germany and Italy declared war on the United States, Laura Ingalls hurried to Washington to see Baron Ulrich von Gienanth. She wanted names of persons "who can continue our work in this country."

A week later she was arrested by the FBI on charges of having failed to register as a paid agent of the Third Reich. She was subsequently sentenced to serve eight months to two years in the penitentiary.

Here are some of the other people who came into positions of leadership or influence in the America First Committee:

> *Ralph Townsend* of San Francisco was a leading speaker for the America First Committee and a member of the editorial boards of *Scribner's Commentator* and *The Herald,* publications sponsored by the Committee.
> Townsend was a paid agent of the Japanese Government. He worked under and got his money from Jikyoku Ilnkai, an agency of Japanese Consulate in San Francisco. After Pearl Harbor, Townsend was arrested in January 1942 by the FBI and subsequently sentenced to serve eight months to two years in prison for failure to register as an agent of the Japanese Government.

> *Rev. John Cole McKim* was Chairman of the Peekskill, New York, Chapter of the America First Committee.
> McKim wrote a regular column for the *Japanese-American Review,* a publication registered with the U. S. State Department as a propaganda agency for the Japanese Government. In this column he praised the writings of Ralph Townsend and other pro-Axis propagandists.

> *Garland Alderman* was Secretary of the Oakland County Chapter of the America First Committee in Michigan.
> Alderman was a member of the National Workers League and, after Pearl Harbor, became Secretary of this Nazi-inspired group. In April 1942, Alderman was indicted by a Federal Grand Jury on charges of sedition and conspiracy to block the execution of laws of the United States.

Dellmore Lessard was Oregon State Chairman of the America First Committee.

Lessard was a pro-Nazi propagandist and an active collaborator with the Silver Shirts. A public scandal forced Lessard to resign from his position as America First Oregon State Chairman after the American Legion disclosed that he had accepted funds for the Committee from the Nazi-controlled *Kyffhaeuserbund* (German War Veterans).

George T. Baker, Samuel L. Brogdon and *Dr. Hugh R. Parkinson* were the three most active members of the San Francisco America First Chapter. Baker was Chairman of the chapter; Brogdon was North California Executive Secretary of the America First Committee; and Parkinson was the regular chairman at America First meetings in San Francisco.

Baker had previously cooperated closely with San Francisco members of the German American Bund. Brogdon had also cooperated with the German American Bund. Parkinson had worked with the Silver Shirts and presided over a number of their rallies. All three of them distributed Nazi propaganda publications such as *Welt-Dienst, Deutscher Weckruf und Beobachter,* and the German Library of Information's *Facts in Review.* (Public pressure eventually forced the resignation of Baker, Brogdon and Parkinson from their executive positions in the America First Committee, but they continued secretly to promote the activities of the Committee.)

Benjamin Franklin Ballard was Chairman of the Los Angeles Downtown Chapter of the America First Committee.

Ballard was the organizer of the American Guard, a Nazi-inspired, anti-Semitic terrorist organization in California.

William P. Williams was head of the North Hollywood Chapter of the America First Committee.

Williams published and distributed pro-Axis, anti-Semitic propaganda pamphlets, advocating the formation of "secret cells." He circulated these pamphlets at America First meetings.

This America First Committee delegation greeted Senator Burton K. Wheeler when he arrived at the Union Station in Los Angeles on September 27, 1941. Senator Wheeler was doubtless unaware that the man standing at the extreme right, against the wall, attempting to conceal his face with a newspaper, was F. K. Ferenz, leading Nazi propagandist on the West Coast. (In May, 1942 Ferenz was indicted by a Federal Grand Jury in Sacramento, California, on charges of sedition.) No doubt, too, the America First delegates did not know that the placards they carried had been painted at the Continental Book Store, 2509 West 7th Street, Los Angeles, a Nazi propaganda outlet, which was owned and operated by F. K. Ferenz.

William Hunt was head of the Glendale Chapter of the America First Committee in California.

Hunt was named by the American Legion in California as an active pro-Nazi propagandist, an associate of Nazi agents, and a frequent visitor to the Deutsches Haus, the headquarters of the German American Bund.

F. K. Ferenz was a key distributor of America First literature and organizer of America First picket lines in California.

Ferenz was an important Nazi propagandist. He handled Nazi propaganda movies and was the chief distributor of written Nazi propaganda in California. Ferenz was indicted in May 1942 by the Grand Jury in Sacramento, California, on charges of sedition.

Ernst Goerner of Milwaukee, Wisconsin, was a key distributor of America First Committee literature, which he received in bulk lots from the Milwaukee America First Chapter.

Goerner was a veteran Nazi agent and a midwest leader of the German American Bund. He was arrested by the FBI on August 9, 1941, on charges of "counselling, aiding and abetting evasion of the Selective Service Act." (After Goerner's arrest the authors sent an investigator to interview Mrs. Goerner. The investigator asked, "Is the America First Committee doing anything to help Mr. Goerner?" To which Mrs. Goerner replied, "Oh, they're a rotten bunch. After all Ernst did to help them, they won't do anything for him now that he's in trouble. I guess they're scared because he's been arrested.")

Ellis O. Jones helped organize America First mass rallies in Los Angeles. He was a key distributor of America First literature on the West Coast and a speaker at America First meetings.

Jones headed a subversive organization which he had named the National Copperheads (in honor of Charles A. Lindbergh). Jones was an intimate of Nazi agents and a regular contributor to the Bund's *Deutscher Weckruf und Beobachter*. On July 20, 1942, Jones was convicted of sedition and sentenced to spend four years in prison. A subsequent indictment brought against Jones charged him with taking part in a conspiracy to sabotage the morale of the United States armed forces.

Robert O. Jordan was a Harlem, New York City, organizer for the America First Committee.

Jordan headed a fascist Negro organization called Ethiopian-Pacific League. He worked closely with German and Japanese agents. This is a characteristic quote from a speech Jordan made in Harlem in October 1941: "I will cut my throat if Hitler doesn't win this war. . . . Hitler has a plan all drawn up; it's a beautiful plan and it was made with the agreement of Japan. . . . Actually, the Japanese want to give you back your culture. . . . I have several hundred tickets [to an America First rally] to give away. They were sent me by the America First Committee. I want all of you to hear Lindbergh at Madison Square Garden." Jordan was arrested in New York City in February 1942 for violating the Alien Registration Act.

Mrs. Joseph Gallagher was in charge of the West Philadelphia headquarters of the America First Committee and was one of the Committee's leading members in Philadelphia.

Mrs. Gallagher was an active worker in pro-Axis and anti-Semitic organizations in Philadelphia and an officer in the subversive Mothers and Daughters of Pennsylvania. She helped arrange the meeting on October 16, 1941, at which the assembled Mothers and Daughters of Pennsylvania sang the Nazi Horst Wessel hymn.

Catherine Curtis was one of the chief America First Committee speakers, sharing platforms with Senator Nye, Mrs. Burton K. Wheeler, Mrs. Champ Clark, and other America First leaders.

Catherine Curtis headed Women Investors in America, an organization named in July 1942 by the Department of Justice as an agency used by fifth columnists in a conspiracy to sabotage the morale of the United States armed forces.

Boris Brasol prepared anti-Administration, anti-Soviet propaganda literature for the America First Committee. He also

wrote for the magazine *Scribner's Commentator,* America First
Committee mouthpiece.

Brasol, an ex-Czarist officer, was an international leader of the
anti-Semitic movement. He brought into the United States the
first copies of the notorious anti-Semitic forgeries, *The Protocols of Zion.* He once boasted: "Within the last year I have
written three books which have done more harm to the Jews
than ten pogroms would have done them." He cooperated
with the Tokyo-supervised Russian Fascist Union in Japan,
as well as with Japanese and German agents in America.
(Some of the propaganda material Brasol turned over to the
America First Committee came directly from Japan.)

Werner von Clemm served as a behind-the-scenes propaganda
strategist in New York for the America First Committee and
also gave it financial support.

Von Clemm was indicted by a Federal Grand Jury on January
28, 1942, on charges of conspiring with the German High
Command to smuggle diamonds into the United States.

V. *Frank B. Burch — A Case History*

It is not difficult to understand why native fifth columnists
aided the Axis in its cunningly devised program to sabotage
United States defense preparations. They were either paid in
cash for their services, or they anticipated loot and Quisling
positions of power in an Axis-conquered America.

But how were the Nazis able to hoodwink or enlist the services of some of the distinguished American citizens connected
with the America First Committee? The case of Frank B.
Burch of Akron, Ohio, illustrates the technique employed
by the Nazi psychological saboteurs in this field.

The America First Committee came to Akron, Ohio, on the
first day of July 1941. One of its founders was the sixty-year-
old Akron lawyer, Frank B. Burch. For many years Burch had
been a distinguished member of the Akron community. He
was elected to the State Senate in 1923, and he later served

as a Republican State Central Committeeman for the 14th District of Ohio. He was a member of the Akron Chamber of Commerce and a leading participant in civic affairs.

Frank B. Burch of Akron, Ohio, was a highly respected American citizen. He would still be if it had not been for his fanatical hatred of Franklin D. Roosevelt. It was this hatred which led Burch into the clutches of Dr. Karl Kapp and the Third Reich.

During the depression years Burch's law practice had suffered like most businesses. He blamed it all on the New Deal and "that man in the White House." His hatred for Roosevelt became an obsession with him. It was all he could think or talk about. It was the main motivating force of his life. Many of his former friends began to avoid Burch, because of his almost pathological, ceaseless attacks on the President. Impelled by his hatred, Burch was drawn to all those who, for whatever motives, expressed animosity towards the President. He began reading the literature put out by Charles Coughlin, William Dudley Pelley, and others like them.

The Akron press reported speeches by Adolf Hitler attacking President Roosevelt in language which echoed Burch's own thoughts. Burch began to think that the Third Reich might have been misrepresented to the American public. He decided to undertake a little research on the subject of Nazism. Early in 1939, he wrote a cautious letter to Dr. Karl Kapp, the German Consul at Cleveland, asking for information on certain questions of Nazi policy. Wasn't the Bund evidence of a Nazi plot against America? What about the concentration camps in Germany? What was the Nazi attitude to the Protestant Church?

The German Consul at Cleveland, like all Nazi diplomats, had been trained in the devices of psychological sabotage. He knew how to spot a potential tool, how to lead him on, and how finally to involve him as an accomplice in Nazi intrigue.

Like a skillful angler, the wily Nazi Consul played the hate-filled Akronite.

Nazi plots in America? Of course not! "The 'Bund' is an American organization," wrote back Dr. Kapp, "and as such the German Government has no influence whatsoever over it." Concentration camps? "Without exaggeration it can be stated that no loyal German has ever served in a concentration camp." Religion in the Third Reich? "Nobody has ever been persecuted on account of his religion." Dr. Kapp thoughtfully enclosed "a few pamphlets and the book 'Hitler Germany'."

Burch entered into a regular correspondence with Dr. Kapp, and before long the relationship had developed into a social one. The Consul was sending his "kindest regards" to "Mrs. Burch," and hoping "to see you in Akron soon." He kept sending Burch Nazi books and pamphlets in which President Roosevelt was described as being under the control of "international Jews." Burch enjoyed reading them, asked for more, and said it was a pity so few Americans knew the "truth." Promptly, Dr. Kapp told his disciple that his office would be glad to supply any number of Americans with the "truth." He asked Burch to whom he should send his material.

Burch named a number of prominent Akron citizens to whom anti-Roosevelt literature might be sent. As time went on, he added names of persons in other cities to the list. He ended by handing over to Dr. Kapp lists of about 50,000 names which he had laboriously compiled from various professional directories and other sources. Burch selected persons, who for one reason or another, he thought would be receptive to anti-Roosevelt, anti-British and general Nazi propaganda. He divided the names into such categories as "Irish-Americans" and "German-Americans."

Burch was very proud of his lists. He wrote Dr. Kapp on August 1, 1940:

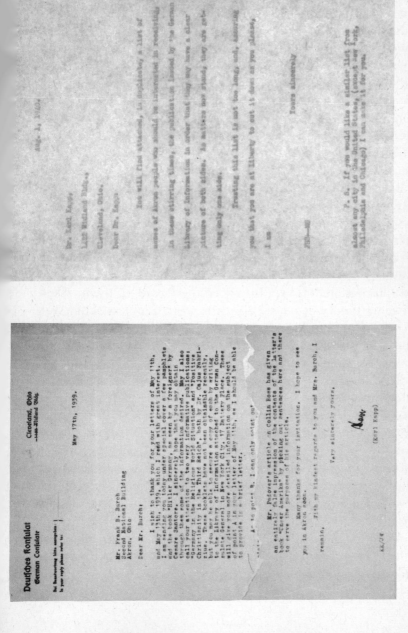

Left: Portion of a letter from Karl Kapp, German Consul in Cleveland, Ohio, to Frank B. Burch, written during the early stages of their relationship, when the Nazi diplomat was describing to the Akron lawyer the virtues of the Third Reich. *Right:* Frank Burch's own carbon copy of a letter to Karl Kapp, written fourteen months later, at a time when the Akron lawyer—now deeply involved with the German Consul—was supplying him with lists of persons to receive German propaganda.

Dear Dr. Kapp:

You will find attached, in duplicate, a list of names of Akron people who should be interested in receiving, in these stirring times, the publication issued by the German Library of Information in order that they may have a clear picture of both sides. As matters now stand, they are getting only one side. Trusting this list is not too long, and, assuring you that you are at liberty to cut it down as you please. . . .

Burch added this postscript:

If you would like a similar list from almost any city in the United States (except New York, Philadelphia and Chicago) I can make it for you.

From the beginning, the Nazi Consul was turning over Burch's lists to George Sylvester Viereck and the German Library of Information for use in the vast campaigns of psychological sabotage they were then conducting in the United States. Burch did not know this at first. By the time he found out, he was already in the pay of the Third Reich.

Compiling lists was not the only work Burch was required to do for his new masters. He was made to serve as a front for Nazi propaganda activity in the Middle West. Large sums of money were turned over to him by Dr. Kapp — always in cash so that the transactions might not be traced. Acting on Dr. Kapp's instructions Burch purchased thousands of anti-Semitic, anti-Administration, pro-Nazi books and pamphlets and distributed them free to the persons named on his lists.

Between January 1, 1940, and July 15, 1941, Frank Burch received $10,000 from the Nazis for services rendered the Third Reich. By no means the least of Burch's services was his work in helping to establish the Akron branch of the America First Committee.

In September 1941, Frank B. Burch was indicted by the Washington Federal Grand Jury investigating Axis propaganda in the United States. Burch was charged with not having registered as an agent of the German Government. Burch pleaded guilty, was fined $1,000, and received, because of his advanced age, a suspended prison sentence of eight months to two years.

VI. *Sabotaging Hollywood*

In the summer of 1939 an impecunious screen writer* suddenly acquired enough money to finance a trip to Nazi Germany. Before he left Hollywood, the screen writer received from a mysterious source a memorandum mentioning the names of certain high Nazi Party officials abroad. Among the names listed were: "Fräulein Reimann, Whitehall 8166 German Embassy (London)"; "Herr Leichtenstern"; and "Herr Bohle." Besides Herr Bohle's name was written the notation, "Speaks English." At the bottom of the memorandum, the screen writer himself jotted down the addresses of several important German government buildings in Berlin.

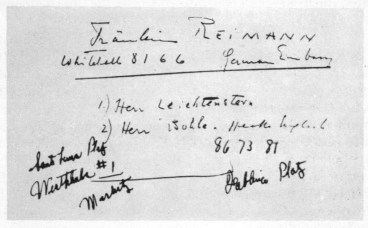

The mysterious memorandum which preceded a certain screen writer's visit to Nazi Germany in the summer of 1939.

Fräulein Reimann was a Nazi espionage agent in England. Herr Leichtenstern was one of Dr. Goebbels' right-hand men

---

*The name of this screen writer is in the possession of the Federal authorities.

in the Third Reich. Herr Bohle was none other than Ernst Wilhelm Bohle, chief of the *Auslands-Organization* and the *Gau Ausland,* and specialist in planning psychological sabotage campaigns in the United States.

The authors do not know what transpired between the screen writer and the Nazi leaders he met with in Europe, but we do know that he returned to the United States supplied with ample cash. We also know that he turned over some money to G. Allison Phelps, head of an organization in Hollywood known as The American Group.

Phelps, who was author of several anti-Semitic and anti-democratic pamphlets, delivered a daily broadcast over the Hollywood station KMTR. Phelps' broadcasts, a number of which were written in collaboration with his friend, the screen writer, hammered away at the theme that Hollywood was controlled by "alien forces" and "Communists" who were producing propaganda moving pictures with the sole aim of involving the United States in the war against Germany.

In the fall of 1940, further fruit of the collaboration appeared in the form of a pamphlet, signed by Phelps and entitled, *An American's History of Hollywood—The Tower of Babel.* Printed at a shop in Los Angeles which regularly handled the printing of the local unit of the German American Bund, the pamphlet repeated the charge that Hollywood had fallen into the hands of aliens and "Reds," and, as proof, included a list of motion picture executives, all of whom had apparently Jewish names. An almost identical list of names had appeared in the January 12, 1940, issue of the official Nazi propaganda news-letter, *Welt-Dienst;* this issue was entitled "Judaized Hollywood."

A year previous to this issue of *Welt-Dienst,* Adolf Hitler, irked by Hollywood's anti-Nazi films, had given notice that he was about to unleash an attack against America's motion picture industry. In his speech before the Reichstag on January 30, 1939, Der Fuehrer declared that Hollywood was a center of anti-Nazism, democracy and Communism, and that this deplorable situation could not be tolerated any longer.

Shortly afterwards, Fritz Kuhn, Fuehrer of the German American Bund, publicly issued a "demand" for the "thorough cleansing of the Hollywood film industry of all alien, subversive elements." William Dudley Pelley printed a six-column article in his Silver Shirt publication, *Liberation*, entitled: "Who's Who In Hollywood — Find the Gentile!" Coughlin repeated the Nazi anti-Semitic propaganda against Hollywood in the pages of *Social Justice*. This psychological sabotage theme was picked up and spread far and wide by every pro-Axis fifth column propagandist in the United States.

Early in 1941, G. Allison Phelps began broadcasting demands for an "investigation" of the motion picture industry. Following a series of such broadcasts, Phelps went to Washington, D. C.

In the Capital, he worked from the office of Senator Robert Rice Reynolds of North Carolina. Providing Phelps with office space was not the only way in which Senator Reynolds assisted his visitor from Hollywood. Senator Reynolds also

This Issue Of

THE AMERICAN VINDICATOR
Sent With

The Compliments Of
Mr. G. Allison Phelps

The printed card sent to G. Allison Phelps' friends with copies of Senator Reynolds' *The American Vindicator*.

THE AMERICAN VINDICATOR

Vol. 2, No. 4

WASHINGTON, D. C., APRIL, 1941

Price 20 Cents

MUST WE FIGHT AGAIN?

Britain Keeps Debt Down As U. S. Piles It Up

America Deeper In the Red Than Warring England

Although the United States will be required to mortgage its future to the extent of 20 billion dollars during the next year and a half to help finance the British in their war, the United Kingdom has been fairly successful in keeping down its own public debt, a comparative fiscal study of the two governments have disclosed.

In the 18 months beginning January 1 the public debt of the United States has been raised by about 20 billions. But in the first 16 months of the European war, the United Kingdom, in the throes of financing the most costly war in history, has raised its public debt only by about 9.6 billion dollars.

U. S. Debt Tops British

Another interesting comparison between the two fiscal positions is that peacetime deficit financing by the administration during the first 16 months of the European war was nearly half as great—4.1 billion dollars to be exact—as the 9.6 billions by which the United Kingdom has had to raise its debt in bearing the burden of a war now costing them about 42 million dollars daily.

The national debt of the United Kingdom today is less than that of the United States, which has not got into real defense financing yet.

On September 2, 1939, one day before Great Britain declared war on Germany, its national debt, including both long and short term obligations and the indebtedness of about five and one half billion dollars to the United States from the old war, amounted to (about 34 billion dollars). On that date the United States had a public debt of 40.9 billion dollars.

English Assets a Mystery

By December 31, 1940, the debt of the United Kingdom, after 16 months of war, had risen only to about 43.6 billion dollars. Our debt by that date had risen to 45 billion dollars, including 1.2 billion for national defense against a national defense cost of 28 to 30 billion dollars just on the basis of plans to date.

Information on the United Kingdom's public debt and fiscal position was obtained from reliable sources in the Treasury, Department of Commerce and Federal Reserve Board.

There is still a great mystery over what has happened to British assets, as their financial statements do no bear out the tremendous dissolution claimed by Secretary of the Treasury Henry Morgenthau jr. in his testimony on the lend-lease bill before congressional committees.

Don't let it happen again

THE THOUSANDS OF AMERICANS WHO DIED IN EUROPE'S LAST WAR

Copyright, 1940, by The Chicago Tribune

Let the Above Be a Grim Reminder of 1917 and 1918

Remember this: If America goes physically into this war by way of the "all out" aid for Britain and we have ships sunk, men drowned, soldiers killed and blood spilt — you may blame it entirely on the passage of H.R. 1776—and you can't place the blame on those Senators who voted against H.R. 1776 because they are the ones who tried to keep the U. S. A. out of war — they are the ones who fought to save your sons! ... *blood spilt in the waters of the Pacific or the Atlantic—which could happen without an actual declaration of war or the sending of an American expeditionary force either to Asia or Europe—but blood spilt, just the same, and when blood is spilt you are actually, and in every sense, in and at war!*

Must Our Youth Again Be Sacrificed Upon Foreign Soil?

How many of the readers of The American Vindicator remember 11:00 A.M. on the morning of November 11, 1918? That was the moment in history when the greatest war the world fought to end all wars, came officially to an end. That was the hour when the Armistice became effective and men ceased to die. That was only twenty-three years ago, and yet, it appears that the American people as a whole have forgotten, have forgotten the blood that spilled, the grief they endured, the money their government spent in those eighteen months of America's participation in the World War. This was evidenced by the tremendous battle over the passage of the Lend-Lease-Give Bill, known as H.R. 1776, which passed the Senate on Saturday, March 8, 1941, *against which passage there were only thirty-one votes*. In other words, this bill, H.R. 1776, was passed by the Senate by a majority of almost two to one, which evidences the fact that the American people had forgotten their sacrifices made during 1917-1918.

The war had hardly ended when the American people said, "Never again." If any public speaker wanted to secure applause he had but to make mention of the fact that in the course of his address that he was opposed to America's participation ever again in any foreign war, and if any national legislator wanted to curry favor of the American people he had but to declare he would never vote for any measure which would take America into another foreign war or place its sons upon foreign shores for sacrifice. *How soon we forget!*

One of the most momentous debates which has ever taken place on the floor of the United States Senate was that pertaining to the Lend-Lease-Give Bill. It is history now, but of course only time will tell as to what legislators were right and which were wrong, as to the votes they cast pertaining to this measure.

On the Democratic side of the Senate Chamber those who opposed the bill selected as their leaders, Senators Burton K. Wheeler of Montana, and Bennett Clark of Missouri, while on the Republican side those who opposed the passage of the bill chose the veteran Senator Hiram Johnson, and Senator Gerald Nye of North Dakota. These four leaders, Democrats and Republicans, selected as the main leader of the Senators opposing the passage of this bill, Senator Burton K. Wheeler of Montana, who, not only debated at length against its passage on the floor of the Senate, but who spoke freely and frequently over the radio and from public platforms.

Some of the proponents of the bill stated it was a measure to keep the United States out of this

(Continued on Page 6)

LET'S STAY OUT OF THIS WAR!

The front page of the April, 1941, issue of *The American Vindicator*, the paper published by Senator Robert R. Reynolds, Chairman of the Senate Military Affairs Committee. (Note that the cartoon is reproduced from Colonel Robert R. McCormick's *Chicago Tribune*.)

inserted excerpts from Phelps' writings into the Congressional Record. Copies of the Senator's own publication, *The American Vindicator,* were mailed to Phelps' friends, with a printed card attached stating: "This issue of THE AMERICAN VINDICATOR Sent With the Compliments of G. Allison Phelps."

Phelps returned to the West Coast with recordings of speeches made by isolationist Congressmen, which he broadcast over his radio program. Continuing his attack on the motion picture industry, he informed his radio audience that he had accomplished a great deal in Washington and that the results of his efforts would soon be apparent.

On August 1, 1941, Senator Gerald P. Nye of North Dakota, at a meeting of the America First Committee in St. Louis, charged Hollywood with being a center of propaganda designed to involve the United States in war. Nye's speech subsequently appeared in the Appendix of the Congressional Record. The speech soon became the basic document of an America First Committee campaign against Hollywood.

At Nye's request, another America First congressional spokesman, Senator Bennett Champ Clark of Missouri, introduced on August 1, 1941, Senate Resolution No. 152.

The experts in the Berlin Psychological Laboratory must have smiled as they filed the text of the Senate Resolution No. 152:

WHEREAS, numerous charges had been made that the motion pictures and radio have been extensively used for propaganda purposes designed to influence the public mind in the direction of participation in the European war; therefore, be it

RESOLVED, that the Committee on Interstate Commerce, or any duly authorized subcommittee thereof, is authorized and directed to make . . . a thorough and complete investigation of any propaganda disseminated by motion pictures and radio or any other activity of the motion picture industry to influence public sentiment in the direction of participation by the United States in the present European war.

The Committee on Interstate Commerce, to which Senator Clark's resolution was referred, was headed by Senator Burton K. Wheeler of Montana, leader of the America First Committee congressional bloc. Wheeler promptly appointed a subcommittee under Clark to "investigate" the motion picture industry.

Just two days after Senator Clark read the text of his resolution on the floor of the Senate, G. Allison Phelps referred in his Hollywood radio broadcast to the forthcoming "investigation" of the motion picture industry and declared: "Now, friends, this is but the beginning. . . . I wish I could read to you, publicly, letters I have received within the last two weeks from certain Senators bearing on the investigation. I wish I could read to you one telegram I received from Senator Charles W. Tobey. . . . This investigation is but the forerunner of the congressional investigation of the entire set-up of the motion picture industry, for which I made a demand in my booklet, *An American's History of Hollywood, the Tower of Babel!*"

Phelps went on to say: "You can never tell whom you will meet when you go to Washington, D. C. I told you I wasn't playing tiddly-winks when I was there two months ago, conferring with Senators and Congressmen. Mr. Smith went to Washington and see what happened to him. G. Allison Phelps went to Washington, and now see what is happening to Hollywood!"

The Nazis, of course, gave the "investigation" an enthusiastic welcome. On August 21, 1941, the German American Bund announced that its "long demanded probe into Jewish Hollywood" was "being undertaken by the Senate."

The
U.S.A.
Is NOT a
"British"
Bolshevik
Nation!

The Free American
and
Deutscher Weckruf und Beobachter

Keep the
U.S.A.
out of
Bolshevik
"Britain's"
Wars!

Vol. 7, No. 13.   New York, N.Y., September 18, 1941   Price 5c.

Producers of Atrocity Films Hire Willkie

Discredited Presidential Candidate Defends the Hollywood Pictorial Dope Industry — Statement of Senator Nye

The Hollywood motion picture magnates are fighting hard to avoid an investigation into their industry of stirring the American people up to a point to consent to a shooting war by doping the public mind with Nazi atrocity films that only vary in method and kind from the British propaganda atrocity tales of the World War. "All of them were admitted to be false, precisely as the films the sons of Israel are forcing the public to see are false."

The preliminary hearing for a Senate investigation started last week. The late Republican candidate for the Presidency has been hired by the Hollywood producers to represent them and in the first skirmish between Willkie and Senator Nye the former indulged in the kind of "campaign oratory" that has made him famous as a belated scion of the school of Judas Iscariot.

Mr. Nye began his prepared statement with a recitation of charges that his conviction was animated by anti-Semitism and his stand on foreign policy by unreason. He declaimed both charges. The Senator was made in many cases, he said, by Jews who were "feeding their prejudices."

He asserted four or five and carefully were 50 per cent of all the theatre capacity.

He said that "each one of them is, I believe, an American citizen, but in the majority born abroad in lands that have been associated with hate, with fear, with prejudice and with persecution.

Besides their political involvement in Old World quarrels because of their European origin, Senator Nye continued, the leading producers have a selfish interest because their sales to Britain often represent just about the difference between a profit and no profit on their entire year's business. If Britain were down, he asserted, they probably would lose these sales and also the money owing them for films previously sold British interests and now in blocked accounts.

Declaring that Lord Northcliffe, British newspaper publisher, realized that Britain owed $160,000,000 in propaganda to get America in World War No. 1, Nye said to list out thousand foreign money is being spent for propaganda through these or radio.

Nye said there are pictures in the making "which now bear well in flashing upon American audiences with the knowledge that they will play a part in making Americans more ready to send their sons abroad."

"Information from inside the moving picture industry is revealing the horror of some of these pictures that are being planned," he continued.

Thus regarded to me by splendid authority would portray a shipload of

British children and pregnant British mothers loaded on board a refugee ship in London, their destination Canada.

"That picture, I am told, will portray the Nazis gleefully wringing their hands and glaying in the opportunity and the plan to destroy the ship and its cargo and thus destroy two generations with one stroke.

"That is the kind of a picture that ought to 'get us.' That is the kind of picture that will 'get' a lot of people who will move into a theatre to be propagandized in this manner. ..... are prepared to give the committee screenshots concerning this particular film, the photograph involving the production be plan for thorough investigation."

Among the pictures which should be investigated, Nye said, are "China

LINDBERGH NAMES THE WAR-MONGERS

They Comprise the British, the Jews, the Capitalists, Communists and the Roosevelt Administration he Declares at Des Moines

In his address at Des Moines, Iowa, September 11, Col. Lindbergh spared no punches in naming the elements that are driving us into war:

"I shall point out some of these groups," he said, "and outline their methods of procedure. In doing this, I must speak with the utmost frankness, for to avoid war we must face them exactly who they are.

"The three most important groups who have been pressing this country toward war are the British, the Jewish and the Roosevelt administration.

"Behind these groups, but of lesser importance, are a number of capitalists, Anglophiles and Intellectuals, who believe that their future and the future of mankind depend upon the domination of the British Empire.

"Add to these the Communistic groups who were opposed to intervention until a few weeks ago, and I believe I have named the major war agitators in this country.

"I am speaking here only of war agitators, not of those sincere, but misguided men and women who, convinced by misinformation and frightened by propaganda, follow the lead of the war agitators.

"Even if America entered the war, she could not win in a short time..."

"England has devoted, and will continue to devote, every effort to get us into the war.

"The second major group I mentioned is the Jewish.

"It is not difficult to understand why Jewish people desire the overthrow of Nazi Germany. But no person of honesty and vision can look on their pro-war policy here today without seeing the dangers involved in such a fuga."

The Greer U-Boat Case in Congress

Two resolutions are pending before the Senate Committee on Naval Affairs to investigate the charge that a German U-boat attacked the American destroyer Greer and the German counter-charge that the U-boat was attacked and chased by the Greer. Senator Walsh, chairman of the committee, introduced his Senate Nye in the author, the other Senator Clark of Missouri, representing both sides of the political complexion of the Upper House of Congress. Senator Nye's resolution calls for an inquiry by the Naval Affairs Committee, with questioning of the Greer's personnel. Senator Clark's calls for the log of the Greer.

Senator Walsh of Massachusetts, chairman of the Senate Naval Affairs Committee, announced that open hearings would be held Wednesday or Thursday of this week, and that Secretary Knox, head of the Navy Department, and Admiral Stark would be asked to testify. The charge that a U-boat attacked the Greer was emphasized by the President in his speech of September 11.

"What's the Matter With You German Americans?"

A Stirring Appeal to His Fellow-Citizens by William Schaumann to Rally to the Defense of the U.S. Against the British Plotters

What is the matter with you Americans of German descent and German birth? Why do you stand the abuse of our country by the "British" and pro-British? Why do you remain passible when American authority, American self-explanation is being gradually undermined by the British imperialists and "world democrats" in the name of "British short of war" and Union (with the British) Now?

You are Americans, citizens of the U.S. of North America, with full rights and a sense of duty peculiar to your blood, yet you see American plutocrats and Americans in these times, when the leaders of international democracy, romance and British imperialism, together with their hirelings, make use

of the radio, press, film, lecture halls and pulpits to propagandize people and build our American people into a war for the interest of British world imperialism?

The German people of Europe are fighting for the same principles that the American plutocracy of whom were people of German blood — fought the British fivicide established in a United States or Empire free of British money plots and industry controllers; to have open wars to all parts of the world without control and decimation of the British.

GERMAN Americans, you know that all the infamous statements about the Germans of Europe of today and those leaders were circulated by every food their souls.

(Continued on Page 6)

Mr. Roosevelt's Ominous War Speech

Threatens to Shoot at Axis Vessels on Sight — Defines no Geographical Limits But Will Sail Defiantly into Blockaded Zones — Speaks for Churchill and Himself in Declaring "We Have a War to Win", Not in the Name of 85 Per Cent of the American People, who are to be Dragged in by the Hair — Senate of Columbian Republic Denies his Charge that Nazis Have Established Air Fields in that Country.

Opinion as to President Roosevelt's speech of Thursday night of last week is divided on the question whether it was a trial balloon to test popular reaction or the inevitable step to involve this nation in Great Britain's war. If the former, the effect was not far fairly estimated at this writing. If the latter alternative is the right one, he leaves the Axis powers no avenue of escape other than to exchange shot for shot. We shall then be in an undeclared war, for he bars no limit but the open seas the world over where Axis craft may be encountered to be fired on at sight and sunk.

This then, is an undeclared war which has not the constitutional authority of Congress and defies 85 per cent of the expressed opposition of the American people against involvement. They are apparently to be dragged in by the hair.

Americans Compared to Moujiks

"Lenin" Baruch vs. "Kerensky" Roosevelt

By B. D. RISSINGER

Has The Revolution started?

Roosevelt threw a monkey-wrench into the Bolshevic Axis when he appointed Wallace head of the Super Defense Board because he stepped on the toes of Baruch who had aspirations to be "the one man" in control of defense hysteria. Wallace will not take orders from Baruch in spite of the fact that Baruch is a Prince of the Golden Fleece, and Baruch knows it. Because Baruch says his plans to juggle prices go a-glimmering, he croaked: "I will KNOCK the everlasting life out of the administration's plan to put a ceiling on prices."

The America First Committee rallied behind the "investigation," and its chapters throughout the country threatened to boycott theaters showing "war propaganda movies and newsreels."

The Hollywood pictures to which the America First "investigators" most strongly objected were the anti-Nazi films: *Confessions of a Nazi Spy, The Great Dictator, Escape, Man Hunt,* and *I Married a Nazi.* At the same time, the "investigators" had not a word to say against the Nazi-produced films which were being currently shown in American cities. Typical of these productions was the UFA *Sieg im Westen* (Victory in the West), a feature-length film of Nazi military victories, which was designed to show the invincibility of Hitler's warmachine. The America First "investigators" were apparently not troubled by this sort of propaganda.

But the campaign against Hollywood exploded in the faces of its promoters. The American motion picture industry refused to be coerced. It struck back at the "investigators." Wendell Willkie took up the cudgels for Hollywood and, in a series of public statements, launched a vigorous counterattack, exposing the true character of the anti-Hollywood witch-hunt. The American public warmly supported Willkie, and things rapidly became too embarrassing for Nye, Clark and Company. The "investigation" was dropped.

VII. *Munich in Wisconsin*

Lake Geneva, the small, quiet, select Wisconsin resort town which calls itself the "Switzerland of America," became the scene of some curious activities during the summer and fall of 1941.

Scribner's Commentator, the slick-paper magazine which ardently promoted the work of the America First Committee, moved its offices en bloc from New York City to Lake Geneva. The publisher of the magazine, Douglas M. Stewart, and the editor, George T. Eggleston, were an enterprising couple of well-to-do America Firsters who had played an important part in steering Charles A. Lindbergh over the first rocky courses of his isolationist career. Lindbergh had great confidence in them, and they regarded him as America's coming Man on the White Horse.

Very soon after Stewart and Eggleston set up their offices at Lake Geneva, the little Wisconsin resort town began buzzing with distinguished new arrivals. The town became the unofficial summer headquarters of the America First Committee. Janet Ayer Fairbank, the National Vice-Chairman of the America First Committee, left Chicago to open a lavish home at Lake Geneva. Urgent conferences were held at her house and at the offices of Stewart and Eggleston. Visitors to Lake Geneva that summer included:

> Charles A. Lindbergh
> General Robert E. Wood
> Senator Burton K. Wheeler
> Senator Gerald P. Nye
> Ex-Senator Rush D. Holt

There were also a number of less distinguished but even more interesting visitors, whose associations and activities were probably unknown to most of the national leaders of the America First Committee.

There was Ralph Townsend, the secret Japanese agent, who came all the way from San Francisco to Lake Geneva to join Eggleston's editorial staff.

There was Louise Carus, who also joined Eggleston's editorial staff. She was the daughter of Edward H. Carus, the German-American industrialist of La Salle, Illinois, at whose home Federal agents finally caught up with the Nazi spy, Dr. Auhagen.

America Has No Enemies In Asia!

□

"Popular rumors from Asia are
very alarming . . . . Analyzed
and compared facts are not."

□

By

RALPH TOWNSEND

Formerly of U. S. Consular Service
in China. Author of *Ways That Are
Dark* and *Asia Answers.*

Price 15 Cents

America Has No Enemies in Asia: one of the many pamphlets written by the Japanese
agent Ralph Townsend and circulated in the United States by the Japanese Chamber of
Commerce of San Francisco and through pro-Nazi German-American bookstores. Ralph
Townsend was a leader of America First Committee activity on the West Coast and later
joined the editorial boards of *Scribner's Commentator* and *The Herald,* two mysteriously-
financed publications edited and published in Lake Geneva, Wisconsin.

And there was Seward Bishop Collins, the wealthy former New York editor, who moved into a large estate at Lake Geneva and began storing thousands of dollars worth of short-wave radio equipment in his spacious garages. In 1938 Seward Collins had provided bail for Mrs. Ignatz Griebl, the wife of the notorious Nazi spy who fled from the United States that year. Collins maintained a bookstore at 231 West 58th Street, New York City, which served as a regular meeting place for fifth columnists. In the midnight mail every Friday a "special release," addressed to Seward Collins at his bookstore, was mailed by the Nazi agent Manfred Zapp, who operated the American branch of Transocean News Service, official propaganda agency of the Third Reich.

In August, Stewart and Eggleston brought out at Lake Geneva the first issue of a newspaper called *The Herald*. A front page article proclaimed:

> Europe Masses to Fight Russian Communists. Seventeen nations join the German Reich in holy crusade against U. S. S. R.

Along with this pro-Nazi propaganda, *The Herald* carried violent "anti-war" editorials, cartoons viciously lampooning the President of the United States, large advertisements for the America First Committee, anti-Semitic subheads and references, and a special column summarizing the speeches of such America First orators as Representative Hamilton Fish, Senators Wheeler, Nye and Walsh, and, of course, Charles A. Lindbergh.

Some time later, when Stewart and Eggleston were facing the Washington Federal Grand Jury investigating Axis propaganda activities, they were asked who paid for the publication of *The Herald*. Stewart and Eggleston said they got $100,000 from Charles S. Payson, a New York millionaire and admirer of Lindbergh. But this money mostly went to finance *Scribner's Commentator*.

The money for *The Herald,* said Stewart and Eggleston, actually came from sources they could not name. One dark August night, they said, "someone" crept up to their open living room window at Lake Geneva and tossed a small bundle into the room. When they opened the bundle they found $15,000 inside. A few weeks later, "a man came up from New York" and handed Stewart a brown paper package. Stewart had never seen the man before and he walked away without a word of explanation. When Stewart opened the brown paper package he found inside sheaves of $20 bills — another $15,000 worth in all. That is how *The Herald,* was financed — according to its publishers. . . .

But there was no mystery about the source of *The Herald's* foreign news. It came straight from the Propaganda Ministries of Berlin, Rome and Tokyo.

A battery of short-wave radio receivers were set up that summer at the Lake Geneva headquarters of Stewart and Eggleston. Companion receivers were built at Seward Collins' estate. Fred Kister, the "radio editor" of *Scribner's Commentator* took charge of the installations.

These short-wave receivers were manned day and night, and kept tuned to Europe and Japan. Messages and official propaganda were constantly coming in from the Axis capitals. The receivers were backed up by costly recording instruments, so that communications could be recorded for translation. Much of the official Axis propaganda received by the secret Lake Geneva radio plants was translated and incorporated into articles and editorials in *Scribner's Commentator* and *The Herald.* These publications were then distributed throughout the country free of charge. They were handed out at America First Committee rallies, and they were circulated on a mass scale to specially prepared America First mailing lists supplied by Lindbergh, Rush Holt, Hamilton Fish, Charles E. Coughlin and Senator Burton K. Wheeler.

A special effort was made to get *Scribner's Commentator* and *The Herald* into the hands of United States soldiers and sailors. Copies of the magazine and newspaper were mailed gratis and unsolicited to Army airfields and Navy airbases, to infantry companies and engineer platoons, to fighting ships and submarines, to Alaska and the Canal Zone, to Midway and Hawaii. Containing official Axis propaganda and material written by expert Japanese and Nazi agents in the United States, and preaching the America First Committee's anti-preparedness doctrines, these publications were regularly forwarded by their publishers to such strategic defense points as:

Ship's Library, U.S.S. *Philadelphia*

Air Base Contractors, Midway Island

Library, Company C, Fourth Infantry, Elmendorf Field, Alaska

Company A, Thirty-third Infantry, Fort Clayton, Canal Zone

Company D, Eleventh Engineers, Fort Davis, Canal Zone

United States Submarine Base, Coco Solo, Canal Zone

Post Library, Fort Sherman, Canal Zone

Commanding Officer, U.S.S. *Lamberton,* Pearl Harbor, Hawaii

Company D, Nineteenth Infantry, Schofield Barracks, Hawaii

Fourth Reconnaissance Squadron, Hickam Field, Oahu, T. H.

Fleet Air Base, Pearl Harbor, Hawaii

Post Signal Fund, Camp John Hay, Mount Providence, Philippine Islands

Commanding Officer, U.S.S. *Gannett,* New York

Crew's Library, U.S.S. *San Francisco*, Pearl Harbor, Hawaii

Crew's Library, U.S.S. *Tennessee,* San Francisco
Ship's Library, U.S.S. *Partridge,* Pearl Harbor, Hawaii
Post Library, Fort Kearney, Saunderstown, R. I.
U. S. Naval Hospital Unit, Bermuda, British West Indies

This was attempted psychological sabotage of the United States armed forces on an ambitious scale.

VIII. *The Third Party*

By the summer of 1941 it was clear that the America First Committee was not going to be merely another pressure group, however powerful. It was growing into a political party. The Lone Eagle and his congressional supporters were stumping the country, not as traditional Republicans or Democrats, but as "America Firsters." They had behind them an enormous propaganda machine and a vast organizational apparatus. They were exploiting issues and slogans of a most extreme and demagogic kind. Nothing like it had ever been witnessed in American politics before.

At Des Moines on September 11, 1941, Lindbergh showed just where all this unusual activity was headed. In language reminiscent of Dr. Goebbels, Lindbergh charged President Roosevelt, the British and the Jews with seeking to involve this country in war. Lindbergh declared that only three groups wanted war — "the British, the Jewish, and the Roosevelt Administration."

The German American Bund's official organ, *Deutscher Weckruf und Beobachter,* proposed Lindbergh for President of the United States.

A month later, Colonel Joseph M. Patterson's *Daily News,* New York's anti-Administration, appeasement-minded newspaper, called for the formation of an "America First Party — signifying a philosophy of keeping our noses out of other people's affairs, especially out of Europe's wars. . . ." Colonel

Robert R. McCormick's *Chicago Tribune* also called for an America First Party.*

In November 1941, the heads of the America First Committee came together in secret conclave in Washington to discuss their future political plans. General Wood presided at the meeting which was attended by Senators Nye, Wheeler, Taft, Representatives Karl Mundt and Day, among others. The general outline of an America First political organization was discussed, and specific plans were drawn up:

1) to launch a campaign to impeach Secretary of the Navy Frank Knox;

2) to align the clergy against aid to the Soviet Union by stressing the "Bolshevik menace";

3) to step up "non-interventionist" propaganda and activity on an even greater scale than heretofore;

4) to set up an America First Party in time for the 1942 elections.†

America First chapters reorganized themselves along congressional district lines. The head of the big Brooklyn, New York Chapter, William T. Leonard, issued confidential instructions to his office staff to make a duplicate file card for every name in his extensive America First Committee mailing list, so that each name could be filed "not only according to name and address, but also according to *election district.*" Other chapter heads issued similar orders. An investigator, who had secured a position in the Brooklyn office of the

---

* In Washington, D. C., the same campaign was carried on by Eleanor ("Cissie") Patterson's *Times-Herald*.

† This America First Party was to have "labor representation" through John L. Lewis, whose daughter, Kathryn Lewis, was a member of the National Committee of the America First Committee. On November 24, 1941, Father Coughlin's *Social Justice* featured a front-page banner headline: "American Labor Stand By Lewis!"

America First Committee, reported to the authors of this book late in 1941:

> The big shots are arranging to compile all names and addresses with political value for use in the 1942 political party which they refer to as the "America First Party" or "The American Party." They're not sure which name they like best. They're even talking about the 1944 campaign already! They've got young Phil LaFollette in mind for President in 1944, Nye for Secretary of State, and Tobey for Secretary of War, and they speak of Lindbergh as "the head of the Party."

An experimental political party was set up by the America First Committee in the second week of November 1941 in Indiana, supposedly an isolationist stronghold. It was called "The American Party" and at its first convention, held at the Cadle Tabernacle in Indianapolis, the chief speaker was Philip F. LaFollette. The National Director of the America First Committee, R. Douglas Stuart, and the National Vice-Chairman, Janet Ayer Fairbank, sat on the platform.

On December 1, six days before Pearl Harbor, General Robert E. Wood, as National Chairman of the America First Committee, announced that his organization was planning to enter the 1942 primary and general elections. The America First Committee, said General Wood, would "mobilize its strength" in an attempt to elect Senators and Representatives pledged to support isolationism.

In one of his last public addresses before Pearl Harbor, Charles A. Lindbergh assured his attentive audience, "We shall clasp hands at the polls in 1942."

CHAPTER ELEVEN

AMERICA AT WAR

On December 12, 1941, five days after Pearl Harbor, the America First Committee officially disbanded. A public statement by its National Chairman, General Robert E. Wood, announced that the Committee was liquidating so that its leaders and members could put all their forces behind the national war effort. Sincere isolationists, who had been members of the Committee, rallied behind the Government. . . .

On December 17, 1941, ten days after Pearl Harbor, a secret meeting was held in a luxurious New York City apartment at 35 Beekman Place. This was the home of Edwin Sibley Webster, Jr., wealthy Wall Street broker and former Executive Director of the New York Chapter of the America First Committee. Webster's guests included Charles A. Lindbergh and a number of key America First leaders in New York.

According to New York newspaper reporters, who discovered and exposed the clandestine meeting, Horace J. Haase, a Brooklyn America Firster, told Webster's guests:

> It is obviously necessary for leaders of America First like Wood [General Robert E. Wood] and Webster to keep quiet. But the organization should not be destroyed. I have never been in the limelight and I have nothing to lose. I can remain active in a quiet way. I should like to offer to keep the files. We must get ready for the next attack which must be made upon this Communistic Administration. . . .

Haase spoke of the day when the America First movement would come to power in the United States:

> If and when the moment comes, I feel sure that our leaders, and especially the Colonel [Charles A. Lindbergh], will take the leadership and lead us to victory.

A few weeks after the meeting in Webster's apartment, Horace J. Haase set up an organization called Americans for Peace. Its membership was composed largely of former America Firsters. The new organization circulated a propaganda bulletin, *America's Hope,* which asserted that the claims of the Axis were just and that the United States had provoked Japan into the war. . . .

Axis psychological saboteurs by no means stopped their work after Pearl Harbor. Their strategy and tactics, however, underwent certain necessary modifications. They now sought to sabotage the United States war effort by: (1) undermining the people's confidence in the wartime leadership; (2) stirring up prejudices against those nations allied with the United States; (3) fomenting disunity among Americans by spreading racial propaganda; (4) creating artificial antagonisms between business and labor.

The Office of Facts and Figures in Washington, D. C., warned the American public against certain disruptive lies which Axis psychological saboteurs and their dupes were spreading throughout the country. Among the Axis propaganda lies were these:

> *American democracy will be lost during the war.*
> *Our leaders are incompetent, our Government incapable*
> *of waging war.*

Stalin is getting too strong, and Bolshevism will sweep
over Europe.
The Chinese and the British will make a separate peace
with Japan and Germany.
The British are decadent and "sold us a bill of goods."
Our armed forces are weak.
The cost of the war will bankrupt the nation.
Civilian sacrifices will be more than we can bear.

The secret war against American morale went on.

Four days after America's entry into the war, two hundred
people held a meeting in the Embassy Auditorium in Los
Angeles and voted to "impeach" a wax-faced dummy of the
President of the United States. Ellis O. Jones, chief of the
National Copperheads, a fifth column organization which had
worked closely with the America First Committee on the
West Coast, told the Los Angeles audience, "The Japanese
have a right to Hawaii! . . . I would rather be in this war on
the side of Germany than on the side of the British!" Robert
Noble, who had been dishonorably discharged from the U. S.
Navy in 1917, shouted from the same platform, "Japan has
done a good job in the Pacific! . . . I believe this war is going
to destroy America!"

In Muncie, Indiana, on January 31, 1942, Court Asher, publisher of the pro-Axis newspaper, *X-Ray*, exulted, "Pearl Harbor sank more than battle wagons; it sank the hopes of Jewry
in this country — and the world forever, Amen and Amen."

In Chicago, Illinois, on February 24, 1942, Mrs. Agnes
Waters who had helped organize subversive women's groups
affiliated with the America First Committee, told a meeting of
We the Mothers Mobilize for America, Inc., that President
Roosevelt should be "impeached." After charging the Presi-

dent with "stripping our country of its defenses," she cried, "He ought to be killed!" One man and several women in the audience shouted, "Let's do it!"

In Nobleville, Indiana, on March 2, 1942, the Silver Shirt chief William Dudley Pelley wrote in his magazine, *The Galilean,* "Germany is coming to the fore all of a sudden because she typifies the best and finest flower of Xanthochroic ('fair white') culture. By the same token, Nippon is coming to the fore in the East because it typifies the best and finest flower of the Mongolian culture."

In Wichita, Kansas, on March 12, 1942, E. J. Garner, publisher of the pro-Nazi propaganda newspaper, *Publicity,* informed his readers, "With your loyal support and distribution to right-thinking Americans the Mongolian Jew Controlled Roosevelt Dictatorship will be smashed."

In San Bernardino, California, in March 1942, David Baxter, head of a secret subversive group called Social Republic Society of America issued a memorandum to his "district memberships" instructing them, "Do not neglect your arsenals. Buy arms and keep them in a place where they are readily accessible. . . . Also keep a plentiful supply of ammunition and do not let it become over a year old or it will deteriorate."

Week after week, in the months following Pearl Harbor, Father Charles E. Coughlin's *Social Justice* continued its propaganda among its 200,000 readers. Coughlin's publication accused the Roosevelt Administration and the "Jews" of getting the United States into the war; maligned Britain, China and the Soviet Union; and proclaimed the "justice" of the Axis cause. Father Coughlin also used *Social Justice* to mobilize the Christian Front movement in an effort to penetrate Civilian Defense organizations. "Join all Patriotic Organizations," read a headline in *Social Justice* on January 12, 1942. An editorial in the same issue told Christian Fronters, *"Social*

Justice advises you to get into every patriotic organization in America," and "capture every office."

The openly seditious propaganda organs were not the only publications that proved useful to the Axis psychological saboteurs in their attack on American morale. Three of the wealthiest and most powerful newspaper publishers in the United States, former supporters of the America First Committee, continued after Pearl Harbor to encourage a spirit of defeatism among the American people. These three publishers—William Randolph Hearst, Captain Joseph M. Patterson, and Colonel Robert R. McCormick—printed in their widely-circulated newspapers an endless series of editorials and articles which could only have the effect of undermining confidence in the United States war effort and arousing suspicion against America's allies. Here are some typical extracts from their newspapers after Pearl Harbor:

> This great war . . . seems to be in the hands of inexperienced civilians who have proved uniformly unsuccessful in managing the country's affairs in time of peace, and are now displaying a more dangerous incompetence in time of war.
>
> *Hearst's New York Journal-American,*
> *March 17, 1942.*

> Of course Russia is not a full partner of the United Nations. She is a semi-partner of the Axis.
>
> *Hearst's New York Journal-American,*
> *March 30, 1942.*

> . . . it is time those who willed the war were driven from their hiding places and sent to the front . . . to share some of the agony they have created.
>
> *McCormick's Chicago Tribune,*
> *February 9, 1942.*

For better or for worse, for good reasons or for bad, we are in
wartime so far away from the position of the Americans who
declared their independence in July, 1776, that the causes
they alleged for dislike of government seem trivial and non-
consequential. . . . Our totalitarian government now lacks only
the abolition of the representative assembly. Remember that
between now and November.

> *McCormick's Chicago Tribune,*
> *July 7, 1942.*

It is said by some and believed by many that this Administration is heavily studded with persons who believe this country
should go Communist, Socialist or anyhow, totalitarian, and
who are trying to use the war as the quickest means of bringing about such a revolution against democracy here.

> *Patterson's New York Daily News,*
> *April 5, 1942.*

So Mr. Roosevelt wants a short name for the war. Why doesn't
he call it simply "My War"? It's certainly all his.

> *One of a series of similar letters*
> *printed regularly in Patterson's*
> *New York Daily News.*

It is worth remembering that before Pearl Harbor these
same newspaper publishers had filled their columns with statements like these:

Certainly it is not Japan which is precipitating this war with
the U. S.

> *Hearst's New York Journal-American,*
> *December 4, 1941.*

What vital interest of the U. S. can Japan threaten? She cannot attack us. That is a military impossibility. Even our base
at Hawaii is beyond the effective striking power of her fleet.

> *McCormick's Chicago Tribune,*
> *October 27, 1941.*

... but for now and the near future it is impossible to see how Hitler is a serious threat to any nation except Russia.

Patterson's New York Daily News,
December 5, 1941.

Three days before Pearl Harbor, when war between the Axis and the United States was clearly inevitable, the Chicago *Tribune* printed certain highly confidential military information which had somehow been obtained from the War Department. This information revealed the projected total force of the United States Army and plans for a possible AEF in Europe.

On December 5, 1941, the day after the *Tribune* printed this report, Secretary of War Henry L. Stimson denounced the publishing of the information as an act of persons "so wanting in loyalty and patriotism" as to reveal military secrets to the enemy.

A few of the Roosevelt-hating Congressmen, whose speeches before Pearl Harbor had been used by George Sylvester Viereck, continued — wittingly or unwittingly — to aid Axis psychological sabotage even after the United States entered the war.

Immediately after the Japanese attack on Hawaii, Senator Gerald P. Nye, who had been one of the top strategists of the America First Committee, excused Tokyo's treachery by saying that the Pearl Harbor assault was "just what Britain planned for us!"

Representative Clare E. Hoffman of Michigan, who had been the congressional spokesman for the "impeach Roosevelt" campaign, carried on after Pearl Harbor with disruptive and inflammatory speeches in the House. On January 27, 1942, Congressman Hoffman delivered an address entitled,

Don't Haul Down the Stars and Stripes or *Roosevelt Is a Judas.* "The Commander-in-Chief, of course, got us into this thing when he himself has failed to prepare to meet it, and here we are," said the Congressman. He ordered 145,000 reprints of this *Roosevelt Is a Judas* speech, and 105,000 franked envelopes to circulate it throughout the country. The chief distributor of Hoffman's scurrilous tirade was Charles B. Hudson, the subversive propagandist of Omaha, Nebraska. Hudson, who was subsequently indicted by the Department of Justice on charges of conspiracy to provoke revolt and disloyalty within the United States armed forces, mailed out thousands of reprints of Hoffman's speech in the Congressman's franked envelopes.

Representative Martin Dies of Texas made virulent attacks against United States Government agencies, charging that they were riddled with "Reds." These charges were picked up and repeated by the Axis Propaganda Ministries. A report made by the Federal Communications Commission on Axis short-wave broadcasts to this hemisphere stated: "Representative Dies received as many favorable references in Axis propaganda to this country as any living American public figure. His opinions were quoted by the Axis without criticism at any time." Vice-President Henry A. Wallace declared that "doubts and anger which statements of Mr. Dies tend to arouse in the public mind might as well come from Goebbels himself as far as their practical effect is concerned."

Typical of the propaganda spread by this small congressional clique after Pearl Harbor was a defeatist address delivered on March 23, 1942, by Representative Harold Knutson of Minnesota, whose speeches had formerly been distributed by Viereck's propaganda machine. Knutson said in his wartime address: "Will Americans graciously bow down to all the totalitarian decrees which will restrict their sugar, their motor cars, their oil, their apparel, their way of life and their pocketbooks, simply to satisfy the ambitions of those who understand victory to be the complete overthrow of their enemies?" *

Continuous "criticism" of the United States war effort and of America's allies was kept up by such Senators as Burton K. Wheeler of Montana and C. Wayland Brooks of Illinois, and by Representatives such as the former America Firsters Stephen Day of Illinois, Dewey Short of Missouri and Paul Schafer of Michigan.

The most important member of Congress to associate himself with disruptive propagandists after Pearl Harbor was none other than the Chairman of the Senate Military Affairs Committee—Senator Robert Rice Reynolds of North Carolina.

Senator Reynolds publicly endorsed the propaganda efforts of Gerald L. K. Smith, ex-Silver Shirter No. 3223 and leader of the Committee of One Million. This same Smith had once bragged in a letter to William Dudley Pelley that he had organized "a uniformed squad of young men composing what I believe will be the first Silver Shirt storm troop in America." Shortly after America entered the war, Smith began publishing in Detroit a magazine entitled *The Cross and The Flag*, which violently assailed the United States war effort and America's allies.

On March 23, 1942, the Chairman of the Senate Military Affairs Committee wrote a letter to Smith praising *The Cross and The Flag* in these words: "Let me congratulate you with my full heart upon your first edition. . . . It is just the right size; it hits the bull's eye with every paragraph; it is straight from the shoulder; it is gotten up in a conservative manner; it should have its appeal; it speaks the truth." This extraordinary letter from Senator Reynolds was later used by Gerald L. K. Smith for promotional purposes. . . .

* It is interesting to note that these identical words appeared on Page 12 of the March 23, 1942, issue of Father Coughlin's *Social Justice*, in an anonymous article assailing the U. S. war effort.

When Senator Reynolds was questioned by Washington newspapermen regarding his endorsement of Smith's publication, the Chairman of the Senate Military Affairs Committee declared, " I have no apologies to offer for endorsing the program of any individual or group standing for the things I have stood for for years."*

---

* Senator Reynolds was not exaggerating. He was himself the, founder and leader of an organization called The Vindicators, and the publisher of *The American Vindicator*, a newspaper widely distributed in the United States by Nazi sympathizers and native fascists, and devoted to attacking the Administration and urging a hands-off policy towards Axis aggression.

Hitler's newspaper, *Voelkischer Beobachter*, had carried an article on February 5, 1939, with the by-line "Senator Robert R. Reynolds, North Carolina." The article, which was in the form of an interview, was entitled "Advice to Roosevelt; Stick to Your Knitting." The same article was printed in the United States in the *Deutscher Weckruf und Beobachter*, official organ of the German American Bund. Hearst's International News Service, which arranged the interview-article, quoted Senator Reynolds as saying: "I can see no reason why the youth of this country should be uniformed to save the so-called democracies of Europe—imperialistic Britain and communistic France. . . . I am glad to be able to state that I am absolutely against the United States waging war for the purpose of protecting the Jews anywhere in the world."

Another Reynolds' quote, from a speech in the Senate in 1938: "Hitler and Mussolini have a date with Destiny. It's foolish to oppose them, so why not play ball with them?"

CHAPTER TWELVE

AMERICA STRIKES BACK

The Axis conspirators, in their plans for world conquest, had dreamed of reducing the United States to a condition of helpless unpreparedness, disunity and indecision. They badly miscalculated. On December 7, 1941, there was no panic in America. Instead, an angered and resolute people was galvanized into a gigantic and unprecedented mobilization of its productive and armed forces against the treacherous Axis foe.

And on the home front, America moved against the Axis psychological saboteurs.

On February 6, 1942, George Hill was sentenced to serve two to six years in prison.

On February 21, 1942, Laura Ingalls was sentenced to serve eight months to two years in prison.

On March 13, 1942, George Sylvester Viereck was sentenced to serve two to six years in prison.

On June 12, 1942, Ralph Townsend was sentenced to serve eight months to two years in prison.

Father Charles E. Coughlin's *Social Justice,* was barred from the mails on April 14, 1942, because of its seditious contents. Similar action was taken against William Dudley Pelley's *The Galilean,* Court Asher's *X-Ray* and E. J. Garner's *Publicity.*

Special Grand Juries were set up in many parts of the United States to investigate enemy propaganda activities. The Federal Grand Jury in Washington continued its extensive investigations in this field.

On July 7, 1942, the New York Grand Jury investigating the German American Bund indicted twenty-six Bund leaders on charges of conspiracy to evade the Selective Service Act. These Bund leaders, and three more, were also indicted on charges of conspiracy to conceal their Bund affiliations on alien registration forms. Among those named in the indictments were Gerhard Wilhelm Kunze, National Director of the Bund; Gustav Elmer, Bund Treasurer; August Klapprott, New Jersey Bund leader; and Herman Schwinn, West Coast Bund leader. Further arrests and indictments followed, as part of a nation-wide campaign "to put the Bund out of business."

On July 23, 1942, the Department of Justice indicted twenty-seven men and one woman on charges of conspiracy to provoke revolt and disloyalty within the United States armed forces. The indictments, which were handed down by the Washington Federal Grand Jury, listed thirty publications as agencies through which the accused had tried to sabotage morale among American soldiers and sailors by picturing the United Nations as weak and ineffective, America's leaders as untrustworthy and the war as a "Jewish plot." Among those indicted were Elizabeth Dilling, author of *The Red Network;* Gerald B. Winrod, publisher of *The Defender* of Wichita, Kansas; Court Asher, publisher of *X-Ray* of Muncie, Indiana; David J. Baxter, organizer of the Social Republic Society of San Bernardino, California; Prescott Dennett, organizer of the Islands for War Debts Committee of Washington, D. C.; William Dudley Pelley, publisher of *The Galilean* of Noblesville, Indiana, and organizer of the Silver Shirts; Robert Edward Edmondson, anti-Semitic pamphleteer of New York City; C. Leon De Aryan, publisher of *The Broom* of San Diego, California; Charles B. Hudson, publisher of *America in Danger!*

of Omaha, Nebraska; Elmer J. Garner, publisher of *Publicity* of Wichita, Kansas; and William Griffin, publisher of *The New York Enquirer.*

Among the thirty publications named by the Grand Jury as part of the conspiracy were the official Nazi news-letter *World Service;* the Bund's *Deutscher Weckruf und Beobachter; Scribner's Commentator;* and *The Cross and the Flag.*

The indictment charged that the conspirators had used the Congressional Record to further their plot against the morale of the armed forces.

The Grand Jury also listed various organizations through which the conspirators sought to sabotage American morale. These included the America First Committee; Representative Hamilton Fish's National Committee to Keep America Out of Foreign Wars; the Silver Shirts; the National Workers League; the Ku Klux Klan; and the German American Bund.

A great educational drive was launched to expose the divisive techniques of the Axis psychological saboteurs.

Government agencies, through radio programs, motion pictures, publications and posters, told the public how to recognize and combat Axis propaganda.

Newspapers throughout the country exposed the machinations of Axis agents, and unmasked fifth columnists in high places.

Labor unions initiated drives against Axis propaganda which sought to create dissension and disunity among America's war workers.

Patriotic and anti-fascist organizations uncovered and combatted Axis-inspired rumors and lies.

All these measures made the work of Axis agents more difficult. Nevertheless, psychological sabotage went on in the United States. It is still going on.

At the time of writing, a number of pro-Axis pamphlets,

news-letters, leaflets, bulletins and magazines are appearing regularly throughout the United States and reaching thousands of Americans with their seditious propaganda.

This is not the only form of wartime psychological sabotage. Referring to that small clique of defeatist newspaper publishers who continue to foster doubts about the United States war effort and America's allies, Archibald MacLeish, Director of the Office of Facts and Figures, told the American Society of Newspaper Editors on April 17, 1942:

> . . . the most pernicious and pervasive defeatism is not practiced by those who violate the statutes of their country openly. It is practiced by those who take scrupulous care to stay within the law—to come, as one of them is reported to have told his staff, "as close to treason as I dare."

And the tiny group of defeatist Congressmen continue their obstructionist work in Washington.

To a great extent, the answer to the problem of wartime psychological sabotage lies with the American people themselves. Public pressure brought about the suspension of *Social Justice*. The same public pressure can bring about the banning of all seditious publications and can stop the spreading of every kind of defeatist propaganda. Through the democratic process itself, the public can use the polls to eliminate all defeatist and obstructionist Congressmen.

The American people know that there is a war of survival to be won. They cannot afford to tolerate the activities of any private individual, politician or group obstructing—for whatever reasons—the winning of this war. In the final analysis, the effect of acts committed by those who assist the enemy unwittingly may be as dangerous to America as the effect of acts committed by those who want the Axis to win.

America's enemies are skillful, powerful and ruthless. For more than ten years they have been building their underground machinery in this country. This vast and intricate apparatus of secret war cannot be smashed overnight, but inevitably it will be smashed by an American people fully aware of the character and methods of the Axis saboteurs and of all who aid them in the United States.

ACKNOWLEDGMENTS

Much of the material for this book has come from the files of *The Hour* and from special reports prepared by our own investigators. We have also drawn heavily upon the public records of the Department of Justice, the State Department and various Congressional Committees.

Among the many books and magazine articles we made reference to in organizing the material for SABOTAGE!, we found the following of special value: *Ambassador Dodd's Diary,* Edited by William E. Dodd and Martha Dodd, Harcourt Brace and Company; *The Brown Network,* Knight Publications, Inc.; "The Case of the Ten Spies," Edward C. Aswell, *Harper's Magazine,* June, 1941; *The Dark Invader,* Captain von Rintelen, Penguin Books; *The Enemy Within,* Captain Henry Landau, G. P. Putnam's Sons; *German Psychological Warfare,* Committee for National Morale, New York; *The German Reich and Americans of German Origin.* Oxford University Press; *Report of Court Proceedings,* Military Collegium of the Supreme Court of the U. S. S. R., Moscow, March 2-13, 1938, People's Commissariat of Justice of the U. S. S. R. Moscow; *Subversive Activities of America First Committee in California,* Americanism Committee, 17th District American Legion Department of California; *Total Espionage,* Curt Riess, G. P. Putnam's Sons; "War Begins at Home," J. Edgar Hoover, *American Magazine,* September, 1941.

We are especially indebted to a number of exposés which first appeared in Walter Winchell's column; to the excellent series of articles on subversive activities, written by Dillard Stokes for the Washington *Post;* to the Flanders Hall exposé by Ray Doyle and William Falvey in the New York *Daily Mirror;* to a series of articles on the abuse of the franking privilege, written by Henry Hoke in his *Reporter of Direct Mail*

Advertising; and to a number of articles which have appeared in *PM* concerning Axis sabotage in the United States. We would like to acknowledge in particular our indebtedness to *PM's* Washington Bureau for its thorough coverage of Senate investigations of Nazi influence in American industry.

We wish to express our appreciation to the Anti-Defamation League of B'nai B'rith for having generously placed at our disposal the contents of its splendid files; also, to the Friends of Democracy, News Research Service, the National Maritime Union, the United Automobile Workers and other organizations which have aided us in the preparation of this book.

M. S.
A. E. K.

INDEX

259